D0903423

The Flexible Constitution

The Flexible Constitution

Sean Wilson, Esq.

LEXINGTON BOOKS
Lanham • Boulder • New York • Toronto • Plymouth, UK

Published by Lexington Books
A wholly owned subsidiary of The Rowman & Littlefield Publishing Group, Inc.
4501 Forbes Boulevard, Suite 200, Lanham, Maryland 20706
www.rowman.com

10 Thornbury Road, Plymouth PL6 7PP, United Kingdom

British Library Cataloguing in Publication Information Available

Library of Congress Cataloging-in-Publication Data
Wilson, Sean, 1967–
  The flexible constitution / Sean Wilson.
    p. cm.
  Includes bibliographical references and index.
  ISBN 978-0-7391-7815-7 (cloth : alk. paper) — ISBN 978-0-7391-7816-4 (electronic)
1. Constitutional law—United States—Philosophy. 2. Constitutional law—United
States--Interpretation and construction. 3. Origin (Philosophy) I. Title.
  KF4552.W57 2012
  342.73001—dc23
                                                                    2012038672

Printed in the United States of America

To the greatest daughter in all possible worlds,

Jocelyn Audrey Wilson

Table of Contents

Citation Abbreviations

(For works cited more than once)

AS-1	Antonin Scalia, *A Matter of Interpretation, Federal Courts and the Law* (Princeton University Press, 1997).
AS-2	Antonin Scalia, "Originalism: The Lesser Evil," *University of Cincinnati Law Review* 57 (1989): 849.
AS-3	Antonin Scalia, "Remarks at Pew Forum Conference, Chicago, Ill.," January 25, 2002 (relevant excerpts cited in *21 Supreme Court Issues Facing America*, (Xulon Press, 2005), 32.
AS-4	Antonin Scalia, "A Theory of Constitution Interpretation," speech at Catholic University of America, October 18, 1996.
B&F	Sotirios A. Barber & James E. Fleming, *Constitutional Interpretation: The Basic Questions* (Oxford University Press, 2007).
DB	David Bakhurst, "Truth, Philosophy and Legal Discourse," *University of Toronto Law Journal* 47, no. 3 (1997): 395-401.
DG	Dennis J. Goldford, *The American Constitution and the Debate Over Originalism* (Cambridge, 2005).
DP-1	Dennis Patterson, "Conscience and the Constitution," *Columbia Law Review* 93 (1993): 270.
DP-2	Dennis Patterson, *Law & Truth* (Oxford, 1996).
DP-3	Dennis Patterson, "Law and Truth: Replies to Critics," *SMU Law Review* 50 (1997): 1563.
GM	George A. Martinez, "The New Wittgensteinians and the End of Jurisprudence," *Loyola of Lost Angeles Law Review* 29 (1996): 545.
GW	Gregoire C.N. Webber, "Originalism's Constitution," in *The Challenge of Originalism, Theories of Constitutional Interpretation*, eds. Grant Huscroft and Bradley W. Miller (Cambridge University Press, 2011).
IB-1	Ian C. Bartrum, "Metaphors and Modalities: Meditations on Bobbitt's Theory of the Constitution," *William & Mary Bill of Rights Journal* 17, no. 1 (2008): 157.
IB-2	Ian C. Bartrum, "The Constitutional Canon as Argumentative Metonymy," *William & Mary Bill of Rights Journal* 18, no. 2 (2009): 327.
IB-3	Ian C. Bartrum, "Constitutional Value Judgments and Interpretive Theory Choice," *Florida State University Law Review* 40, no. 2 (forthcoming, 2013); UNLV William S. Boyd School of Law Legal Studies Research Paper. Pagination is to the SSRN paper, available: http://ssrn.com/abstract=2035936 (accessed June 12, 2012).

JA	J. L. Austin, *The Province of Jurisprudence Determined, and the Uses of the Study of Jurisprudence* (Hackett Publishing Co., 1998).
JB-1	Jack Balkin, "Abortion and Constitutional Meaning," *Constitutional Commentary* 24 (2008): 291.
JB-2	Jack Balkin, "Original Meaning and Constitutional Redemption," *Constitutional Commentary* 24 (2008): 427.
JB-3	Jack Balkin, "Framework Originalism and the Living Constitution," *Northwestern Law Review* 103 (2009): 549.
JBr	John Brigham, *Constitutional Language: An Interpretation of Judicial Decision* (Greenwood Press, 1978).
JE-1	Joseph Ellis, *Founding Brothers* (Vintage, 2002).
JE-2	Joseph Ellis, *American Creation: Triumphs and Tragedies at the Founding of the Republic* (Vintage Books, 2007).
JE-3	Joseph Ellis, *Patriots, Brotherhood of the American Revolution* (Barnes & Noble, 2004).
JE-4	Joseph Ellis, *His Excellency George Washington* (Vintage, 2004).
JF	John Ferling, *Adams vs. Jefferson: The Tumultuous Election of 1800* (Oxford University Press, 2004).
KW-1	Keith E. Whittington, *Constitutional Interpretation: Textual Meaning, Original Intent and Judicial Review* (University Press of Kansas, 1999).
KW-2	Keith E. Whittington, "The New Originalism," *Georgetown Journal of Law & Public Policy* 2, no.2 (Summer, 2004): 599.
KW-3	Keith E. Whittington, *Constitutional Construction: Divided Powers and Constitutional Meaning* (Harvard University Press, 1999).
LS-1	Lawrence B. Solum, "What is Originalism? The Evolution of Contemporary Originalist Theory" in *The Challenge of Originalism, Theories of Constitutional Interpretation*, eds. Grant Huscroft and Bradley W. Miller (Cambridge University Press, 2011).
LS-2	Lawrence B. Solum, "Semantic Originalism" (Draft of May 5, 2008), Illinois Public Law and Legal Theory Research paper Series No. 07-24. Available at SSRN: http://papers.ssrn.com/sol3/papers.cfm?abstract_id=1120244 (accessed June 12, 2011).
LW-1	Ludwig Wittgenstein, *Philosophical Investigations*, 3rd ed., trans. G.E.M. Anscombe (Prentice Hall, 1958).
LW-2	Ludwig Wittgenstein, *Aesthetics, Psychology and Religious Belief*, ed. Cyril Barrett (University of California Press, 2007).
LW-3	Ludwig Wittgenstein, *Tractatus Logico-Philosophicus*, trans. C. K. Ogden (Barnes and Noble, 2003).
LW-4	Ludwig Wittgenstein, *Zettel*, eds. G.E.M. Anscombe & G.H. von Wright, trans. G.E.M. Anscombe (University of California Press, 1967).
LW-5	Ludwig Wittgenstein, *Culture and Value*, trans. Peter Winch (University of Chicago Press, 1984).
LW-6	Ludwig Wittgenstein, *Last Writings on the Philosophy of Psychology*, vol. 1, ed. G.H. von Wright and Heikki Nyman, trans. C.G. Luckhardt and Maximilian A.E. Aue (University of Chicago Press, 1990).
LW-7	Ludwig Wittgenstein, *Philosophical Grammar*, ed. Rush Rhees, trans. Anthony Kenny (University of California Press, 2005).
LW-8	Ludwig Wittgenstein, *On Certainty*, ed. G.E.M. Anscombe and G.H. von

Wright, trans. Denis Paul and G.E.M. Anscombe (Harper Torchbooks, 1969).

LW-9 Ludwig Wittgenstein, *Last Writings on the Philosophy of Psychology, The Inner and the Outer*, vol. 2, ed. G.H. von Wright and Heikki Nyman, trans. C.G. Luckhardt and Maximilian A.E. Aue (Blackwell Publishing, 1992).

LW-10 Ludwig Wittgenstein, *Philosophical Remarks*, ed. Rush Rhees, trans. Raymond Hargreaves and Roger White (University of Chicago, 1975).

LW-11 Ludwig Wittgenstein, "The Nature of Language: Philosophical Investigations (excerpts)," in *Philosophy of Language: The Central Topics*, eds. Susana Nuccetelli and Gary Seay (Rowman & Littlefield, 2008), 19-21.

LW-12 Ludwig Wittgenstein, "Chapter 11: Philosophical Investigations, Sections 65-78," in *Foundations of Cognitive Psychology: Core Readings*, ed. Daniel J. Levitin (MIT Press, 2002), 271-276.

LW-13 Ludwig Wittgenstein, *Remarks on the Philosophy of Psychology*, vol. 1, ed. G.E.M. Anscombe and G.H. von Wright, trans. G.E.M. Anscombe (University of Chicago Press, 1988).

LW-14 Ludwig Wittgenstein, *The Wittgenstein Reader*, 2nd ed., ed. Anthony Kenny (Blackwell Publishing, 2006).

MB Mitchel Berman, "Reflective Equilibrium and Constitutional Method" in *The Challenge of Originalism, Theories of Constitutional Interpretation*, eds. Grant Huscroft and Bradley W. Miller (Cambridge University Press, 2011).

OV Ozan O. Varol, "The Origin and Limits of Originalism: a Comparative Study," *Vanderbilt Journal of Transnational Law* 44, no. 5 (2011): 1239.

PB Paul Brest, "The Misconceived Quest for the Original Understanding," *Boston University Law Review* 60 (1980): 204.

PBt-1 Philip Bobbitt, *Constitutional Fate* (Oxford, 1982).

PBt-2 Philip Bobbitt, *Constitutional Interpretation* (Blackwell, 1991).

RB-1 Randy E. Barnett, "The Original Meaning of the Commerce Clause," *University of Chicago Law Review* 68 (2001): 101.

RB-2 Randy E. Barnett, "An Originalism for Nonoriginalists," *Loyola Law Review* 45 (1999): 611.

RB-3 Randy E. Barnett, *Restoring the Lost Constitution* (Princeton, 2004).

RC Ron Chernow, *Alexander Hamilton* (Penguin Press, 2004).

RD-1 Ronald Dworkin, *Law's Empire* (Harvard University Press, 1986).

RD-2 Ronald Dworkin, *A Matter of Principle* (Harvard University Press, 1985).

RD-3 Ronald Dworkin, "Comment," in *A Matter of Interpretation, Federal Courts and the Law*, by Antonin Scalia (Princeton University Press, 1997): 115-127.

RD-4 Ronald Dworkin, *Life's Dominion* (Vintage Books, 1994).

RD-5 Ronald Dworkin, "The Model of Rules," in *Philosophy of Law, Sixth Edition*, eds. Joel Feinberg and Jules Coleman (Wadsworth, 2000).

RD-6 Ronald Dworkin, *Freedom's Law: The Moral Reading of the American Constitution* (Harvard University Press, 1996).

RD-7 Ronald Dworkin, *Taking Rights Seriously* (Harvard, 1977).

RM-1 Ray Monk, *The Duty of Genius* (Penguin Books, 1990).

RM-2 Ray Monk, *How to Read Wittgenstein* (W.W. Norton & Co., 2005).

SK Saul Kripke, *Naming and Necessity* (Harvard University Press, 1980).

SP Steven Pinker, *Words and Rules: The Ingredients of Language* (Perennial,

1999).

SW   Sean Wilson, *The Influence of Language Upon Supreme Court Voting In Civil Liberties Cases,* WVU Electronic Theses and Dissertations (2004), http://alturl.com/eqget (accessed June 12, 2004).

Citation Form and Style

§ 1. Internal Citation

Chapters are divided into sections. When the book cites to itself, it refers to this logic, not the pagination. So, for something found in Chapter 3, Section 2, Subsection (a), the citation is [9:§2(a)]. Only the appendix is different. It is written in Wittgensteinian format, with each remark numbered. A citation to remark 47 appears as: [App: 47]. Table 0.1 summarizes the format:

Table 0.1: Citation Format	
Citation form:	*Translation:*
[3:§3]	Chapter 3, Section 3.
[9:§2(a)]	Chapter 9, Section 2, Subsection (a)
[App]	The Appendix
[App: 32]	Appendix, remark 32

§ 2. External Citation

For publications that are cited more than once, I use a system of abbreviations based upon author initials. If an author is John Doe, for example, the abbreviation is [JD]. For more than one publication, it would be [JD-1] and [JD-2], etc. The abbreviations are listed in alphabetical order on the previous pages. The reader is advised to have the table handy. I use this system for its great efficiency.

Preface

I offer an original work in legal theory. The method is philosophical. I do not offer an encyclopedic survey of the views of any one field or concern. But I do pay close attention to research and perspectives from many different fields as I present my thesis.

It took me nearly four years to complete this book. I started in November of 2008 and finished in mid-August, 2012. I was motivated to work on the problem because of the suffocating nature of the existing discourse. I wrote the book with hopes that certain kinds of conversations about "the true meaning" of the Constitution would be quieted.

I've had persistent battles with how to organize the material. At first, I only set out to write a book about the troubles with originalism. But when presenting these, I had no choice but to show what I thought to be a proper resolution. Hence, out came the Wittgensteinian constitutional perspective. Prior drafts had this perspective emerging toward the end of the book, the way a movie ends its plot. But the organization proved too chaotic. I finally settled for flipping it around. I front-loaded my constitutional views and put the originalism critique in the back. At that point, the work became something different. The indictment of originalism was no longer the headline: it was a mere conclusion of everything else.

If you really want to know what I believe about the Constitution that differs from my peers, you should go directly into Chapters 5, 6 and 7. They encapsulate the heart of the matter. I also caution against neglecting the chapter endnotes. They often complete the understanding of the main text.

If I could offer one word of advice for people writing in this field, it is that they do their jurisprudence with examples rather than "systems of thought." So much confusion can be avoided if we do philosophy on the ground.

Regards and thanks,

Dr. Sean Wilson, Esq.
August 14, 2012

Acknowledgments

I thank the following people for their contributions to this work.

Commenters

Mark Tushnet was the first person to provide helpful and substantial comments. It is because of him that the organization of the book changed dramatically. He opened my eyes to how terribly chaotic the earlier drafts were. He was the first to suggest frontloading the case for a flexible constitution and moving the originalism material to the back.

Ian Bartrum was the first to provide a truly extensive review. He commented upon each chapter. It is because of him that the text is more readable. I lessened the presence of jargon and substantially reformed the appendix. Ian also suggested that my views on connoisseur judgment might be more in spirit with Philip Bobbitt's actual sentiments then perhaps the manuscript might indicate. I added an additional footnote in Chapter 7 because of his concern. I thank Ian for all of his comments and will always remember his encouraging help at a time when I greatly needed it.

John Brigham also was invaluable. Along with being supportive during the process of finding a publisher, he helped me see that the tone of my sentences on occasion was too authoritative, not leaving enough to the reader. I thank him for that, for I could not see it. And, along with many insightful comments, he had the most amusing remark for why he didn't like the term "connoisseur judgment." He was reluctant to involve French words in matters of the American Constitution.

Valuable comments were also provided by Aaron R.S. Lorenz, Francis J. Mootz ("Jay") and George Martinez—all of which resulted in an improved text. Aaron helped me see that an earlier draft was too repetitive. One of Jay's many interesting comments was that originalists might plead guilty to the charge of a flexible constitution, but still argue for their beliefs purely for the pragmatic reason of wanting flexibility curtailed. I confess that my book does not anticipate instrumental reasoning. My concern is only with the way the Constitution is, not with the ways we could deny that. But I thought his point quite clever.

Finally, I must mention Stuart Mirsky, author of historical fiction and passionate advocate in the area of philosophy of mind. His proofing of the text for typos and grammatical errors was quite helpful. Any errors that remain are, indeed, my own.

Publisher

I thank Lexington Books for publishing my work. I thank Melissa Wilks, who showed great confidence in this project and proved to be a wonderful editor. And I thank Alison Northridge, another wonderful editor who had to put up with my numerous e-mails and concerns. I am very grateful of the way Alison couriered the project and helped me. And I thank production editor Lindsey Frederick for the fantastic job she did on the final proofread and for also being a superb editor.

Permissions

I thank the following for granting me permission to quote extensively: Philip Bobbitt, from his extremely important work, *Constitutional Interpretation*; and ABC-CLIO, from John Brigham's vital publication in 1978, *Constitutional Language*.

Personal

I thank Mark Graber for always giving me advice whenever I would bother him, which was frequently. And I thank my daughter, Jocelyn Wilson, who was the first person to endure several poorly-written chapters of an early draft during her freshman year of college. The chapters were dense in format and relied upon a convoluted system of symbolic notation. Jocelyn remains the only person who found the notation easy to digest. Because her opinion was outnumbered by the rest of humanity—including my father—I removed the symbols from the book.

I also thank the following people for agreeing to read the manuscript, although time did not permit them to make comments: James Tully, Steve Griffin, Gary Lawson and Peter J. Smith.

Finally, this being my first book, I thank the professors who have meant the most to my development: Robert DiClerico, Stephen Hetherington and the late John Jacobsohn. Each left an important and distinct impression. I also thank my family and Wright State for their support. And as to the most important influence in my intellectual life, I thank Ludwig Wittgenstein.

The Conclusion

Those who read this book and understand it properly will be left with three conclusions:

1. We cannot behave toward the Constitution in the way originalists want without also changing what the act of legislation is as a *behavior*. In other words, originalism asks us to be incongruent with our current legal forms.

The only way to see originalism clearly is to see it as a legal ideology that has political objectives in mind. This book does not say these things; it shows them.

2. No judge can validly use history to say what the American Constitution means, unless he or she: (a) compares this understanding to other means of knowing; and (b) finds it to be superior for reasons *other* than history.

Another way of saying it: history only works if it is still "good."

3. When saying that x is "constitutional" (or not), a person makes an *artisan* judgment, not a statement of fact. The ultimate truth of the American Constitution rests with the best of its *connoisseurs*.

Introduction

This book is divided into two philosophical investigations. Part I concerns how to interpret the American Constitution. The point is to understand not only what it means to "follow it," but how to do that *well*. This is covered in Chapters 2 through 7. Each chapter works its way, developmentally, to its ultimate conclusion. Part II is an attempt to understand the philosophy of originalism and why it is incompatible with the American legal system. This occurs in Chapters 8 through 13. It, too, proceeds developmentally toward its conclusion.

The book starts with a literature review, titled, *Chapter 1: Wittgenstein, Law and Originalism*. The point is to fit the book into existing scholarship.

Part I: Interpreting the Constitution

Part I begins with *Chapter 2: Obeying Flexible Commands*. The point is to explore what it means to follow a flexible rule. I present an abstract framework that reforms the way Ronald Dworkin approaches the issue. The discussion is important for understanding how a flexible constitution can be "obeyed."

Whether the Constitution has a "definite meaning" is taken up in *Chapter 3: Is There a Fixed Meaning?* This question is contemplated from the standpoint of text, history, grammar and levels of meaning (abstract/concrete). The chapter also examines the views of several important scholars.

Next, I explain how the cognition of ordinary language works in *Chapter 4: Public Meaning v. Meaning as Use*. This is important because the Constitution is composed with plain words. I rely upon linguistic research and the views of Ludwig Wittgenstein. And I criticize something originalists call the "public meaning" of words.

Perhaps the most important chapter in the book is *Chapter 5: The Flexible Constitution*. It investigates what any constitution written in plain language necessarily means in a legal system like America's. The point of the Constitution is for generations to arrange ways to follow flexible ideas. So long as the framing generation could understand what we have done with the words, the document has been "obeyed."

The issue of where the Constitution's flexibility ends is taken up in *Chapter*

6: Structuralism and Polysemy. My views about ordinary language constitutions, I contend, are not "willy-nilly." There are meaningful limitations placed upon judges from any historical era who claim to follow the same plain-worded document. Importantly, some of these limitations arise from language itself.

The conclusion to Part I comes in *Chapter 7: Law as Connoisseur Judgment.* The chapter proposes criteria for what constitutional judging is as a *behavior*, and what makes one decision better than another. The chapter relies heavily upon Wittgenstein's views about "aesthetics." Making good constitutional judgment is no different than making good music. They both require a culture of appreciation for the thing in question and for connoisseurs to define what is "correct." Therefore, the Constitution ultimately means what its best connoisseurs determine, not what history says apart from that.

Part II: Understanding Originalism

Part II begins in *Chapter 8: The Philosophy of Framers' Intent.* The chapter investigates "old school originalism." It sets forth an analytic framework, distinguishing between arguments are text-free, text-centered, devotional or formalistic. All of arguments, I contend, share one thing in common: a belief that the wishes of an imagined personification must be obeyed.

A critique of the old originalism is presented in *Chapter 9: Why Framers' Intent is Flawed.* Every argument against the old view is listed in an organized fashion. Toward the end, readers also learn what alternatives exist. Different and new models of interpretation are then presented.

In *Chapter 10: The New Originalism*, I explain how a new generation of conservative thinkers tried to reinvent their belief system. I present a detailed analysis of the maneuvers they make and compare them to the old styles of belief. Special attention is paid to their positions on "authorless texts."

A novel kind of originalism is then explored in *Chapter 11: The Constitution as Old Society.* This view claims to find "the true Constitution" in the beliefs that society held about the provisions when they were being passed into law. The chapter investigates how this belief system works and offers a short critique.

I continue the discussion of past society in *Chapter 12: Cultural Construction.* I present a hypothetical involving time travelers from the framing culture who are summoned to help modernity decide two big cases: abortion and sodomy. Everything the travelers put forth is inherently *opinionated* and culturally constructed. The chapter ends with a summary of how American constitutional practices have developed over time.

Part II concludes in *Chapter 13: What Originalism Really Is.* A formal definition is offered that places originalism *between* positivism and natural law, having certain affinities with both. The new and old forms of belief are also differentiated along novel lines. And I argue why originalism cannot be compatible with the American legal system.

The book concludes with a thought experiment in the Appendix, titled, *The Philosophical Investigation*. The experiment involves the 1960s generation creating a Declaration of Justice (DoJ) that sets forth the right way to live. The DoJ is passed onto children, who claim to accept it. However, the children, known as GenerationX, turn out to be materialistic and wealth-maximizing. The question is then posed: are they violating the document? The parents take the position that they are; the children say they are not. The question ultimately turns upon the wording of a specific provision and arguments about its meaning. In the end, the arguments of the parents are not accepted.

Chapter 1:

Wittgenstein, Law and Originalism

§ 1. Law and Wittgenstein

This book confronts two areas of scholarly literature: works that mix Ludwig Wittgenstein with jurisprudence and scholarship about originalism. I discuss the former first.

(a) John Brigham

In 1978, John Brigham authored a book that was inspired by Wittgenstein. It was titled, *Constitutional Language, an Interpretation of Judicial Decision*. The book tried to show that the decisions made by judges (and lawyers) about the meaning of the Constitution are inherently tied to, or structured by, the document's language and grammar.[1] The book had theoretical aims that were both broad and experimental.[2] And it was written primarily with social science in mind—particularly, the study of judicial decisions by professors of politics.[3] The book relied upon Wittgensteinian ideas about language—only slightly from the Tractatus[4] and overwhelmingly from later works[5]—and also incorporated numerous other views, including Frederick Waismann, Stanley Cavell, Gilbert Ryle, Barry Stroud and even A.J. Ayer.

Although my efforts do not have judicial behaviorism specifically in mind, they nonetheless share an important affinity with Brigham's publication. The most important can be seen in the following three passages. In each, Brigham stresses that the Constitution is a plain-language document. As such, it obtains its meaning from the use and grammar of ordinary expression. He writes:

> [A]lthough it is a legal document, much about the Constitution can be studied in the same fashion as ordinary language. It is in this sense that the linguistic

capabilities of a native speaker of English are a guide to the judicial decision [JBr, 56].[6]

The language of law is not purely legal; it emerges from ordinary discourse. Ordinary language is essential for discussion of legal concepts. It has an on-going significance in their development [JBr, 115].

[I]n considering the linguistic aspects of the Constitution, it is important to demonstrate simply that the meaning of some words emerges from the way we have come to use them. . . . Hence, the use of the ordinary words in the Constitution can be explained in terms of the principles of ordinary language use . . . [JBr, 29-30].

My hope is to build upon these important insights, but in a slightly different way. Compared to Brigham, I place more explicit emphasis upon the Wittgensteinian ideas of family resemblance [4:§2-3] and connoisseur judgment [Chapter 7] when describing constitutional interpretation. And I offer my own thesis for what any judge of a plain-language document, at any point in history, must do to be faithful to its words [6:§3-§4]—something Brigham wasn't attempting.

Also, there is a slight tension in a few areas of Brigham's work that I have attempted to address. The issue concerns the role that legal norms are said to play in constitutional meaning. Do the norms merely *influence* system participants—i.e., affect the way lawyers and judges read the Constitution—or do they reveal the document's "true meaning"? The former is a behavioral thesis; the latter is prescriptive.

Throughout most of Brigham's work, he adheres to the behavioral thesis. He claims, for example, that we can only understand what judges do by understanding the norms and practices of legal culture. Brigham sees legal craft as something that *structures* the behavior of participants when they decide what the Constitution means [6:§1]. He writes:

The law also uses ordinary English, but in a special way. The specialized vocabulary of law evident in the Constitution includes words such as "judgment," "offense," "jurisdiction," "witness," and "probable cause." . . . These words, when interpreted in the Constitution, depend to some degree for their meaning on the tradition in law of the special use to which these English words have been put [JBr, 30-31].

Examples of the grammar of constitutional law which distinguish it from other spheres of language are evident in . . . legal practices such as the case or controversy requirement, the appellate process, the issue of retroactivity, and the legal guarantees of the Bill of Rights . . . [JBr, 93].

But there are other times when Brigham seems to make *prescriptive* claims. He sometimes suggests that the words and phrases in the Constitution (secretly) mean the technical things that lawyers share when using those words together as a community. This claim is different from the one above, because it is not trying to explain why participants behave. Rather, it is trying to say something about the truth of a text. One can see the shift of emphasis in this passage:

> A notion of law, apart from the way law is used, i.e., the way things are re-
> ferred to in law, makes no sense. Since the reference to things in constitutional
> law is basically a linguistic activity, meaning in constitutional law can only ex-
> ist as a result of the way the concepts, principles, and maxims that constitute
> this tradition are used. . . . If meaning in language can only be understood in
> terms of prior examples and the conceptual possibilities they reveal, then the
> same may be true of constitutional law [JBr, 77].[7]

I call this argument the *professional-sense thesis*. In a nutshell, it says that
we have no choice but to give certain words and phrases in the Constitution the
meaning that lawyers have shared when speaking about them in prior conversations. My inclination is to reject this thesis on two grounds.

First, the meaning of plain words can never be automatically closed off
(fixed) merely because of the prior conversations of any group of people [4:§1,(a)-
(c)]. Rather, meaning is fixed only by whatever could be understood when the
words in question are injected into those language games. I call this the *intelligibility thesis* [5:§2]. It says that meaning is always that which *could* be successfully spoken about, not merely those things that already have been.

Second, we cannot treat the enacted law as a private conversation. It's a
public declaration of what the law is. And I contend that American legal culture
treats enacted law as speaking solely for itself—that is the way the philosophy
of legislation works [3:§3; 13:§2]. Therefore, if any generation wants future inhabitants of the country to read certain words in the Constitution with a lawyerly
understanding (only), that generation must make this idea clear in the text of the
document. This could be done with a definition section or with sufficiently precise nomenclature [3:§2]. Otherwise, the judges are forced to pick the best sense
to give the words—whether that results in a lawyerly vernacular or not.

(b) Postmodern Scholars

There have been several scholars since Brigham who have claimed Wittgenstein as a key influence for their jurisprudential views.[8] These scholars are
often called "postmodern."[9] My effort is not in agreement with a good bit of
their critique.

To understand what postmodern scholars have advocated, one must consult
an example. Imagine a lawsuit claiming that the Free Speech Clause[10] protects
the right of corporations to make unlimited campaign donations.[11] Postmodern
scholars approach this constitutional issue like they would any other. The first
maneuver is to claim that there is no correct or superior answer to the question—
the argument begins with a skeptical premise.[12] This is because, they say, constitutional issues cannot be proven true or false in the way that claims of science
can—they can't, in short, be "externally verified."[13] As Dennis Patterson says,

"The problem with virtually all constitutional theory, and much of general jurisprudence, is the continuing need to legitimate the law by resort to some external
source" [DP-2, 136, note 36].

The next maneuver is to claim that "truth" in law is ultimately a function of
having put your argument in the right style. You must affirm or dispute the issue
in the way that the legal culture does. Hence, whether the Speech Clause is
properly taken to give corporations the unlimited power of donation (or not) is
simply a matter of whether the argument for or against comes in the recognized
format—no matter which side wins.

The father figure for this view is Phillip Bobbitt, although Dennis Patterson
has become an equal voice. Bobbitt argues that there are only six acceptable
forms of legal argument, depicted in Table 1.1 [PBt-2, 12-13]. He calls them "modalities." He doesn't anoint the six a priori; he believes they are embedded in the
cultural practices of American lawyering.[14] Because of this, he unfortunately
deduces that no other style of argument is permissible.[15] Or as Dennis Patterson
explains: "[T]here is nothing more to constitutional argument than the six modalities. As [Bobbitt] argues repeatedly . . . the forms of argument answer any
question concerning what is being done" [DP-1, 294, note 78].[16]

I call this view *format-static skepticism.*[17] It claims that the meaning of law
reduces *only* to the (sociological) norms that constitute past legal practice. The
meaning of any clause in the Constitution, therefore, is revealed simply by learning to mimic (or combine) the six ways for creating a position concerning it, no
matter which way the position rules. Another way of saying it: constitutional
analysis is what constitutional culture *does*—the whole thing is just an activity,
like a style of dance [IB-3, 52].

Table 1.1: Bobbitt's Six Styles of Legal Craft	
Mode	**Description**
Historical	Relying on the intentions of the Framers and ratifers of the Constitution
Textual	Looking to the meaning of the words of the Constitution alone, as they would be interpreted by the average contemporary "man on the street"
Structural	Inferring rules from the relationships that the Constitution mandates among the structures it sets up
Doctrinal	Applying rules generated by precedent
Ethical	Deriving rules from those moral commitments of the American ethos that are reflected in the Constitution
Prudential	Seeking to balance the costs and benefits of a particular rule

My efforts oppose this idea on several grounds. I take up the taxonomical
question of what constitutional judgment is in Chapter 7. But, for now, the best
way to show my objection is with an example. So I now turn to the case of
Brown v. Board of Education,[18] which shows not only what is wrong with Bobbitt's vision, but why Wittgenstein shouldn't be associated with it.

(c) Format and Innovation

Examine Table 1.1 and ask yourself a question: what other styles of argument are missing? That is, how is it possible to argue constitutionality *without* appealing to history, text, institutional logic, doctrine, ethics[19] or rule-balancing?[20] One answer, it seems, is to appeal to *science*. And this is precisely what the Warren Court did in *Brown v. Board of Education*, when it relied upon an approach called "sociological jurisprudence."[21]

The approach asks that lawyers and judges consult empirical science when deciding constitutional cases.[22] The Court in *Brown* purportedly did this when it relied upon "doll studies" conducted by Kenneth Clark to show that state-sponsored segregation helped cause an inferiority complex in African American children.[23] This meant that the very *idea* of an "equal separation" could be seen as defective, because it produced a psychological caste as a byproduct—even if equal physical materials (money, supplies, etc.) would have been awarded.

To understand why format-static skepticism is problematic, consider Bobbitt's position on sociological jurisprudence. He says that judges cannot use "coordinate disciplines" like philosophy, psychology or economics to create legal rules. This is because doing so would de-legitimate and impoverish legal analysis[24] and would replace "the legal approach with one for which there is no constitutional authority."[25]

Compare this, however, with John Brigham's view. He has no trouble with judges appealing to "coordinate disciplines," because whatever they appeal to is only for the purpose of keeping constitutional *text* culturally relevant (meaningful). The forms of argument become useless if they discredit the text they serve.[26] The rhetorical style of a brief is therefore never "unto itself." It exists merely as a social practice for saying something about *plain text*. As such, the argument in *Brown* simply allowed an ordinary sense of the term "equal" to triumph, allowing the claim to be *intelligible* to legal culture. Brigham writes:

> To the extent that the claim was "intelligible" in 1954, it depended on a reconstruction of the . . . possibilities in the idea of equality. A new sense was imparted by the Warren Court in its treatment of the issue by the introduction of the psychological evidence presented by the NAACP. It was the intelligibility of the claim imported from ordinary use—that the Constitution prohibited racially segregated educational facilities in spite of particular outcomes to the contrary—which made such an appeal to the Constitution reasonable. Knowledge of the concept and the room to maneuver were fundamental to raising an intelligible claim in this context [JBr, 100].

Importantly, note how Wittgenstein fits into this. Not only does Brigham rely upon an argument about the ordinary use of the term "equal"—which is, of course, a plain and common sort of word [4:§2-4]—but he also relies upon the idea of "grammar." But his version is *not* something static or rule-bound. Like Wittgenstein,[27] Brigham sees grammar as that which allows something to be *intelligible*. Grammar isn't a straitjacket; it's like Play-Doh™.[28] Brigham writes:

> There is an important difference between a statement that a claim in law has a poor chance of being ruled on favorably and a statement that a claim makes no sense at all, i.e., that it is unintelligible. The difference exists because some . . . practices . . . can be designated by rules, while the role these practices . . . play in our lives, i.e., the kind of practices which they are, depends on grammar [JBr, 94-95].

By contrast, note how differently Dennis Patterson approaches this issue. He seems to have Brigham's point backward. He appears to believe that how one can acceptably talk about equal protection is predetermined by the way lawyers have argued in the past. He thinks the briefing behavior is a law unto itself because of something he calls "grammar."[29] He writes, "The practice of law is conducted in the language of the forms: without them there is no law. . . . The forms of argument are the legal grammar of meaning-making. We use the forms of argument to show what the legislatively produced text means."[30]

My efforts wholeheartedly endorse Brigham's views in this respect. Patterson's position on grammar is neither believable nor Wittgensteinian, as other scholars have noted.[31] The forms of argument lawyers make have never been unto themselves. The way that lawyers and judges argue about fundamental law (constitutionality) is itself dependent upon intellectual culture [12:§2]. This means that legal craft changes and develops over time. One of the central flaws of format-static skepticism is that it cannot account for these dynamic features.[32] Not only have other scholars made this point [GM; and IB-1, 159], but even Dennis Patterson himself has acknowledged it.[33] In fact, Patterson has offered an adaptation to Bobbitt's views that addresses this problem, which I consider in a moment.

But my point for now is simple. It is neither true nor Wittgensteinian to say of the ordinary words in the Constitution, that they must somehow depend upon past styles of legal argument for their meaning. The meaning of those words amounts only to the successful things that could be spoken with them in a shared language culture [Chapters 4, 5].[34]

(d) Beyond Skepticism

When postmodern scholars are confronted with the various problems of their orthodoxy, they offer supplemental positions. I want to briefly explore them, because they, too, involve Wittgenstein. The problem is quite practical: how are judges supposed to make decisions in a world where the skeptical thesis is true? What would postmodern scholars have judges do, and why?

Bobbitt's position is interesting. It has the most integrity, because it does not hedge from his central thesis. He argues that judicial choice is ultimately a function of "conscience."[35] This maneuver appears influenced by Tractarian Wittgenstein in the way it commits the ultimate resolution to the realm of the unspeakable (mystical). We could never prove which ruling is truly "correct," so we simply pass over our respective judgments in silence and commit them to our devout inner feelings.

Patterson, however, doesn't like this. He dismisses Bobbitt's conclusion for relying upon a "hidden realm" [DP-2, 142-146, 171]. Instead, Patterson favors an approach that would allow one to "debate-score" legal rhetoric by certain criteria. The arguments lawyers make, he says, can be differentiated by how disruptive they are to the stipulations we want to keep around in the legal system. In short, the better arguments are those that are least disruptive to the assumptions we want to keep in the Legal Complex. He writes, "In choosing between different interpretations, we favor those that clash least with everything else we take to be true. . . . In law, we choose the idea that best hangs together with everything else we take to be true. . . . the degree to which it can be made to cohere with everything else we take to be true about legal texts" [DP-2, 172, 173].

On the surface, Patterson's idea seems to be influenced by Wittgenstein's concern for "assertability conditions." Trouble is, in the end, it only amounts to a proposal for how to become a debating judge. Patterson even uses debate language, saying we can analyze arguments by their "grounds" and "warrants" (and so forth). He even argues that the majority opinion in the famous case of *Riggs v. Palmer*[36] is inherently superior to the dissent for reasons similar to that which a debate coach might offer [DP-2, 172-174].

However, it seems to me that that the activity of judging debates is very different from making constitutional judgments. They are not the same *behavior*. Imagine if the recent health care case was decided using debate criteria from the oral arguments.[37] This isn't what legal judging is. (In Chapter 7, I take up the issue of what constitutional judgment really is, as a behavior).

Another trouble with Patterson's solution is that it no longer bears any relationship to either his or Bobbitt's initial critique. It no longer advocates for skepticism, and it doesn't seem to be static. It also is neither Wittgensteinian nor postmodern. And it seems to render a large gap between the original bark and what is now the bite.

I simply cannot accept the way Bobbitt and Patterson have come to see the issues of truth and grammar in constitutions. Indeed, one of the central features of Wittgenstein's work that has been completely ignored is his views on connoisseur judgment [7:§1]. Constitutional judgment is not unlike a kind of art-appreciation—it's an "aesthetic" in a Wittgensteinian sense. This means it is quite possible to say which renditions of the craft are better than others.[38] The implication here is bold: the Constitution ultimately means what its proper *connoisseurs* say.

And this idea, properly understood, means that the answers to constitutional questions are *not* subjective. They are "correct" in the way that any specimens of a craft or genre are—no matter whether it is cutting hair or making music. There is a learned way to appreciate the constitutional craft that is *not* measured ultimately by past sociology (norms) or even politics—but by good connoisseurs who properly cultivate the aesthetic. Just as certain performances in theater can be remarkably better than others, so too can certain decisions of the Court amount to a superior rendition of the craft [7:§3(a)-(c)].

So, this is the way that my book fits into the existing law-and-Wittgenstein scholarship. And now, I discuss how it affects the literature on originalism.

§ 3. Originalism

The ideas that I propose are in direct conflict with the published views of Keith Whittington,[39] Larry Solum,[40] Randy Barnett,[41] Supreme Court Justice Antonin Scalia[42] and others. Because the language of the Constitution is ordinary [5:§1], it has what Ludwig Wittgenstein called "family resemblance" [4:§2-3]. This means that the text is flexible and requires readers to select *arrangements* for it [5:§1(a)-(c)]. The whole point of a plain-language constitution, in fact, is for different epochs to arrange better ways to follow flexible ideas. There is a different way to follow any provision in the Constitution [5:§2].

Originalists often say that constitutional text acquired a "fixed meaning" at the time it was enacted [LS-1, 33; LS-2, 3]. However, because the document was written in plain language, the only fixed aspect consists in those things that people who use the words could successfully speak about in a shared linguistic culture [5:§1(a)-(c)]. Therefore, so long as the framing generation could understand what we have done with the document's language—so long as we could successfully converse about it—the Constitution has been "followed." I call this the *intelligibility thesis* [5:§2].

The beauty of having a flexible constitution is that it allows judges to shift the sense of ideas to better suit contemporary situations [5:§1(a)-(c)]. It allows them to give the document a distinct vernacular and grammar [5:§4]. Yet, when doing this, I argue that there are important limitations. Judges must avoid "cognitive polysemy" [6:§3(a)-(d)] and must make exemplary judgments predicated upon the best thinking that intellectual culture has [6:§2,4; 7:§3(b)-(c)].

This approach spells trouble for those who want to speak of the Constitution as having "an original meaning," an expression quite popular among American legal thinkers of late.[43] This is because all of the arrangements that could fit the flexible text are "truthful;" none are more linguistically precious [3:§5; App]. So it makes no sense to speak as if the first one is "the real one."

And all of this has implications for several other originalist doctrines. I propose that we reject the false distinction between interpretation and construction [5:§3]. And that the idea of "public meaning" is confused [4:§1(a)-(c)]. I also contend that the position taken by Whittington and Stanley Fish about authorless texts is, at heart, a theology [10:§1(a)]. And I offer several new models of interpretation that break away from the trappings of "speaker's meaning" [9:§2(d)].

Using a philosophic approach, I also offer a framework for classifying the *kinds* of originalism that can exist [Part II]. And the arguments I make about flexible text having a three dimensional structure help, I hope, reveal the inherent complexity in statements about "what the Constitution means" [2:§1-2].

And I offer a new, technical definition for the term "originalism" that I hope will give structure to our future conversations [13:§1(a)].[44] I place the belief system *between* the ideas of natural law and positivism, having affinities and differences with both [13:§1(b)]. This is a breakthrough, I hope, in the common thinking, which treats originalism as being a positivistic school of thought.[45]

Finally, I make the case that originalism is inherently incompatible with modern American legal culture [13:§2]. This is because it does not allow the enacted law to speak solely for itself. Legislative and administrative text in America is linguistically pedantic. It uses language that specifically directs its adherents. This is what makes the law sound "legalistic." Yet, the Constitution exhibits none of these linguistic properties, despite the fact that it sits atop of the American legal system. The document doesn't even contain a definition section.

Because of this, originalism asks us to use history to create a *pretend* constitution. But we cannot do that, because it would alter what legislation is as a *behavior* in the system. It would make lawyers behave as though the document is a religious text. In short, if the framing society had wanted a determinate and stern constitution, it needed to legislate better. Lacking that, we are left with the Constitution that we have.

Notes

1. The term "grammar" refers to the things that make any use of language intelligible. In short, it refers to the assertability conditions that are inherent whenever any ideas are spoken of. Ludwig Wittgenstein introduced the concept to replace the role that the word "logic" had once served in his beliefs [RM-1, 293, 322-23].

2. [JBr, vii]. The preface refers to the "speculative nature" of the work. Also, Brigham writes, "The work employs an approach not yet fully integrated into the study of politics to examine a realm of action not always recognized as political. It is thus speculative on two accounts" [JBr, 3].

3. His book had a very important message for judicial behaviorists in Chapter 3, titled "Beyond the Behavioral Model of Judicial Decision." Brigham writes:

> This chapter concentrates on the attitudinal dimension evident in recent studies of judicial decision making. . . . The intention here is to attack this method not for any failure to accomplish what it sets out to do, but rather for its limits on what is explored. Thus, even with its considerable success in achieving its research goals its value in the study of politics and the legal process is limited [JBr, 36].

The study of language takes for its data an entirely different sphere from that of behaviorism in law. Where behaviorism has been primarily concerned with the attitudinal differences among judges when they dissent on a case, the study of legal language explains the widespread similarities in judicial decision [JBr, 41-42].

4. In Chapter 2, Brigham discusses how aspects of Tractarian Wittgenstein and its offspring can be used to approach certain kinds of words in the Constitution. But he then quickly becomes critical of "the empiricist theory of language," stating:

A modern linguistic perspective on the meaning of words shows the limitations of the approaches which have been derived from the empiricist position. Recent developments in the study of language, which have come from structural linguistics and ordinary language philosophy, challenge the empiricist theory of meaning on the basis of the claimed word-object relationship and the account of language learning by ostensive definition [JBr, 26].

5. The most heavily quoted and cited of Wittgenstein's ideas comes from post-1932 remarks in *Philosophical Investigations* and *The Blue and Brown Books*.
6. Brigham continues:

According to the philosophy of language, one might view the words of the Constitution, like the words of ordinary language, as meaningful not because they refer to specific elements of the world but because their use is governed by conventions akin to grammar. It is not prescriptive rules which determine the relationship between the word and the thing signified, but it is the place the word occupies in the grammatical structure of language which gives meaning to words. The goal here is to show the ways in which words occupy places in these grammatical or linguistic structures. Since the focus is on constitutional law, the function of grammar is shown by examining the way in which linguistic considerations reveal the meaning of the Constitution [JBr, 58].

7. In another passage, Brigham talks about how lawyerly understandings must "necessarily influence" the meaning of the Constitution. He writes:

Law has its own technical vocabulary and also uses ordinary language in a special way. Many crucial words in the Constitution derive their meaning from the legal tradition. . . . [S]uch words as "indictment," "jury," "trial," "case," . . . belong to legal practice and describe the unique practices, institutions, and processes that are peculiar to legal activity. . . . When these words are also used in the Constitution, their meaning is necessarily influenced by the way they have come to be used by lawyers and judges [JBr, 30].

The key issue is whether Brigham is saying that, if a slightly different sense of these words developed outside of legal circles, that it would be necessary for the lawyerly sense to dominate the Constitution. It is one thing to say judges will generally prefer a legal sense because of the way they are trained. That's a behaviorist concern. But it's another to say that the legal sense must be given preference or else the interpretation is "wrong." That's a whole different can of worms. My view on this is clear: if any generation wants the future inhabitants of the country to read any words in the Constitution with a lawyerly sense, the dictates of modern legal culture require that the generation specifically codify that sense in the body of the document, using appropriate nomenclature. Otherwise, judges are free to select the *best* sense of the idea, which may or may not be the lawyerly one.

8. These scholars were unfortunately called "The New Wittgensteinians" in legal circles in the 1990s [GM], but they are not to be confused with another group of scholars outside of legal philosophy who are also called that name (today) for other reasons. The real New Wittgensteinians are those who came to re-evaluate certain standing notions in Wittgenstein studies over the last fifteen or so years. They stress the therapeutic and anti-programmatic aspect of his philosophy and find more connection between Tractarian and later works (than previously thought). Two popular examples of such scholars are Cora Diamond and James F. Conant. The term is only a convenient one, however: none of the scholars have identical views. See Alice Crary and Rupert Read, eds., *The New Wittgenstein* (Routledge 2000).

9. This is the label that Dennis Patterson prefers [DP-2, 151-179]. But it is not without some controversy, as David Bakhurst notes in the following passage:

> Yet in some respects *Law and Truth* is not postmodern at all. Patterson operates with a traditional image of scholarship as a movement from obscure and misconceived theories to transparent and enlightened ones. The book is structured around a "grand narrative," the story of our casting off the yoke of the philosophical misconceptions of modernity to attain an undistorted vision of our practices. . . . Moreover, as I have stressed, Patterson retains a remarkable confidence in the efficacy of philosophical reflection. Postmodernists typically aim to embarrass philosophers by arguing that the discipline has failed miserably in its effort to create a tribunal to assess the knowledge claims of other disciplines. So much for the Queen of the Sciences! Patterson somehow wants to embrace these criticisms, yet keep the philosopher on a pedestal. He is happy for the philosopher to lecture us about how there are philosophical reasons why we cannot ground our practices and why we must rest content with describing or illuminating them. But those of a genuinely postmodern disposition will find this philosopher as tedious a reformed alcoholic denouncing the evils of the bottle. The solution, they will say, is to cut out all these meta theoretical ruminations and get on with illuminating the practices at issue [DB, 400-401].

10. The Clause reads, "Congress shall make no law . . . abridging the freedom of speech, or of the press; or the right of the people peaceably to assemble, and to petition the Government for a redress of grievances." U.S. Const. Amend I

11. See *Citizens United v. Federal Election Commission*, 558 U.S. 50, 130 S.Ct. 876 (2010).

12. See these quotes from Dennis Patterson and Philip Bobbitt respectively:

> The key is to see that the practice of judicial review—or, more broadly, constitutional law—requires no justification. The answer to the skeptic's question of what justifies judicial review is "Why nothing, of course" [DP-2, 136].
>
> What is the fundamental principle that legitimizes judicial review? . . . There is none. It follows from what I have said thus far that constitutional law needs no "foundation" [PBt-1, 237].
>
> Clear, consistent rules can generate equally plausible claims for mutually exclusive results; they may be used to legitimate a variety of actions. In this apparently contradictory method, not in spite of it, our values are created, endure, and prevail [PBt-2, 183].

13. The terms "true" and "false" normally refer to binary outcomes. For example, "the light is red" is a statement that can, in many circumstances, be true or false. But whether the Free Speech Clause protects campaign donations is not something that can be true or false in the same way (the same sense).

But this should not be germane to the issue. All that this does is change the *sense* within which one might discuss a legal result being true. You cannot complain that the terms "true/false" have different assertability conditions in science versus law without first showing that the *sense* of "truth" spoken of in constitutional scholarship fails for its *own* purpose—the way, e.g., that Wittgenstein showed Moore that his sense of "know" was useless for the claim, "I know I have a hand" [LW-8].

Also, the dwelling upon the ideas of real/unreal and true/false creates a false problem—one that Wittgenstein reminded us to avoid. He writes:

> One man is a convinced realist, another a convinced idealist and teaches his children accordingly. In such an important matter as the existence of non-existence of the external world they don't want to teach their children anything wrong. . . . What will the children be taught? To include in what they say: "There are physical objects" or the opposite? . . . But the idealist will teach his children the word "chair" after all, for of course he wants to teach them to do this and that, e.g., to fetch a chair. Then where will be the difference between what the idealist educated children say and the realist ones? Won't the difference only be one of battle cry? [LW-4, §413-14].

14. Bobbitt writes, "This book is a collection of agreements about the use of the American constitution in practice. It describes, by examples, what sorts of combinations and strategies are possible [PBt-2, 182-83].

15. Bobbitt writes,

> The modalities of constitutional argument are the ways in which law statements in constitutional matters are addressed. . . . There is no constitutional legal argument outside these modalities. Outside these forms, an idea about the U.S. constitution can be a fact, or be elegant, or be amusing or even poetic, and although such assessments exist as legal statements in some possible legal world, they are not actualized in our legal world [PBt-2, 22].

16. Patterson continues:

> There is nothing more to constitutional law (or any other body of doctrine) than the use of the six modalities of argument. For jurisprudence, both constitutional and general, the lesson is clear: the essential task of jurisprudence is the accurate *description* of our legal practices of argument and justification. Theory is banished not because it is wrong, but because it is irrelevant. If law is an argumentative practice composed of the six modalities of argument, then the key to understanding law lies in understanding how these forms are deployed in legal argument [DP-1, 294-95]. (Note 80 on same page: "theory means 'a sublime explanatory mechanism,'" citing PBt-2 at 24).

17. The term "skepticism" is used in philosophy to mean certainty isn't possible for the question at hand and that no better answer exists. See Peter Klein, "Skepticism," *The Stanford Encyclopedia of Philosophy* ed. Edward N. Zalta (Summer 2011 Edition) http://plato.stanford.edu/archives/sum2011/entries/skepticism/ (accessed June 12, 2012).

18. *Brown* was decided in 1954; it outlawed racial segregation in public schools.

19. Bobbitt's true position here doesn't really endorse ethical arguments per se, but rather only those arguments that are predicated upon what he calls an "American ethos." He does not mean "moral argument generally," but rather those things which seem "beyond the power of government to compel" by virtue of the way the Constitutions config-

ures liberty/power [PBt-2, 20-21]. He uses an example of a man opposing state-mandated castration under the argument that "the decision to have children is deeply rooted in the American notion of autonomy" [PBt-2, 21]. Another example is the belief in limited government, which means "all residue authority remain[ing] in the private sphere" [PBt-2, 20]. Hence, he writes, "[W]hile the American cultural ethos may encompass cheeseburgers, rock and roll, and a passion for Japanese electronics, the American *constitutional* ethos is largely confined to the reservation of powers not delegated to a limited government" [PBt-2, 21].

20. Note that Bobbitt's system *has* to cut off some forms of argument or else his system of belief fails. For if *any* mode of argument worked, keeping a list of them would become a lexicographic task rather than an act of canonization. This is the way that dictionaries work when they catalogue and update word sense. An open list would say that modalities simply are whatever they do, which is the way that language itself works [Chapter 4]. This, I contend, is what a real Wittgensteinain account of modalities would look like. But Bobbitt's account wants to draw a line between what can properly be said and what cannot in a legal opinion. His views, therefore, are more reminiscent of a Tractarian approach.

21. See Suri Ratnapala, *Jurisprudence* (Cambridge 2009), Chapter 7.

22. The argument is that the law should avoid "legal fictions." Decisions about constitutionality simply shouldn't be predicated upon states of affairs that cannot be validated by empirical studies.

23. I have reproduced Footnote 11 in Warren's opinion, so that one can see the studies it refers to:

K.B. Clark, *Effect of Prejudice and Discrimination on Personality Development* (Mid-century White House Conference on Children and Youth, 1950); Witmer and Kotinsky, *Personality in the Making* (1952), c. VI; Deutscher and Chein, "The Psychological Effects of Enforced Segregation: A Survey of Social Science Opinion," 26 *J.Psychol.* 259 (1948); Chein, "What are the Psychological Effects of Segregation Under Conditions of Equal Facilities?," 3 *Int.J.Opinion and Attitude Res.* 229 (1949); Brameld, *Educational Costs, in Discrimination and National Welfare* (MacIver, ed., 1949), 44-48; Frazier, *The Negro in the United States* (1949), 674-681. And see generally Myrdal, *An American Dilemma* (1944).

24. This view, on its own, sounds very formalistic. There have been many before Bobbitt who have objected to the style of the decision in *Brown*. But one must remember that Bobbitt's critique comes from an anti-formalistic framework. And to understand what separates the one from the other in this situation, one must always focus upon this article of faith: what lawyers have done in the past, behaviorally (culturally), they cannot change in the future. Meaning is always the replication of past behavior. If legal culture innovates, it isn't being "legal" anymore. (I criticize this argument shortly).

25. His point appears to be that, when judges import other disciplines, they are not engaged in the business of *doing* those disciplines. As such, they miss the point of what they *are* in the business to do: make a decision of conscience upon legal arguments that have a proper format. He writes:

What is the proper use of these coordinate disciplines? . . . [D]oing law by reference to the standards of a coordinate discipline, like economics, say, is not doing economics; . . . someone doing law, with the assistance of arguments stolen from other disciplines, is not acting within those other disciplines. Lawyer's history is not just shoddy history; it is the use of historical methods that have been fabricated, re-made for a purpose that is not the historian's purpose. . . . If we import a model—economic, political, etc.—into law we invariably carve away those aspects of the legal situation to which the model is inapplicable. . . . In this way we do not enrich legal analysis by resort to coordinate disciplines; we impoverish it. . . . For if it were taken as the [rule of decision,] it would de-legitimate the analysis, replacing the legal approach with one for which there is no constitutional authority [PBt-2, 173-74].

But notice that Bobbitt also leaves room for the possibility of a new legal world to emerge, so long as it doesn't indulge "the ideal" or "a theory of justice." Such sins come about when we use principles of efficiency, utility (economics) or empirical science to provide analytical support for a rule of law. Instead, Bobbitt prefers things like poetry and drama. He writes:

Does this mean we can be educated to do better, make wiser and more just decisions? Yes: it is only if one conflated legitimacy and justification (perhaps by narrowing one's focus to a single mode) that one would conclude that this was the best of all possible worlds. But let us be clear about how this improvement might come about. The study of history . . . poetry and fiction, drama and biography, enriches the daily experience of legal practice. But the latter is the soil from which justice must grow. Our consciences did not arise from the ideal and they cannot be replaced by it. A theory of justice is a wonderful artifact, like a vase. Any case it could decide would be a travesty of human responsibility [PBt-2, 179].

26. Brigham writes:

In considering the charge that the Brown decision was a sociological and not a legal one, Pritchett agrees that it could not be "legal" because the precedents were against it. . . . It seems possible, however, that if the legal considerations are viewed in terms of the arguments presented, these arguments may be said to follow an established pattern. Although both sides of the argument are presented, the fact that the appeals are made with regard to what makes sense shows the importance of a tradition [that reveals] limits [in] the meaningful use of a concept. It is in this regard that the "grammar" of constitutional language indicates the role of "law" in constitutional interpretation. The linguistic dimensions of law influence the decision-making of judges [JBr, 100-101].

27. Wittgenstein writes, "Grammar does not tell us how language must be constructed in order to fulfill its purpose, in order to have such-and-such an effect on human beings. It only describes and in no way explains the use of signs. . . . The rules of grammar may be called 'arbitrary,' if that is to mean that the *aim* of the grammar is nothing but that of the language" [LW-11, 19, §496-97].

28. Consider these thoughts from Wittgenstein in *Philosophical Grammar*. He writes:

Why don't I call cookery rules arbitrary, and why am I tempted to call the rules of grammar arbitrary? Because I think of the concept "cookery" as defined by the end of cookery, and I don't think of the concept of "language" as being defined by the ends of language. You cook badly if you are guided in your cooking by rules other than the right ones; but if you follow other rules than those of chess you are playing another game; and if you follow grammatical rules other than such and such ones, that does not mean you say something wrong, no, you are speaking of something else [LW-7, 184-185].

His basic point is that we make meaning through "grammar" (assertability conditions). His point is *not* that our behavior must accord to a predetermined set of rules. Lawyers who offer science in legal briefs are not "violating the grammar of law." To the contrary, they are merely using an innovative rhetorical tool that allowed legal culture to make better sense of constitutional words.

29. Ian Bartrum's latest work characterizes Bobbitt's views about grammar in similar terms. He writes of Bobbitt, "Thus, the Constitution can *have no meaning* if not embedded in a shared practice of interpretation, and what legitimates a particular act of interpretation is the *form or grammar* of the argument that it rests upon" [IB-3, 2]. At the end of the article, he writes, "To understand the law is thus to *know how to practice it*, and so to understand the Constitution is to be able to make legitimate assertions about its meanings within the existing grammatical forms. . . . The meaning of a term derives from its proper use within a particular argumentative modality" [IB-3, 52].

30. [DP-2, 178]. He continues on page 142, "Bobbitt's singular contribution to constitutional jurisprudence is in drawing attention to the fact that the modalities are the argumentative grammar of constitutional law. The six modalities are the ways in which ideas of constitutional law are shown to be true or false."

31. There have been persistent criticisms of those who co-opt Wittgenstein as a champion for destructive purposes. Consider Newton Garver's critique of Dennis Patterson's *Law & Truth*. After claiming that Patterson's treatment of Quine is too simplistic, Garver offers this critique of Patterson's treatment of Wittgenstein:

> If the presentation of Wittgenstein is a fair example, what readers learn may sometimes be superficial. Patterson remarks that "in the *Philosophical Investigations* Wittgenstein still toys with the idea of a distinction between the grammatical and the empirical, between non-philosophical and philosophical inquiry" (p.160n). The rhetoric here is partisan and prejudicial. Wittgenstein insists on grammatical ideas being a different use of language than empirical ones, but he nowhere speaks of "the grammatical" as a body of knowledge or a subject matter. And that is just the point: although philosophy is a distinctive activity, it is not a science or an inquiry, in part because neither the grammatical nor philosophical remarks have a distinctive matter or content. Wittgenstein's distinction between grammatical and empirical ideas escapes Quine's strictures just because it is a distinction between uses of language, or what he calls "language-games," rather than between kinds of truth-claims.
>
> Wittgenstein's early work fares no better. Patterson cites a substantial portion of the *Tractatus*, claiming the "picture theory provides us with one expression of the dominant, modernist view of language as representational medium" (p.164). What Patterson does not tell us is that the *Tractatus* also says that logical symbols do not refer, that logical ideas are meaningless or *sinnlos*, and that anyone who understands Wittgenstein will realize that his whole book, which is surely part of language, is nonsense or *Unsinn*. What holds for logic and philosophy also holds for ethics and law: their symbols do not refer and therefore their ideas lack truth-false bipolarity. So a deeper inspection reveals that Patterson distorts both the early and later work of Wittgenstein to suit the brisk rhetoric of his book. Newton Garver, "Book Review," *The Journal of Value Inquiry* 32 (1998): 418.

Similarly, philosopher David Bakhurst offered this comment in a book review of *Law & Truth*: "Patterson does make much of the idea that the forms of argument constitute the 'grammar' of the law. Here again his inspiration is Wittgenstein. Patterson obviously admires Wittgenstein's thought; unfortunately, however, he is prone to invoke Wittgensteinian slogans without adequate explanation" [DB, 399].

32. Ian Bartrum has proposed that Bobbitt's critique should be supplemented with the idea of "metaphorical thinking," based upon the work of Ivan Richards and Max Black [IB-1].

33. Patterson sees this problem through the work of William Eskridge, who introduced a path-breaking approach to statutory interpretation. The approach argued that the meaning of a statute can change over time. When noting this innovation, Patterson remarks, "What is left out of [Bobbitt's] account is any notice of the fact that, within law, participants contest the adequacy of the forms of argument themselves" [DP-1, 295, note 79]. He cites to Eskridge's "Dynamic Statutory Interpretation," 135 *U. Pa. L. Rev.* (1987): 1479.

34. I never take legal meaning to be a static picture (closed). Meaning is use, not merely certain prior uses. Language could never be language and be static. Cognition—how the brain understands something—is as much a part of the idea of grammar as is anthropology.

35. Bobbitt writes, "The recursion to conscience is the crucial activity on which the constitutional system of interpretation that I have described depends. . . . The cultivation of our constitutional traditions requires, as I have endeavored to show, the cultivation of our consciences . . ." [PBt-2, 177]. He continues, "We are incapable of making something that will obviate (rather than suppress) the requirement for moral decision. . . . [E]ach person must . . . defend what he wants to survive ultimately when the one thing he knows for certain is that he himself will not ultimately survive" [PBt-2, 186].

36. 115 N.Y. 506 (1889). This is a famous case involving a grandson who killed a grandfather to keep the latter from cutting him out of the will. The statutory law that governed the case seems to have allowed the murderer to inherit, if read literally, because the lawmakers did not foresee this issue when drafting the text. The true question in the case is whether the Court could repair the statute creatively or whether it was stuck with what appeared to be its fixed and vacant parameter. The majority was persuaded by ethics and made creative arguments that allowed the judges the freedom to deny the inheritance. The dissent argued for brute positivism: the judges are stuck with a bad law and can do nothing to change it. Patterson believes that the majority's argument for construing a statute with an absurd result was not met with sufficient counter-point, and that, as such, we can say who "won" [DP-2, 173-174].

37. It is interesting to note that some thought the government's case poorly argued. *NFIB v. Sebelius* was decided on June 28, 2012, when this book was in its final stage. See http://msnbcmedia.msn.com/i/msnbc/Sections/NEWS/scotus_opinion_on_ACA_from_m snbc.com.pdf.

38. This book, in fact, takes great pains to demonstrate that originalism is an inherently problematic idea—one that amounts to a very serious confusion.

39. [KW-1, KW-2, KW-3].

40. [LS-1, LS-2].

41. [RB-1, RB-2, RB-3].

42. [AS-1, AS-2, AS-3, AS-4].

43. To see this point clearly, examine the following titles, culled from only a cursory search on Google for articles containing the term "original meaning," which I have for-

matted in all capitals for emphasis. (The author's name appears at the end because the title of the piece is the most important information):

- "Abortion and ORIGINAL MEANING," *Constitutional Commentary* 24 (2007): 291, Jack Balkin.
- "ORIGINAL MEANING and Constitutional Redemption," *Constitutional Commentary* 24 (2007): 427, Jack Balkin.
- "The Meaning of ORIGINAL MEANING," *Georgetown Law Journal* 86 (1998): 569, Mark D. Greenberg & Harry Litman.
- "The ORIGINAL MEANING of the Constitution's "Executive Vesting Clause"—Evidence from Eighteenth-Century Drafting Practice," *Whittier Law Review* 31 (2009): 1, Robert G. Natelson.
- "Delegation and ORIGINAL MEANING," *Virginia Law Review* 88 (2002): 327, Gary Lawson.
- "The ORIGINAL MEANING of the Ninth Amendment," *Columbia Law Review* 90 (1990): 1215, Thomas McAffee.
- "Integrating Normative and Descriptive Constitutional Theory: The Case of ORIGINAL MEANING," *Georgetown Law Journal* 85 (1996-1997): 1765, Michael C. Dorf.
- "Land Use Law in the Early Republic and the ORIGINAL MEANING of the Takings Clause," *Northwestern University Law Review* 94 (1999-2000): 1099, John F. Hart.
- "The Lost ORIGINAL MEANING of the Ninth Amendment," *Texas Law Review* 83 (2004-2005): 331, Kurt T. Lash.
- "Sources of Federalism: An Empirical Analysis of the Court's Quest for ORIGINAL MEANING," *UCLA Law Review* 52 (2004-2005): 217, Peter J. Smith.
- "The ORIGINAL MEANING of the Fourteenth Amendment: Panel VI-Did the Fourteenth Amendment Incorporate the Bill of Rights against States," *Harvard Journal of Law & Public Policy* 19 (1995-1996): 443, Akhil Reed Amar.
- "The ORIGINAL MEANING of 'Unusual': The Eighth Amendment as a Bar to Cruel Innovation," *Northwestern University Law Review* 102, no. 4 (2008): 1739, John F. Stinneford.
- "Taking Text Too Seriously: Modern Textualism, ORIGINAL MEANING, and the Case of Amar's Bill of Rights," *Michigan Law Review* 106, no. 3 (Dec., 2007): 487-543, William Michael Treanor.
- "Does Due Process Have an ORIGINAL MEANING? On Originalism, Due Process, Procedural Innovation . . . and Parking Tickets," *Oklahoma Law Review* 60.1 (2007): 1-52, Lawrence Rosenthal.
- "Jack Rakove's Rendition of ORIGINAL MEANING," *Indiana Law Journal* 72 (1996-1997): 619, Raoul Berger.
- "The ORIGINAL MEANING of the Recess Appointments Clause," *UCLA Law Review* 52 (2004-2005): 1487, Michael B. Rappaport.
- "The ORIGINAL MEANING of the Establishment Clause and the Impossibility of Its Incorporation," *University of Pennsylvania Journal of Constitutional Law* 8 (2006): 585, Vincent Phillip Munoz.
- "Juriscentrism and the ORIGINAL MEANING of Section Five," *Temple Political & Civil Rights Law Review* 13 (2003-2004): 485, Rebecca E Zietlow.
- "Symbolic Expression and the ORIGINAL MEANING of the First Amendment," *Georgetown Law Journal* 97 (April, 2009): 1057, Eugene Volokh.
- "The ORIGINAL MEANING of the Establishment Clause," *William. & Mary Bill of Rights Journal* 14 (2005-2006): 73, Robert G. Natelson.
- "The ORIGINAL MEANING of the Establishment Clause and Its Application to Education," *Regent University Law Review* 13 (2000-2001): 111, William F. Jr. Cox.

- *The Fourth Amendment: Origins and ORIGINAL MEANING 602-1791* (Oxford University Press: 2009), William John Cuddihy.
- "ORIGINAL MEANING, Democratic Interpretation, and the Constitution," *Philosophy & Public Affairs* 21, no. 1 (Winter, 1992): 3-42, Samuel Freeman.
- "The ORIGINAL MEANING of "Democracy: Capacity to Do Things, not Majority Rule," *Constellations* 15, Issue 1 (March 2008): 3-9, Josiah Ober.
- "The ORIGINAL MEANING of an Omission: The Tenth Amendment, Popular Sovereignty and 'Expressly' Delegated Power," *ExpressO* 2008. This work is available online: http://works.bepress.com/kurt_lash/2, Kurt T. Lash;
- "New Evidence of the ORIGINAL MEANING of the Commerce Clause," *Arkansas Law Review* 55 (2002-2003): 847, Randy Barnett.
- "The ORIGINAL MEANING of the Commerce Clause," *University of Chicago Law Review* 68 (Winter 2001): 101, Randy Barnett.
- "Trumping Precedent with ORIGINAL MEANING: Not as Radical as It Sounds" *Constitutional Commentary* 22 (2005): 257, Randy Barnett.
- "The ORIGINAL MEANING of the Necessary and Proper Clause," *University of Pennsylvania Journal of Constitutional Law* 6 (2003-2004): 183, Randy Barnett.
- "The ORIGINAL MEANING of the Judicial Power," *Supreme Court. Economic Review* 12 (2004): 115, Randy Barnett.

44. I hope to have the same effect that Austin's treatment of the word "law" had upon those who, when discussing that subject, had been talking past themselves [JA]. The Austinian idea of law—a command from a sovereign—gave people a sharp boundary that was useful and distinct from more grandiose senses ("the law of science"). My definition of originalism will likewise provide more structure to the discourse.

45. See, e.g., Richard Fallon who writes:

[O]riginalists appear to assume that if we are bound by the Constitution at all, we must be bound in the way that the framers and ratifiers wanted, intended or understood us to be bound. This assumption fits naturally with, and indeed is supported by, a traditional strain of legal "positivism"—a general legal theory asserting that questions of law are a species of questions of fact—that equates law with the "commands" of a sovereign, such as the framers and ratifiers. If the Constitution necessarily derived its status as ultimate law from the commands of a sovereign lawgiver, than no other norms, including interpretive norms, could attain the status of ultimate law unless they, too, traced to the same source of sovereign authority. Richard Fallon, *Implementing The Constitution* (Harvard University Press, 2001): 18.

Part I:

Interpreting the Constitution

Chapter 2

Obeying Flexible Commands

§ 1. Three Levels of Analysis

How can a person "follow a rule" that is set forth in flexible language? I contend two things. First, Ronald Dworkin's views on this matter need to be reformed. Second, there are three basic levels of analysis to consider, as indicated in Illustration 2.1. Before one can claim to follow the Equal Protection Clause,[1] for example, one must make (or endorse) three *kinds* of choices: conceptual, criterial and instantial.

Illustration 2.1: Hierarchy in Meaning

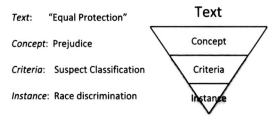

Text: "Equal Protection"

Concept: Prejudice

Criteria: Suspect Classification

Instance: Race discrimination

To understand this better, I now explain the levels of analysis, using the Equal Protection Clause as a vehicle. After this, I explain why Dworkin's position needs to be altered.

(a) Conceptual Analysis

I can think of at least three concepts[2] that compete for the soul of the Equal Protection Clause. The first is a literal or idealistic view. It believes that government must treat every person equally, period. I call this *Even-Steven*.[3]

Imagine a state having two universities, Alpha and Beta, which are identical in the challenges they face regarding student drinking and driving. However, imagine that the police decide to set up a random check-point for DUI violations on thoroughfares located next to Alpha, but not Beta.[4] Although Beta should be every bit as susceptible to receiving this treatment, it isn't being targeted.[5] Does this sort of claim violate equal protection? According to *Even-Steven*, it surely could be *argued* that it does. The matter would ultimately depend upon the criteria selected to implement the concept.

But let's suppose that, upon further reflection, one rejects this as a poor concept. It can't be what the law is all about. Instead, the major concern is for prejudice in democracy. Because majorities historically enact laws that discriminate against certain kinds of people, there is a flaw in the way democracy works. Prejudice comes about from a kind of social pathology—an animus, insecurity or ignorance—toward groups of people in and of themselves. And it can seriously injure. Therefore, the idea that the Equal Protection Clause exists specifically to eradicate this kind of evil, I call *Prejudice*.[6]

But there is yet a third concept vying for consideration. Imagine one who argued that the law required nothing more than for each person to be subject to the same exact rule. So, for example, government could forbid people of different races, or of the same gender, from marrying, so long as each person was being governed by the same rules.[7] Each must be living under the same set of laws.[8] The only thing that is forbidden, therefore, is if a king emerged in the system and declared himself above the law—having rules unto himself—or if slaves were declared unfit for the ordinary social order ("below the law"). This is another way of saying that equal protection only means that the rule of law must exist.

I name this concept *Vacuous*. The reason is because the American legal system already had the rule of law before it enacted the Equal Protection Clause. Hence, *Vacuous* seems to render the clause meaningless (superfluous). In a manner of speaking, it erases it.

(b) Criterial Analysis

After making a conceptual judgment, one must make criterial choices. If *Prejudice* is the main idea, for example, the next issue is how to implement it. Do laws that forbid women from administering estates count?[9] To answer this, we need criteria.

Consider these. "Women cannot claim to be victims of government prejudice because they: (a) are a majority of the voting-age population; and (b) have free and unobstructed access to the vote."[10] Therefore, the Equal Protection Clause can't apply to women. I call this *Formalistic-Numerosity*. The alternative argues that prejudice isn't about having a certain number of members, per se; it is about how power is socially constructed—wealth, education, social norms, etc. Thus, if any group becomes unfairly castigated by "power-groups" within government, they can seek redress. I call this *Suspect-Classification*.[11]

(c) Instantiations

The last unit of analysis concerns winners and losers. The term "winning" here means only that the *facts* in the case become acknowledged as a rightful example of the concept and criteria. Losing means the opposite: the facts are not so regarded. So, when bans on interracial marriage were struck down,[12] interracial marriage became a winner for the Equal Protection Clause.[13] I call this an *instantiation*.

Imagine one day that a police officer is fired for having long hair. Imagine further that he claims a violation of equal protection, under the concept of *Prejudice* and the criteria of *Suspect-Classification*. His argument is that long-haired males receive a kind of power-group abuse in certain government industries and jobs—and that history will come to see this as resulting from an improper impetus. The point: a judge now must decide whether this particular item (long-haired male police officers) should be a winner or loser. When this judgment is made, an instantiation occurs.[14]

§ 2. Decision Trees

The levels that I just described are pictured as a *decision tree* in Illustration 2.2. The tree contains three potential concepts vying for consideration, each facing its own criterial needs and structuring its respective instantiations.[15]

Illustration 2.2: Three Levels of the Decision Tree

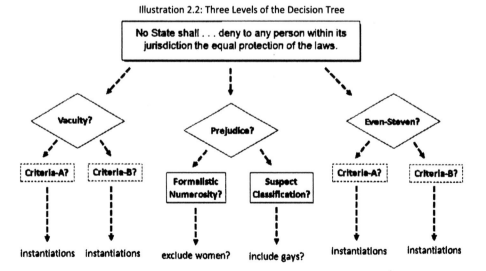

Real legal decision trees are no doubt more complicated. The additional complexity involves *sub-criteria*. These are the same sorts of things that criteria are, only they descend in the tree from themselves. As such, even with complex trees, one can still speak of three basic *kinds* of things.

Also, a tree could exist for a court as well as for each individual justice. It works for any entity claiming to "state the law."

(a) Interrelation

But how does the tree work? Do judges work upward or downward? Presumably, this has to do with the type of cognition (thinking) being used. Perhaps, on occasion, an instantiation is made for the sole purpose of creating or adjusting concepts/criteria (result-oriented). On other occasions, perhaps not. Surely there are examples from the bench, and elsewhere, that can fit either modus operandi.

The fact is that the role of the instantiation in the tree is complicated. In some cases the factual scenario that wins could be fairly said to be predetermined. In this situation, judges have articulate criteria in hand and see no need to make alterations. But in other cases, the winning scenario could usher in major new adjustments to criteria or even the governing concept.

There is, however, an important enthymeme here. It is not possible to use any part of the tree without implicating other parts. And so, every concept requires at least *some* criteria for the law to be administered. Every litigant seeking an instantiation has no choice but to advocate for some combination of concept/criteria. So, all three levels of analysis are interconnected—none can operate autonomously or without consequence upon the others.

This becomes important when considering a position that Jack Balkin espouses. Balkin apparently believes that lawmakers can intend a specific concept, like *Prejudice*, when setting forth the Equal Protection Clause, but are not allowed to intend criteria for it. I criticize this view in the next chapter [3:§4, note 35]. The counterview comes from McGinnis and Rappaport, who argue, in essence, that how *Prejudice* would have been articulated in specific cases "will often be some of the best evidence of what that meaning is."[16]

The difficulty with Balkin's position is that he appears to see concepts somehow operating autonomously, detached from their tree.[17] If, however, it is normal for the implementation of the law to adjust and change when being brokered against a new instance—so that specific cases sometimes cause criteria to change or shift—then one cannot simply dismiss instantial preference. The question of what any person in history meant when espousing a concept, therefore, may have to account for what he or she would have done when encountering this or that instance. This, after all, is what casuistry is all about [7:§3(a)-(b)].[18]

Having just explained how levels of analysis work, I now move on to discuss Ronald Dworkin.

§ 3. Reconsidering Dworkin

Ronald Dworkin has controversial views about how to follow flexible rules. He appears to frame the problem as having two, not three, dimensions. He also seems to believe that obeying a person's concept makes for a "better following," perhaps not seeing the issue of rival concepts. And he thinks that a flexible rule is followed best when all parties agree with the judgment after the fact.

To begin, consider Dworkin's famous distinction between a concept and its "conception." He describes a parent who tells his children not to treat others unfairly. Dworkin sees two basic levels at which "fairness" can be understood: as a concept (in general) and as specific examples. He writes:

> Suppose I tell my children simply that I expect them not to treat others unfairly. I no doubt have in mind examples of the conduct I mean to discourage. But I would not accept that my "meaning" was limited to these examples, for two reasons. First, I would expect my children to apply my instructions to situations I had not and could not have thought about. Second, I stand ready to admit that some particular act I had thought was fair when I spoke was in fact unfair or vice versa, if one of my children is able to convince me of that later; in that case I should want to say that my instructions covered the case he cited, not that I had changed my instructions. I might say that I meant the family to be guided by the *concept* of fairness, not by any specific *conception* of fairness I might have had in mind [RD-7, 134].

Here is the difficulty. If the father admits that one of his instantial preferences turned out to be "wrong," the issue turns on what he and the child share in common that allow for this agreement. It could be that: (a) the father's concept of fairness changed; (b) new criteria were adopted; or (c) poor information existed for that instantiation [2:§3(a)]. So the question of whether the boy followed the father's instructions is complicated. If the father and the boy agree after the fact, we can only admit of their happiness. Nothing more can be said. For it is quite possible for them to have disagreed over the concept, criteria or instantiation—with the boy still properly claiming to have "followed."

To see this more clearly, consider Dworkin's discussion of how a manager should follow his boss's command. In this situation, unlike the one above, disagreement with the choice seems likely after the fact. There is no harmony. Dworkin writes:

> Suppose a boss tells his manager (without winking) to hire the most qualified applicant for a new job. The boss might think it obvious that his own son, who is an applicant, is the most qualified; indeed he might not have given the instruction unless he was confident that the manager would think so too. Nevertheless, what the boss *said*, and *intended* to say, was that the most qualified applicant should be hired, and if the manager thought some other applicant better qualified, but hired the boss's own son to save his own job, he would not be following the standard the boss had intended to lay down [AS-1, 116].

I contend that this view is confused. The issue is not what the boss intends to say in language, versus what he[19] expects to result. It is what the boss intends for his central concept; what criteria are in mind and what instantiations are expected. All three levels of analysis are in play. We cannot speak as though only the boss's concept is his language ("semantic intent").

Note that this poses a more daunting challenge to the idea of "intention." It's quite reasonable to assume that, in many cases, the specifics of one or more of the three levels are incomplete.[20] And it's not that they are incompletely communicated; it is that they are incompletely *intended*. In this situation, the only thing we could speak of as a universal are the various behaviors that the utterance could support in the language culture— i.e., its grammar—and the way that this particular language game is expected to be played [6:§1, note 4].

The truth is that this example is no different from the one of the parent (above). If the boss and manager happen to agree after the fact, all that can be admitted is that their outcome was happy. Nothing more can be said with respect to rule following. This is because, if they disagree, the manager can properly claim to have "followed the order" in one of three different ways, which I now venture to show.

(a) Three Levels of Analysis

The most obvious reason for the boss and manager to reach different results is simply because of differences in hiring *criteria*. Imagine a committee of five people charged with hiring the best college professor. The majority stresses publication and teaching; the minority, teaching and collegiality. The different criteria could, quite obviously, produce different recommendations.[21]

But note that even those sharing perfectly *identical* criteria may not pick the same person, simply because of *informational* problems. When hiring someone, you never know how good the person is; you only get an idea of it. Hence, even among those having "clone criteria," there could be factual disagreement about which candidate best meets them. Differences like these are only *instantiating,* because they purport to select different winners or losers while sharing an identical overall outlook.[22]

But what about conceptual disagreement? Where is that one? At first blush, it is difficult to see any rival concepts. But ask yourself: what is the basic *behavior* required to carry forth this task? On one hand, it seems to require an aesthetical or connoisseur judgment [7:§1]. That is, it seems to tell the manager to become a knowledgeable industry employment critic. It tells him to formulate a conception about what is "the best" for this occupation.

Yet, upon further reflection, it isn't clear that this is required at all. Note that the boss *already has* criteria in mind: he thinks it "obvious" that the son is most qualified. If one pictures the boss to be an oaf, that is one thing. But let's assume the boss is sufficiently learned in these matters, and that his sentiment is considerate. Indeed, perhaps the son is quite a good specimen who was groomed for this work.

So, if the boss already has good criteria in mind for an aesthetical judgment, does the command "hire the most qualified" order you to *validate* those criteria (second guess them)? Or does it simply require you to implement the boss's *sense* of best? That is, are you to *justify* his criteria or simply *fetch* them?

Note that when two connoisseurs are charged with making a choice, there is a different problem in the *theory* of choice than when the matter is between connoisseur and not [7:§1]. Assuming the boss is an expert in these matters, his sense of "best" might only ever be disputable in the way that those who pick academy award winners might disagree. And the difficulty with *you* choosing job criteria from one expert in the field over what your boss has in mind is that the grounds for the switch may be like picking Beethoven over Bach. And this simply may be difficult where the person in authority has already suggested to you that Bach-like things are "best."

And so, there are two options here. You could take the boss's command *literally* (and detached), or you can read it as being *perspectival*. If you feel forced to select the best, period, this position is called *Sanctified*. It makes *you* the connoisseur: you pick the criteria. But if you simply go with the boss's considerate criteria, knowing that any difference here only amounts to reasonable disagreement, this makes you a simple administrator. This is called *Servitude*.

And the point is that this dilemma involves *conceptual disagreement*. There is now more than one concept vying for consideration.[23] Each constitutes a different sort of *behavior*. One tells you to be a connoisseur; the other tells you to be an administrator.[24] Illustration 2.3 shows the problem.[25]

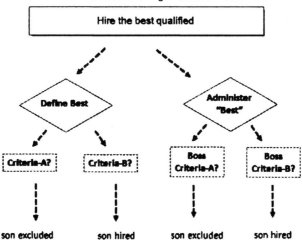

Illustration 2.3: Following a Boss's Command

(b) Conclusion

The point of this is to show that Dworkin's hypothetical presents a three-dimensional conundrum. One can imagine different people claiming to validly obey the boss's order by following one of three different things (concepts, criteria or instantiations). And every person who followed each one differently could all claim to have carried out the very *same* order.

And the question that haunts us is: what is the real order here (the real following)? And should it be troubling to us if, in fact, "the following" is allowed to be *all* of the examples? For isn't it the truthful case that no one in the scenario I just described failed to obey the order? No matter if they followed different concepts, used different criteria or simply had instantiating differences—all of them could rightfully be said to have "followed."

And if, by accident or training, the parties are in agreement after the fact, all that we can admit to is their happiness. We cannot say that this state of affairs constitutes "the real following." For it only constitutes what it is: two people being happy, either by accident or training.

Notes

1. To begin, consider what it says: "No State shall . . . deny to any person within its jurisdiction the equal protection of the laws."

2. The Wittgensteinian in me would rather refer to these as *pictures of account*, not concepts. For that is what they really are. However, because philosophers with certain kinds of orientations have chosen a certain way to speak about the matter, I feel forced to wear someone else's shoes.

3. I'm naming the concepts so I can depict them in Illustration 2.2.

4. Assume for purposes of the discussion that the police do not rotate their location: they don't, for example, police Alpha this month and Beta next month. Hence, how they behave toward Alpha bears no relationship to how they behave toward Beta.

5. I've left it purposely ambiguous as to who is complaining. One could imagine different kinds of complaints coming from (say) the drinkers or bar owners in Alpha versus the community residents of Beta. If there are consequences for enrollment, one could imagine administrators having certain complaints.

6. Note that the central difference between it and *Even-Steven* boils down to who the customer of the right is. Alpha and Beta seem to be out of the concern now, because they are not victims of social prejudice (discrimination) in the sense that is suggested. Their issues are no different from anyone else who has to deal with how the sheriff allocates policing units (or which houses the post office delivers to first). Fundamentally, the universities are "out" because the idea is no longer that government must be angelic or free of favor. Rather, it is only that government must be free of a kind of pathological orientation toward groups of people in and of themselves.

7. This was argued in *Loving v. Virginia*, 388 U.S. 1 (1967):

[T]he State argues that the meaning of the Equal Protection Clause, as illuminated by the statements of the Framers, is only that state penal laws containing an interracial element as part of the definition of the offense must apply equally to whites and Negroes in the sense that members of each race are punished to the same degree. Thus, the State contends that, because its miscegenation statutes punish equally both the white and the Negro participants in an interracial marriage, these statutes, despite their reliance on racial classifications, do not constitute an invidious discrimination based upon race.

8. Similarly, if the law says that police have discretion when deciding where to locate DUI check-points (the Alpha/Beta example above), the law, again, is being applied equally to everyone—because each university is living under the risk of the police using its discretion in the way it does. Therefore, so long as no one is living under a different set of laws, the Equal Protection Clause is not violated.

9. *Reed v. Reed*, 404 U.S. 71 (1971).

10. See *Adkins v. Children's Hospital*, 261 U.S. 525, 553 (1923): "But the ancient inequality of the sexes, otherwise than physical . . . has continued "with diminishing intensity." In view of the great—not to say revolutionary—changes which have taken place . . . in the contractual, political and civil status of women, culminating in the Nineteenth Amendment, it is not unreasonable to say that these differences have now come almost, if not quite, to the vanishing point."

11. Note that the idea of a "suspect class" tries to differentiate situations where power groups are *rightfully* allowed to etch their preferences into law. For example, children are denied the right to do certain things. College students are also not allowed to do certain things. And young adults age 18 to 20 cannot consume alcohol. Are any of these situations an example of power-group abuse? The answer depends upon whether children, college students or 18-year-olds are socially castigated and receiving substantial injury as a result of a prejudice or pathos that history will come to vindicate. Current trends in thinking would seem to say "no."

12. *Loving v. Virginia*, 388 U.S. 1 (1967) (Interracial marriage violates both the Due Process Clause and the Equal Protection Clause).

13. Notice that winners can become quite hairy to define when the area of law is complicated. Take, for example, gender discrimination under the Equal Protection Clause. It's not exactly clear when gender discrimination is allowed. So, it would be incorrect to say that "gender" itself is a winner. Rather, only the facts that have prevailed for any specific case wins. In *Reed v. Reed*, e.g., the winner was women administering estates. 404 U.S. 71 (1971).

14. Also, it isn't possible for every scenario to win; the law has to have losers. Once one situation wins, this creates the grounds for another to come along. And if that wins, still another. At some point, litigants have to lose or else the law seems not to have parameters. And so, in the case of Equal Protection, one has to decide whether to give protection (and how much) for all sorts of scenarios alleging discrimination on account of race, gender, sexual orientation, poverty, national origin, alienage, hair-length (and others).

15. Note that if any two concepts happen to conflict or are contradictory, the selection of one would cause the other "branches" to be "clipped." Therefore, one might think of Illustration 2.2 as showing *potential* branches (choices). Trees are allowed to have more than one branch if they do *not* conflict. For example, the Due Process Clause has

both a substantive and procedural component.

16. John O. McGinnis and Michael Rappaport, "Original Interpretive Principles as the Core of Originalism," *Constitutional Commentary* 24 (2007): 371, 378. See also, Keith Whittington, who argues that, "If the founders gave examples of how they thought the constitutional principle would work in practice, then that is helpful to understanding what the constitutional principle is that they adopted . . ." [KW-2, 517].

17. Balkin is concerned with the issue for this reason. He likes the rhetoric used by certain members of Congress when passing the Equal Protection Clause—talking about ending castigation in America—but doesn't like the fact that those same people would not have applied the idea to, e.g., homosexuals. The philosophic question becomes whether the drafters are contradicting themselves or simply have a different cultural construction of the concept in mind (different criteria) [3:§4].

18. Casuistry is a term that describes a type of moral reasoning. It refers to the consideration of morality one case at a time ("case-based moralizing"). The basic idea is that morality is a function of its circumstances, which are announced and differentiated one problem at a time. Implicit in the idea are two notions. The first is that concrete problems should inform abstract ideas, and that induction is more helpful to morality than deduction. The second is that the task involves comparison-and-contrast reasoning. For more on casuistry, see Albert R. Jonsen, Stephen Edelston Toulmin and Stephen Toulmin, *The Abuse of Casuistry: A History of Moral Reasoning* (University of California Press, 1990).

19. Dworkin's hypothetical has the participants being male. I've kept it that way only for consistency's sake.

20. One could even imagine specifics being incomplete, to some extent, for *all three* levels. A person might have vague ideas for one or another concept, and not have thought much about criteria. Or perhaps one has very specific things in mind for all three levels, but has not been very articulate. Still yet, a person might only have a sole instantiation in mind and wish you to construct the concept and criteria for it—to validate it, so to speak. The thesis that I espouse throughout this book is that, very often, ordinary language games involve more than just language; they involve people learning to complete the messages of others for them, as a kind of assistance. For this is what communication is in this context: a request for assistance [4:§5; 6:§1, note 4].

21. The same goes for sub-criteria: if members disagree about what constitutes (say) a "good publication," the different sub-criteria could produce different results.

22. What is really happening is that people are using different methods for *weighing* the information. For example, one might be using a gut feeling about (say) the evidence for collegiality, while another is using the memory of a past experience. These might be thought of as *intervening criteria*, because they arise from ideas different from the ones that the committee is charged to implement. That is, they stem from beliefs about how to weigh certain evidence, not from the idea of what constitutes "the best candidate." However, because everyone agrees, in theory, what constitutes a best candidate, they are all "on board" at least for the order they are charged to implement. As such, their differences are only instantiating; they are not conceptual or criterial.

23. Some may argue that, if a person followed *Servitude,* no issue would exist with criteria, since that only requires one to follow the boss's criteria. Hence, the idea of a concept and criteria are superfluous. The reply here is straight-forward. The boss's criteria are not explicitly provided for (in the hypothetical). One needs to ask: "What sorts of things does the boss have in mind?" And this is as much of a *criterial problem* as if one

were to pick criteria irrespective of the boss's desires.

Another argument is that the *Servitude* and *Sanctified* are simply criterial disputes hiding in disguise, making the idea of "concept" superfluous. This also misses the key point. To carry out the boss's directive, the first question that must be answered is: how do I behave? Do I administer, or do I (myself) define? This initial step is what structures the criteria I will need to pick. Hence, step 1 is different from step 2.

24. Some may present the *cynic's argument*. It goes something like this. There are not, in reality, three levels of problems here—there are only ever instantiating problems. The other two are false. This is because ideas and criteria are constructed *after the fact* and, therefore, come about reflexively. The cynical argument says, in essence, that one hires the employee as a "brute matter"—impressionistically, politically (perhaps)—and tidies up the reasons after the fact.

This is a poor argument for two reasons. The idea that an expedient, poor, devious or shorthand thinker can somehow threaten an otherwise cautious or contemplative thinker is not a convincing idea. And if the argument is saying that our very form of life (existence) is so brutish and dismal—or that the world is so corrupt—that none of us could ever truly have "principles," one needn't concede this as a *thesis*. For if such a thing was ever true, it would only be so as a *case*. And this is because it would take far more *thinking* on behalf of the cynic to build this case into a reliable generality than the very thesis itself allows. And as such, any thinking at the *level* of a thesis has no choice but to admit of our genuine thinking capacities, lest its own very claim lay in the same ruins it heaps upon others.

25. Note that the illustration shows that it is possible to use the boss's own criteria, yet still not hire his son. There are two reasons why this is possible. First, the boss may simply be mistaken as to the strength of the applicant pool: there might be a "ringer" that is better, even under the boss's own expectations. Secondly, it could be that trying to follow the boss's own criteria is difficult. One could easily imagine two people disagreeing about what they think the boss likes. In the hypothetical, of course, one cannot ask the boss for help, because the scenario is not meant to illustrate a managerial problem—it's meant to show a conundrum for philosophy of law.

Chapter 3

Is There a Fixed Meaning?

§ 1. The Baptismal Thesis

Larry Solum is a philosophically-oriented legal scholar and key proponent of originalism. He believes the law acquires a "fixed meaning" when it is enacted. Therefore, for Solum, the Constitution became vested with a definite understanding at the point of its passage. He writes:

> [M]ost or almost all originalists agree that original meaning was *fixed* or determined at the time each provision of the Constitution was framed and ratified. We might call this idea *the fixation thesis.* . . . The idea that meaning is fixed at the time of origination for each constitutional provision serves as the common denominator [for originalism]. Thus, *the fixation thesis* might be described as a core idea, around which all or almost all originalist theories organize themselves.[1]

Note that Solum's thesis is predicated upon a key legislative behavior: when members officially record their approval of a bill. Or when, as they say, "the ayes have it."[2] It is at this point when the law officially receives its "blessing," an act which, for Solum, christens a definite understanding of some sort. It's not, of course, that such an understanding failed to exist before the blessing; it's that it wasn't *law* until this occurred. Therefore, because the ritual of adoption is the central feature in the argument, one can understand Solum as espousing a *baptismal* account of meaning.[3] Of course, it's not just Solum who espouses this; Keith Whittington is also a key proponent.[4]

But what, actually, becomes "baptized?" What becomes fixed? Note how this idea changes remarkably depending upon whether we are talking about the *document* or a specific *provision*. As a document, the Constitution might be taken to say something about, e.g., classical liberalism and Enlightenment political thought, setting forth a plan of government to provide for the general welfare.[5] But when saying that a specific *provision* means something fixed, the issue seems to be of a markedly different kind.

But here is the critical point. For the baptismal thesis to say anything meaningful about any single *provision*, it must say that a specific concept, criteria or instantiation[6] has *already* been legislated upon, to the exclusion of rivals, for the given piece of text. Otherwise, if all that the baptismal account said is that, "the language is spoken," it would seem to be a vacuous thesis. It must, therefore, *select* something at some unit of analysis. It must posit that a specific concept, criteria or instantiation has already been legislated upon to the exclusion of rivals, for the given text. And the next question becomes: how?

§ 2. Language Rigidity

One of the obvious ways that legal language could specifically enact any concept, criteria or instantiation is to simply state them clearly in the body of the text. Quite often, in legal culture, one finds language that is specific, directive, complicated, dense or "legalistic." When composition is like this, it is helpful to think of the text as having *rigidity*.[7] The key feature is the removal of *rivals*.

When legal language is rigid, it removes rival meanings along three potential units of analysis. First, if the text specifies only one concept to use—meaning it is impossible to use a rival concept and still claim to be compliant with the language—it has *conceptual-level rigidity*. The discussion of Dworkin's boss in Chapter 2 showed the difficulty of obtaining this state of affairs even with the simple statement, "Hire the most qualified person" [2:§3]. The Fourth Amendment discussion later in this chapter shows something similar [3:§4(b)]. One way that the law can provide conceptual rigidity is to provide a definition section, so that ideas like "unreasonable search" or "most qualified" are better defined.

Secondly, if the law specifies criteria for any concept—if the criteria are already laid out for us to the exclusion of rivals—legal text has *criterial rigidity*. This, of course, can be full or partial if the law only sets forth *some* of the criteria. A good example might be found in administrative regulations. They often fill in the gaps of the ideas found in statutes, so that the administration of the law is more directive (concrete).

Thirdly, if legal text specifically codifies a single instantiation, it is rigid at the level of a specific judgment. To see an example of this, consider rules 401 and 411 of the Federal Rules of Evidence, which read as follows:

> "Relevant evidence" means evidence having any tendency to make the existence of any fact that is of consequence to the determination of the action more probable or less probable than it would be without the evidence. Rule 401 (2009)
>
> Evidence that a person was or was not insured against liability is not admissible upon the issue whether the person acted negligently or otherwise wrongfully. Rule 411 (2009)

In this situation, the law sets forth the idea of "relevance," and then proceeds to enact a *judgment* for it. Whether a person has liability insurance cannot
be relevant evidence to show that a person acted negligently—it can never be a
"winner" for this area of law. This is an example of the text specifically enacting
an instantiation.

Also, one could think of examples where the law fixes certain instantiations
by disallowing people to litigate claims. Consider a Bill of Attainder.[8] This is a
law that tries to make one or more specific litigants win or lose, without the
benefit of a trial. Another example is a law that strips jurisdiction from the
Court, such as when Habeas Corpus jurisdiction is revoked. Both of these have
the effect of trying to rig certain case results, when the law might otherwise have
resulted differently—which is why the legislature wants to close the courtroom
doors. Immunity laws that bar certain tort lawsuits do the same sort of thing.

So my point, then, is to show how legal language can be rigid at three distinct levels of analysis. The enacted law can speak at the level of concepts, criteria or instantiations. But as I will soon argue, the Constitution doesn't have
significant rigidity in its text [Chapters 4, 5]. The provisions simply have too many
missing "blanks." And that causes a problem for the baptismal thesis. For if the
text of the Constitution is not rigid, how can the law (silently) enact the meaning
needed to make its language useful?

§ 3. History as Law

Is it possible for history to tell us what is missing from the Constitution?
One of the interesting problems with this idea is what it believes about philosophy of legislation. When legislators pass a law, what, exactly, becomes enacted?
I contend that only two possibilities exist. Either the language itself is enacted,
or a cultural orientation becomes prescribed, for which the text serves only as a
celebration or gesture. The question is whether the text is taken to say something, on its own, or merely to point to it, as though it were a kind of toast.

My contention throughout this book is that modern American legal culture
is "positivistic." When I use this word, it is similar to what other people mean
when they say "hyperlexis."[9] It means that the lawyering culture requires everything to be spelled out. It is characterized by comprehensive codes, "statutification,"[10] dense administrative regulations, definition sections, elaborate and thick
contractual clauses, fine print, exceptions, wherefores and whatnot. Lawyering
in America is simply linguistically *pedantic*. That is the way that the language
games are set up. And this is because modern American legal culture treats the
enacted law as speaking solely for itself. This is, in fact, what makes the language become "legalistic" [13:§1-§2].

Keith Whittington does not agree with this idea. He believes that constitutional provisions are not allowed to become "autonomous." For him, the Constitution always silently enacts its authorial, linguistic and social context (revealed

through history).[11] But this view, I contend, flirts with an idea of "constitution" that is not legalistic and contradicts his other claim that the *text* must be regarded as "fundamental law."[12] If the text merely celebrates and points to a specific historic outlook, arrangement or understanding, the fundamental law would become only the homage owed to that cultural or historic setting.[13] In essence, the Constitution would become something sacramental; it would become a *gesture*.

Whittington also thinks that what makes the Constitution "legal" is the simple fact that majorities legislated upon something—that they etched their will into a public writing. He therefore speaks of the document as being an act of popular sovereignty, where a society bound its progeny to an expressed desire.[14] However, I contend that modern positivistic legal culture doesn't take the act of passing the law to say, "I legislated you," as in, "I dominated." Rather, it only takes it to say, "Follow these words." And by virtue of the way legal culture reads language, the only way one's will can dominate another is if the effect of the text is to say, "My words have pinned you, cognitively."

This is why, in fact, legal language is so pedantic. The law has to be dense, defined and full of legalese to reduce the wiggle room of the people it wants to regiment. As such, legislation cannot stand in a symbolic way to any people's historic wills, cultural practices or outlooks: it must explicitly state the behavior prescribed. Otherwise, people can validly claim not to be bound in courts of law. That is what it means for something to be "legalistic" [13:§1-§2].

Therefore, one of the central problems with originalism in a modern legal culture is what it believes about how legal text acquires meaning [13:§2]. Simply put, it isn't possible for any concept, criteria or instantiation to already be enacted unless the *language* used for that provision made no other inference linguistically possible. In other words, for these things to already "be there," the text must specifically state them.

In American legal culture, lawmakers only ever enact the text itself. Legislation is only ever its *language*. As such, if legislative bodies—including constitutional conventions—want to try to mandate principles, force criteria or rig the specific winners and losers in the courts, they have to pass articulate nomenclature. They have to pass, in short, definition sections, detailed clauses and sentences—something the Framers of the Constitution never did.

§ 4. Abstract Principles?

Another idea for how the provisions of the Constitution might be fixed comes from so-called "liberal scholars" like Jack Balkin. They believe that certain "abstract principles" are clearly embedded in the text of the document. Therefore, they believe that some provisions are conceptually rigid. If true, this would mean that the very top of law's "decision tree" [2:§2] is already provided to judges, at least for some issues. This would leave judges the task of filling in only criteria and drawing instantiations—or, perhaps, supplying additional concepts that do not conflict with the ones already believed to be "there."

I contend that this view is problematic. Merely because it stops at the top of the decision tree does not make it immune from the same objections I levied against Solum and Whittington. Whether constitutional text is conceptually rigid is a function of its language, not of history. This means that, if it is *linguistically* possible to assert a rival concept for the text—if the language culture could support that way of talking—there is no basis to say that the rival has already been legislated upon (excluded).

At times, Balkin flatly rejects this. The view he announced in two popular law review articles essentially reduces to the following idea: where the Constitution uses general phrases like "due process" or "equal protection," it is permissible to use *history* to reveal the intended concept, but not its criteria or instantiations.[15] The only difference between this claim and the ones espoused by conservative originalists, therefore, is how much specificity history is allowed. Conservatives would use the past to tell them criteria and possibly instantiations [8:§3(b), note 15]; "liberal originalists," by contrast, would use it only for concepts.

For example, Balkin takes the position that certain speeches or debates from the Senate in 1866 show that the Fourteenth Amendment[16] enacted an "antisubordination principle" that was against class and caste legislation.[17] From this, he builds an argument that the "original meaning of the amendment"[18] protects abortion rights, even though the same speechmakers would disagree. He also says that it protects gays from discrimination even if "nobody" would have approved of that.[19] Properly reduced, his view seems to be that any special concept he can find in various speeches can function as though it were text in the Constitution itself.

I contend that this view is seriously confused. First, the speeches of legislators are not what are legislated upon. Secondly, because the text that *is* legislated upon doesn't say what Balkin wants (exactly), he cannot treat the provision as having been silently rewritten.[20] The reason is because it upsets the way that modern American legal culture works. Balkin's idea would make the Constitution a celebration or gesture to some other event in history—in this case, the speeches—rather than a document that spoke solely for itself [13:§1-§2].

I also can see absolutely no basis for discriminating among levels of analysis in meaning while using an argument predicated upon authorial intent. If the argument is premised upon what lawmakers intended the law mean (the speeches), it makes no sense to treat a large principle as gospel while ignoring the intended criteria or instantiations for it.[21] Stealing a concept from the floor of the Congress, treating it as the text, and retrofitting it into a new cultural arrangement, seems to steal something out of context.[22] And that, in fact, is exactly what Whittington's argument is all about.

But my point is that *both* Balkin and Whittington are wrong. When the Equal Protection Clause was passed—without a definition section or rigid nomenclature—it potentially enacted *all* senses of "equality" that could be linguistically understood. What it put forth was the idea that an equality program of some kind had to be culturally administered. The question of how to administer it—what concepts, criteria and instantiations it should have—thus became a separate question from what was legislated upon. If we can all agree that we cannot take the Congress in 1868[23] as having legislated upon Balkin's concept— i.e., if we can all agree that the law is the simply the text—then we can move on to discuss Ronald Dworkin.

(a) Dworkinians

Dworkin is different because he doesn't rely upon history to establish his constitutional views. As such, he doesn't claim that certain concepts are already legislated upon and doesn't use the phrase the "the original meaning." Instead, he properly sees that the role of the judge is to make the best sense of what the text could be *taken* to mean—which involves selecting the best meaning to *give* to it [RD-1, 176-275; RD-2, 146-66].

This, I think, is the best way to handle the issue of concepts and principles. It is much better to simply say that, if any principle or idea makes *the best sense* for a provision, it should be chosen by a judge because of this quality [B&F, 10-11, 31-32]. You can't pretend that the language *itself* already covers it—because, if that was true, it would not even require an argument: the language would be plainly communicative. The idea has to be that, among the potential concepts available to the provision, one of them is urged as doing it the most *justice*. Dworkin therefore does not purport to vindicate an "original meaning;" he purports to vindicate a state of cogency (or supremacy) in the constitutional idea he is defending. This is also the view adopted by Dworkinian scholars Sotirios Barber and James Fleming,[24] with some minor exceptions.[25]

This is a very important distinction. As I show in Chapter 13, it determines whether one is an originalist [13:§1-§2]. Dworkinians are not originalists because they freely admit that *judges* must complete the law[26]—giving it a cogent and integrous account.[27] This view has the Constitution being handed to its judges for "finishing" in the way that a product in a factory might.

It's almost as if the difference between Dworkinians and originalists boils down to this. One believes the *best* expositor for the Constitution is something that lies in epistemology, metaphysics, good reasoning or empathy; the other believes that the *true* expositor lies in history. The former merely tries to give legal text its best "face" (cosmetic); the latter purports to say what it really means as a *fact*—a view that I am quite critical of throughout this book.

And so, the basic point comes down to this. If any liberal scholar believes that any provision of the Constitution *enacts* any concept or abstract principle to the exclusion of a rival, he or she would have to show how this is true *linguistically*—which, if true, wouldn't need to be "shown," because it would be plainly evident. Short of this, all that the scholar can offer is the promise that the concept he or she wants to vindicate will make the Constitution a better document.[28]

(b) Example: "Unreasonable" Searches

To understand this issue better, consider the Fourth Amendment's Search and Seizure Clause. It protects against unreasonable searching and seizing. But what, exactly, does this fix?[29] Given the way that the cognition of the word "unreasonable" works, the law only sets forth a *chameleon concept*.

Here's how it works.[30] The word "unreasonable" can mean something that is verb-possible or adjective-opposite. One of the linguistic features that may encourage this is the fact that the prefix and suffix specify logical operations, but provide no indication of what order they are to be performed. Consider the meaning of the prefix and suffix:

- *Prefix*: "un" means opposite; (To be unlocked is to be open).
- *Suffix*: "able" means possible; (One can lock that which is "lockable").

Any word that starts with "un" and ends with "able" can have a different idea depending on what order the mind performs the opposite and possibility functions. One way to interpret unreasonable—let us call it x—is as follows:

1. *un* = opposite
2. *unreason* = opposite of reason
3. (unreason) + able = possible to opposite reason.
4. Therefore, x = something which can be opposite reasoned.

Hence, if it is possible to counter-reason something—if there are two equally cogent justifications—the thing in question must be unreasonable. Literally speaking, one is able to "unreason" the result.

To understand how x would impact the Fourth Amendment, consider this hypothetical. A murder has just occurred in a neighborhood, and police are looking for the assailant. An officer then sees gun ammunition on the floor board of a car late at night as a motorist exits his vehicle to pump gas in an area proximate to the crime. The ammunition looks like the kind of slugs used at the crime scene, and the person is wearing ragged clothing. Would acting upon this information be unreasonable given the interpretation in x?

Well, it would be if one found an equally valid counter-theory. Let's suppose that many people in the area are avid hunters; the ammunition is common for hunting deer; it is open season; and hunters wear dingy clothing under their orange vests. So, one has two assertions, P and Q, each of which has a certain degree of speculative force. One says that the person may be linked to a murder; the other says that he or she is linked to hunting. If one reads the word "unreasonable" to mean "that which cannot be opposite reasoned," one must find any seizure on this basis to violate the text of the Fourth Amendment.

But not so fast. Consider now a different order of operations. Another way to "calculate" the meaning of the word unreasonable—let us call it *y*—is as follows:

1. *able* = possible
2. *reasonable* = possible to reason
3. *un* = opposite
4. un + (reasonable) = not possible to reason
5. Therefore, *y* = something which cannot be reasoned (arbitrary).

Under this interpretation, unreasonable means that which cannot be reasoned at all. Decisions for which no reason can be offered are said to be *arbitrary*. If the Fourth Amendment protected only against arbitrary searches, then the government could search whenever it had some simple basis capable of articulation. It would not matter whether a counter-basis existed—any minimal chain of inference would do. This standard seems to allow the officer in the hypothetical to search the car and seize evidence.

Note how fascinating this transformation is. In both situations there is a kind of indisputable logic. Both syllogisms, *x* and *y*, purport to be deductive. Yet, one says that unreasonable means that which can be opposite-reasoned, while the other says it means that which is not possible to reason at all (arbitrary).

What is also interesting is how the meaning of unreasonable varies from something akin to *x* and *y* in tort versus criminal-procedural law. In torts, "unreasonable" means a risky violation of the relevant custom (a stronger standard). But for police officers it largely means arbitrary conduct (a weak standard). Indeed, if doctors were allowed the same latitude in medical treatment that police officers are allowed in searching and seizing, it would be quite difficult to find rule violations in medical malpractice cases.

But the point here is *not* to argue for a uniform standard; that would be idiotic. The point is simply to show that that the term "unreasonable" is *chameleon*. It offers one of two concepts that significantly changes its meaning. Therefore, judges have no choice but to select the one they believe is most suitable to the situation.[31]

This example was meant to show the difficulty with the notion that the Search and Seizure Clause was given a fixed meaning at the time of its passage—even in terms of an abstract principle. For there seems to be no specific concept, criteria or instantiation enacted into law. Rather, the only thing that appears "fixed" is the text itself, which is the same as saying, "at the time of the founding, the provision was stated."

§ 5. Original Meaning?

But notice that the term "unreasonable" does offer fixed content in this sense: it offers a choice between the two basic concepts, x or y. This is the view that I adopt in Chapter 5 [5:§4]. It merely says that the term has a certain *grammar*.[32]

But note that this doesn't help the baptismal thesis. The point of that thesis was not to christen all of the possible things constitutional words could say in the language culture—for this is what lexicography does (dictionaries). You don't need a baptism for that. Rather, the point was to christen *specific* meaning—i.e., to show that rivals were somehow excluded at any unit of analysis.

Therefore, if scholars only mean that an English expression has an intelligible grammar on its face—that "unreasonable" means x or y—two things follow. First, the scholar is *not* an originalist,[33] because history is not being summoned to eliminate rival concepts, criteria or instantiations for text in need [13:§1].[34] Second, merely knowing the basic grammar of something shouldn't be called its "original meaning." When we teach English as a foreign language to students, we don't call it "the original meaning class." We don't call dictionaries "the original meaning books" [6:§3(d)]. And even in cases where a scholar *does* intend to refer to specific meaning, the phrase is *still* problematic. As I contend elsewhere [App: 17-20, 22-24, 63-68], it is simply better to say "the first construction" or "the first arrangement," even when speaking only about concepts, as Balkin wants.[35]

Having just shown the difficulty of the baptismal thesis for any unit of analysis, I now move on to discuss what language meaning really consists of.

Notes

1. [LS-2, 3; LS-1, 29]. Keith Whittington also argues, "The first contention needed to build this argument is that only a fixed text can provide judicial instruction and therefore be judicially enforceable against legislative encroachment" [KW-1, 54].

2. Of course, it doesn't become law until the president signs. So one may want to include this gesture as well. I'm side-stepping this issue because I don't need this additional complexity to make my point.

3. I've changed Larry's terminology here for this reason. The term "fixation" commonly has a psychological grammar, meaning something like "obsessed," "preoccupied," "fixated," "neurotic," etc. In chemistry, however, it can mean, "the reduction of a substance from a volatile or fluid form to a nonvolatile or solid form." *Collins English Dictionary—Complete and Unabridged* (HarperCollins Publishers 1991, 1994, 1998, 2000, 2003) http://www.thefreedictionary.com/fixation (accessed June 12, 2012).

Because the focus of Larry's thesis is upon the christening of meaning, I have tried to pick a term that best captures this idea without causing other difficulties. I note that

Larry once changed one of my expressions for the better, and I ended up adopting it in this book [App: 11, note 4]. If others find my name for his thesis unfortunate, I would encourage an equal amount of license in them.

4. He writes, "[O]nly a fixed text can provide judicial instruction and therefore be judicially enforceable against legislative encroachment. The judicial requirement of a fixed text not only authorizes judicial review but also limits it within the context of determinate meaning" [KW-1, 54]. He continues, "The second aspect of accepting a written constitution as law is that only a fixed text can be adequately ratified, that is, legislated into the fundamental law" [KW-1, 55].

5. U.S. Const. pmbl.

6. This talk of "concepts, criteria and instantiations" is explained in Chapter 2.

7. I'm borrowing this expression from Saul Kripke [SK].

8. This is an act of a legislature that declares a person or group of persons guilty of a crime, without benefit of trial, due process, etc. See, e.g., John R. Vile, *A Companion to the United States Constitution and its Amendments* (Greenwood Publishing Group, 2010), 48.

9. Bayless Manning, "Hyperlexis: Our National Disease," *Northwestern University Law Review* 71 (1977): 767.

10. William D. Popkin, *Statutes in Court: The History and Theory of Statutory Interpretation* (Duke University Press, 1999), 115.

11. [KW-1, 59-60, 76, 84, 93-99, 175-79, 182-87, and 210-11].

12. Whittington writes, "In order to realize the fundamental law as a judicially enforceable instrument to restrain the legislature, the unwritten principles behind government had to be fixed in writing. As a fixed and written text, the supreme law of the Constitution can be self-consciously considered and properly ratified and can have the specificity to provide judicial instruction" [KW-1, 53-59].

13. I consider this idea in several places. The appendix uses an interesting thought experiment. It shows the difficulty with the idea that a generation could enact its social context using only simple sentences composed of plain language. Chapters 11 and 12 also spend great effort showing why any specific past social context could never be what the American Constitution legally passes along to future generations. Finally, the issue culminates in [13:§1-§2].

14. [KW-1, 110-159]. Whittington writes on page 153: "The embodiment of the sovereign will in a constitutional text creates an independent law that is binding on the government. Rather than govern by its own hand, the popular sovereign must rely on agents who hold political power in trust and on rules that authorize and bind those agents."

15. Balking provides an analysis of how to read the Fourteenth Amendment [JB-1, 303-19].

16. The relevant portion of which reads:

All persons born or naturalized in the United States, and subject to the jurisdiction thereof, are citizens of the United States and of the State wherein they reside. No State shall make or enforce any law which shall abridge the privileges or immunities of citizens of the United States; nor shall any State deprive any person of life, liberty, or property, without due process of law; nor deny to any person within its jurisdiction the equal protection of the laws. U.S. Const. amend XIV, §1.

17. He relies almost exclusively upon a speech by Senator Jacob Howard, who said

that the Fourteenth Amendment was designed to "abolish[] all class legislation in the States and do[] away with the injustice of subjecting one caste of persons to a code not applicable to another." And that the amendment "establishes equality before the law, and it gives to the humblest, the poorest, and the most despised of the race the same rights and the same protection as it gives to the most powerful, the most wealthy, or the most haughty" [JB-1, 314-15].

18. It's unfortunate that Balkin is using the expression "original meaning" here. His argument is really a straight-forward Framers' intent argument. I discuss this in Chapter 8. The argument that Framers intended only a concept for a provision of law, and that the concept should therefore be taken as *being* the law, is called text-centered, formalistic OI in the third degree [8:§3(a)-(c), Table 8.3].

19. The full quote is as follows:

I think the principle against class legislation might protect homosexuals from discrimination even if nobody knew there were such things as homosexuals in 1868, or, if they knew what homosexuals were, would have opposed the extension of the principle to that social group. One doesn't need a "new" principle for this case; rather one needs to apply the class legislation principle correctly to present-day circumstances given present-day understandings [JB-2, 488].

20. The appendix presents a good account of this. Generation X's reading of the Free Spirit Clause clearly has different principles in mind.

21. Cf. the example in the last chapter involving Dworkin's boss [2:§3]. It would be the same as if the manager had believed his role was to accept the boss's criteria for "best," but then decided not to use them. If you accept the *Servitude* concept, you wouldn't change the boss's criteria; you'd try to fetch them. That's what servitude is all about. But if you believe the command requires the *Sanctified* concept, you'd construct your own criteria. Balkin appears to believe that the provision in question requires servitude to another's concept, but wants to construct the criteria for himself.

22. This may be why Balkin later decided to back off authorial intention as a vehicle. He writes: "I do not believe that the principles underlying the Constitution may include only those 'the framers and ratifiers actually sought to endorse.' Nevertheless, I think it is very important to look to history to derive underlying principles, even (and perhaps especially) principles that nobody in particular intended" [JB-2, 487]. What isn't clear, however, is how a principle that nobody in particular (in history) intended gets to be treated as being "the original meaning" for a provision. Perhaps this argues for a view I consider in Chapter 11: historic societal preference.

23. The Fourteenth Amendment was passed in 1868. The speech that Balkin primarily relies upon was given in 1866, when the Amendment was introduced to the Senate [JB-1, 313].

24. [B&F, xiii, 155-56, 161-63, 168-70, 189-92].

25. Barber and Fleming emphasize that, in making constitutional ideas "the best," they would look to moral reasoning, social science, and the goals of the document's preamble: to provide for general welfare, establish justice, ensure domestic tranquility and secure the blessings of liberty [B&F, xiii-xiv, 155-56, 169].

26. Dworkin writes in *Freedom's Law:*

Where do we stand? The most natural interpretation of the Bill of Rights seems, as I said,

to give judges great and frightening power. It is understandable that constitutional lawyers and teachers should strive to tame the Bill of Rights, to read it in a less frightening
way, to change it from a systematic abstract conception of justice to a list of discrete
clauses related to one another through pedigree rather than principle. These efforts fail,
however . . . [RD-6, 81].

27. The difference between my own view and the Dworkinians is discussed at the
very end of Chapter 6 and in Chapter 7. For now, all that needs to be emphasized is that I
see the selection of any concept, criteria or instantiation (for text in need) as being a
connoisseur judgment rather than a moral problem. One of the key differences is the
emphasis of culture.

28. One criticism of my approach may be that it seems exclusively text-based. Very
often, scholars make the argument that the Constitution has *meta-principles* which are not
clause-bound. A popular example is the principle of "separation of powers," which exists
in the absence of a specific separation-of-powers clause [JB-1, 305, 306].

My view is that meta-principles are still *inferential.* They come from examining a
blueprint. Instead of reading from a clause, you read from a design. Even a doctor who
reads an X-ray forms an idea in the mind. Hence, even though the skills needed might be
somewhat different—you are, in essence, reading a picture—the matter still seems to be
like reasoning from text.

A similar criticism can be found in arguments for *holistic judging.* This idea says
that legal judgments must not merely be integrous for any specific provision, but across
all provisions [RD-6, 80]. Because holistic judging is not specifically clause-bound, some
may argue that it poses some difficulty for my approach. But my position, once more, is
that it does not. Holistic judging only affects what is *chosen,* not what you choose *from.*
As such, when a judge selects a concept, criteria or instantiation, he or she has no choice
under Dworkin's account but to choose from things that would be available had *no* holistic judging occurred. All that holism does is narrow those options further.

Dworkin himself makes this point when he says that judges must preserve the integrity of text when selecting its best meaning. He writes regarding the interpretation of
statutes, "Integrity requires [Hercules] to construct, for each statue he is asked to enforce,
some justification that fits and flows through that statute and is, if possible, consistent
with other legislation in force. This means he must ask himself which combination of
which principles and policies . . . provides the best case for what the plain words of the
statute plainly require" [RD-1, 338].

29. The clause reads: "The right of the people to be secure in their persons, houses,
papers, and effects, against unreasonable searches and seizures, shall not be violated."
U.S. Const., amend. IV.

30. This account originally appeared in my dissertation [SW, 50-54].

31. To see an interesting example of this, compare the meaning of an unreasonable
seizure in *Browner v. County of Inyo*, 489 U.S. 593 (1989), to what is normally regarded
as unreasonable police conduct. Browner is a tort case. It involves the police trying to
stop a criminal who was fleeing in a stolen car. The officers set a road block that ultimately killed the driver. Evidently, the defendant could not see the road block because it
was constructed at a bend in the road. As the driver made the turn, he encountered the
traffic obstructions too late to safely stop. He died in the crash. His heirs sued for inten-
tionally violating the defendant's Fourth Amendment right against unreasonable seizures.

The issue in the case is simply whether the "seizure" of the defendant—i.e., forcefully stopping his car on the road—was "reasonable." If so, no possible violation of the Fourth Amendment occurred and recovery is barred. But if not, the heirs have the right to go to trial and recover damages (so long as they prove that the violation was intentional). The question, then, is simply whether "wrongful roadblocks" constitute a valid theory for lawsuits claiming a tortious violation of the Fourth Amendment. The plaintiff's counsel argued, obviously, that a reasonable police department would not have set up the road block that way—they would have been more cautious of the harm involved (not placing it around a bend).

The decision in the case is interesting. The Court held that the tort theory was *valid* and that the case could not be dismissed as a frivolous lawsuit. Hence, the Court apparently held that what can be an unreasonable seizure under the Fourth Amendment can be a higher standard in tort than for criminal cases, even though it involves *the same exact conduct and the same exact provision of law.* After all, does anyone really think that, if the victim lived, he could have suppressed his evidence in a prosecution for fleeing under claim that the road block was an illegal seizure? Defendants who survive such "seizures" cannot show a violation of the Fourth Amendment when they are prosecuted for their crimes. But if they die—who knows?—maybe it violates for other purposes.

32. The term "grammar" has senses. It can refer, as it does above, to the many things a word can mean—the x and y. Or it can refer to just one of them. For example, one could say that the term "unreasonable" sometimes takes on the grammar of arbitrariness (just y). For more on grammar, see Chapter 1, note 1.

33. This point also leads me to reject the term "abstract originalists" put forth by Barber and Fleming (with reservations). They write: "[I]f a constitutional provision is written in general terms, abstract originalism construes those terms to refer to general ideas or concepts. Thus, 'due process' is taken to refer to *due process*, not anyone's conception of due process. . . . '[D]ue process' must refer to *due process itself*, not this or that conception of due process" [B&F, 99].

34. There are times when Balkin's position here can be unclear. He writes, "In drafting constitutional rights provisions, constitution makers may not do much more than provide a constitutional grammar and vocabulary, a set of basic principles and textual commitments, and a practice of constitutional argument in which people reason about their rights." It isn't clear in this passage whether he believes that history selects the concept, like he does in other passages [JB-2, 460-61].

35. There are times when Balkin's use of the term "original meaning" is peculiar. He uses the phrase to refer to historic evidence that can be found only for the generality of a constitutional idea. In this situation, he calls the general idea, "the original meaning." But then, he does not allow himself to speak this way if historic evidence reveals something criterial or instantiating. This, he says, is "original expected applications." So for him, meaning is only spoken of at one unit of analysis, at least where the provision is composed of general words [JB-1, 293; JB-2, 449].

The problem here is twofold. Meaning can be spoken of for any unit. It's awkward to say that only generality is "meaning," even for general words. One could have in mind something very specific when using the word "speech," for example. Just as one could have a very particular arrangement in mind when using the word "liberty." Also, one is still being "applicatory" when selecting among rival concepts. C.f. The "originally expected concept." It simply doesn't make sense to speak only of the historical concept being "the meaning," but then speak of historic criteria or instantiations as being "the non-meaning" (the applications).

Therefore, in this book, the term "original meaning" refers to the idea that history has removed rivals at *any* unit of analysis, resulting in specific meaning. And of course, I take the position that the use of the term (as such) is confused for the reasons I indicate. We should pick a better expression that does not mislead. We could say, for instance, "the first arrangement" or the "the first construction."

Chapter 4

Public Meaning v. Meaning as Use

§ 1. "Public Meaning"

There are many originalist scholars who believe that the Constitution amounts *only* to its language. Larry Solum is one who champions this mantra [LS-2]. These scholars, however, talk curiously about "the public meaning" of the document's provisions.[1]

At the outset, I want to note that the phrase "public meaning" is a peculiar expression.[2] If I say that something has a "private meaning," I mean it is idiosyncratic among a small number of people (a secret code or an alias). But for all other words not like this, I do not describe the meaning as "public." Instead, *senses* are described—the use might be archetypical, idiomatic, colloquial, archaic, technical and so forth.

When American legal scholars refer to the public meaning of the Constitution's text, they espouse a problematic idea. It is the view that plain words have fixed and substantive content,[3] revealed through a rule of some kind (e.g., majority preference). Below, I examine three incarnations of this view, and then show why it is problematic.

(a) Majority Preference

It is not uncommon to hear originalists claim that the true meaning of a word or expression in the Constitution amounts only to what relevant majorities believed about the same when the provision became enacted. Consider the views of Justice Scalia. He believes that the meaning of "cruel and unusual punishment" in the Eighth Amendment[4] is governed by the judgments the framing society would have made for the idea.[5] He writes:

> [T]he Eighth Amendment is no mere "concrete and dated rule," but rather an abstract principle. If I did not hold this belief, I would not be able to apply the

Eighth Amendment (as I assuredly do) to all sorts of tortures quite unknown at
the time the Eighth Amendment was adopted. What it abstracts, however, is not
a moral principle of "cruelty" that philosophers can play with in the future, but
rather the existing society's assessment of what is cruel. . . . otherwise, it would
be no protection against the moral perceptions of a future, more brutal, generation. It is, in other words, rooted in the moral perceptions *of the time* [AS-1, 145].[6]

Likewise, Jack Balkin believes that the true meaning of the word "commerce" in Article I, Section 8[7] is something very broad, because the Federalist-
minded First Congress apparently behaved this way when passing laws concerning Native Americans.[8] For Balkin, therefore, the "true meaning" comes from a
majority of views of a more narrowly tailored public.

My contention is that both of these positions rest upon a fallacy about language. The true meaning of the words "commerce" and "cruel punishment" is
never what the majority of *any* public thinks. Rather, the true meaning is merely
that which can be linguistically understood when the words are exchanged in
that language culture. Therefore, Balkin and Scalia are confusing the *sense* of an
idea that supposedly came to dominate a given public (or institution) with the
meaning of a word or phrase that has more than one sense or arrangement available to it.

The meaning of a word is always *all* of its understandable arrangements.
And if any public wants only one particular sense or idea to always prevail
throughout history when others read the text of the Constitution, that public is
forced to legislate better. They must define the term or use more articulate nomenclature that speaks to the specific desire. This is what modern legal culture
requires. But if any public *fails* to do such a thing—if they only enact general
words—then future generations are allowed to make different arrangements of
"cruel" and "commerce," so long as the same can be understandably spoken of.

Note how strange it would be to say of the dictionary that new entries
should be voted upon by the public. The idea is problematic because it sets forth
political criteria for meaning. People have *no control* over whether something is
communicative (intelligible). You cannot legislate away the fact that expressions, when exchanged, cause meaning in others. If people can use terms in
ways that can be understood, that understanding is part of the language culture,
which is why lexicographers exist to record such things, rather than majorities to
prescribe them.

Imagine someone saying that the public meaning of "marriage" is matrimo-
ny "between a man and a woman." What does this actually say? All that it really
says is that a majority are (or were) against the social policy of allowing gays to
marry. It doesn't actually say anything about the meaning of "marriage." This is
because, even among those who agree with the mantra, no choice exists but to
understand someone who said, e.g., "I'm married to my job." Or, "You should
see my dog and cat—they seem like they are married." Because these *senses* of
marriage are readily understood, they are part of the language meaning—which

is something that one cannot disavow with a vote or campaign. And so, if someone said that two men should be able to marry, the idea wouldn't violate the meaning of "marriage"—either public or otherwise [App: 58-62].

Does that mean, then, that if a constitution enacted a provision granting the right to marriage,[9] that it would have to allow the right to "marry a job" or to have a dog and cat commingle in certain ways? Note that I have said *nothing* (yet) of how a judge should or should not choose. I've merely said that what is on the table to choose from is not precluded by anything artificial, like a public vote—from the past *or* present—that would constrict the way ordinary language comes to be understood in the language culture. So the point is not whether it would ever be good or bad to choose even an exotic or a strange sense[10] of any word in the Constitution; the point is that such choices are not automatically precluded by some artificial rule that cuts off the way the speaking of such language works in the culture.

(b) Historical Stereotypes/Archetypes

Aside from majority preference, there is a second way that public meaning can artificially truncate ordinary expression. It concerns the use of historical archetypes or stereotypes.[11]

For example, consider the First Amendment's protection of "religion." Imagine someone claiming that a Satanist, a practitioner of Voodoo, or a worshipper of tree spirits was forbidden from practicing his or her religion because the same was not commonly thought of as being "religion" in December of 1791, the year the Bill of Rights was passed. The argument is that, because most people did not commonly associate Voodoo (etc.) as "religion"—at least not, perhaps, without thinking about it—the "public meaning" of the term must therefore preclude Voodoo from being protected by the Constitution.

Note that there are two claims here: empirical and linguistic. The empirical claim is that, if you asked people to rate examples of religion on a scale of one to ten, they would rate Christianity, Islam and Judaism higher than they would the worship of tree spirits or the practice of Voodoo. We have every reason to believe that this is empirically true.[12] Likewise, if you asked people from 1791 what kinds of things commonly "popped in the head" when the idea of religion was spoken of (an open-ended question), similar results would surely be obtained. The point: Voodoo simply isn't a popular cultural image for "religion" (either then or today).

But what does this show about *language*? All that it shows is that the hypothetical 1791 community possesses a *stereotype* for religion. It might also show that the most popular image(s) that comes to mind could be spoken of, in some circles, as an archetype or exemplar. But no matter what label is applied to the favorite items, the question remains: what does this say about the meaning of the term, "religion?" Does it mean that only the favorite items, stereotypes or dominant cases count when the term is used in the language culture—either in 1791 or today?

The answer quite clearly is "no." Archetypes and stereotypes are only *examples* of the idea; they are not, themselves, the only possibilities. Otherwise, there would be no need to speak of them as being "stereotypical" or "archetypical." The very fact that the examples carry these designations is evidence that they share some relationship to other kinds of examples (border cases).

Also, if two people could argue across time about whether Voodoo counts as "religion," the argument would not be about what religion meant (linguistically). Rather, it would be an argument about the *sense* of religion the discussants favored—and, perhaps, the cases they preferred [5:§1]. The fact that both could even *have* the argument shows that the word "religion" is being understood at some basic level, as far as *language* goes.[13]

And so the point always boils down to the same thing. If any generation wanted the Constitution to protect only a particular *sense* of religion for all future generations—if it wanted certain cases excluded—it is required to pass language that specifically states this desire. If lawmakers in 1791 (or today) wanted to make only "stereotypical religion" from the perspective of a Christian-dominant community protected in the First Amendment, they would need to legislate better. And if they do not—which they didn't—no choice remains but for the *judges* to select the *sense* of the idea and which examples count or not. And though one might be able to argue that a judge should or should not read the term "religion" this or that way, one *cannot* argue that certain senses are automatically *precluded* from consideration merely because they fail to be stereotypical or archetypical cases in 1791 cultural psychology (or even today).

(c) Aggregated Historical Behavior

Yet another way that public meaning can truncate ordinary language is by appealing to historical behavior that was dominant in the American past. Consider this example. Suppose someone said that the term "liberty" in the Fifth Amendment of the Constitution[14] had to primarily mean "protecting property rights," because that is the way people in 1791 behaved under warrant of the idea. In short, the word is taken to mean the cultural program that was celebrated [App: 12-32].

The same sorts of arguments that are made against stereotypes/archetypes apply here as well. The naked word "liberty" doesn't have to be wed to a property-centric cultural arrangement. This is only one example of the idea. Just as "liberty" needn't entail owning slaves[15] or keeping women in patriarchy—other arrangements from the American past—so too can it adorn many unforeseen forms. For example, the idea can be arranged around a sense of individual autonomy for the body, which is what basically happened in the 1900s in the aftermath of the New Deal.[16] Or, in societies less enamored with John Locke and more with Jean-Jacques Rousseau, "liberty" can be constructed around certain communitarian objectives—e.g., the right to government-paid tuition and health care.

All of this is possible, of course, because "liberty" is simply an ordinary word, like "lunch," that has many different social arrangements. It can crisscross grammar with "freedom" and can even have a high disregard for the idea of equality, as libertarians could surely attest.

And so, if the framing culture wanted to prescribe a certain *sense* of liberty in the Constitution, it was required to *explicitly* do so, with appropriate language. One can make an argument that some provisions venture down this road. The document, for example, protects property with due process of law, provides compensation for "takings"[17] and obliges contracts.[18] This is an example of how the law can more specifically protect something with a word other than "liberty."

§ 2. Family-Resemblance—Wittgenstein

The central problem with all the views I have considered thus far is that they prescribes *statist* criteria to police the free markets of language. Meaning is only limited by what "capital" one can redeem from trading it in any market. If the trading of words is successful, whatever "stuff" those trades supply becomes admitted to the lexicography of the term. The meaning is inventoried by linguists as *senses* of the word. There are two consequences here: (a) language is a *behavior*; and (b) its meaning is simply any successful *usage* in the culture [LW-1].

Ludwig Wittgenstein is the philosopher who showed that ordinary words have what he called "family resemblance."[19] The idea, in its simplest sense, is that the mind associates meaning in loose bundles or *frameworks*. Members of the bundle all bear some resemblance to one another, much in the way that a family might. Illustration 4.1 depicts an example, using the word "chair."[20]

Illustration 4.1: The Family Resemblance of "Chair"

Linguists and philosophers frequently refer to this idea as a "cluster concept." Membership clusters together without the benefit of a bright line showing which items count and which do not. Another way of saying it: the border cases become admitted for want of an actual border.

A good way to conceptualize a cluster is to imagine a set of traits, {a b c d e}.[21] Now imagine only a *handful* of those traits being placed into a small bag. In the simile, the bag is the word. One use of the word might "bag" traits {a b c}, while another might have {a d e}.[22] It is up to the brain's cognitive faculties to figure out what assortment the bag carries each time the word is deployed.[23]

A common misreading of Wittgenstein is to think that this idea is limited to words like "chair" or "game."[24] This isn't true. The phenomenon applies to any word where more than one sense develops in the language culture, and where those senses become bundled together, cognitively. Also, Wittgenstein's basic point is about meaning being use, not about any specific words having a given cluster. If meaning is use, the use has no choice but to cluster in some respect.

It is more beneficial, therefore, to focus upon Wittgenstein's idea of "word sense."[25] The whole point of saying that a word has "sense" is to qualitatively differentiate the ways in which the word is deployed. We might say, e.g., that a chair in the sense of an exemplar is something different from a chair in an extended sense (a living-room beanbag). Or, that a chair in the sense of a seating device is different from a "chair" in the sense of an executive (chairperson).[26] How senses relate to one another tells us something qualitative about the usage.

And so, the fundamental point is this: Wittgenstein's idea concerns more than just words like "game" and "chair," though these are popular examples. It applies to any word that takes on more than one sense, where those senses form a bundle or framework in the mind.[27] This includes pretty much every ordinary word one can think of. It is extremely difficult to find words that do not develop multiple senses that bear some cognitive association to one another.

In fact, the only words that escape a family of senses are those where the cultural learning is specifically meant to resist this phenomenon. These tend to be certain kinds of scientific jargon (e.g., acidosis).[28] Philosophers sometimes call these words *rigid designators* [SK]. Although even these words may not be completely immune from developing multiple senses, it is fair to say that the way sense occurs in them is much more limited—which means their families, if any, are affected. It is important to remember, however, that these words need constant social policing and indoctrination to keep people doing the right sort of behavior-reaction when encountering them—which is why they tend to sound technical or jargonized and are used by social organizations (e.g., science) for specific purposes [App: 45-46, 48-49, 54-57].

§ 3. Family-Resemblance—Pinker

Famous linguist Steven Pinker endorses Wittgenstein's notion of family resemblance.[29] He writes, "Many experiments have confirmed that everyday concepts act like family resemblance categories."[30] He describes the idea as having: (a) fuzzy borders (is a scorpion a bug?);[31] (b) stereotype membership (grandmothers are old and gray, and make good chicken soup);[32] and (c) exemplar membership (a robin is better example of "bird" than an ostrich).[33] Linguists have even found evidence of family resemblance in natural-kind words like "disease," "fruit," and "insect,"[34] and in words one might commonly assume to have a clear boundary, such as "odd number" and "woman."[35]

Pinker has an interesting theory about what causes this. His argument is that the brain has two cognitive pathways for processing language.[36] The brain can either type its surrounding or calculate from it. It is the former that causes family resemblance and the latter that causes words to have "sharp boundaries," an idea considered in a moment.

First, when the brain is said to "type" something in its environment, it pictures commonality. This is the way stereotypes and similar kinds of associations arise. Pinker refers to this as a "pattern associator" [SP, 278]. It is this feature that allows one to say that a throne is a "chair" or that pat-a-cake is a "game."

Pinker argues that this aspect of cognition is functional to our form of life. It's the way our species makes efficient sense of repetition in the environment.[37] It allows us to put the world into a framework.[38] Otherwise, our experiences would seem random or arbitrary. Imagine, for example, how a computing form of life is experienced (being a processor). It occurs in serial, alphabetical or numerical bundles. If we had to organize our experiences this way, we simply could not make sense of our existence. Hence, that is why we have a pattern associator that works hand-in-hand with our language.

§ 4. Sharp Boundaries

The mere fact that a word has family resemblance doesn't preclude the use of a sharp boundary. Pinker notes that people have the ability to impose sharp boundaries if they wish.[39] Hence, if asked whether a dolphin is a mammal, one might say, "yes," because of the definition: it breathes air, nurses young, has warm blood, etc. One who did this would be treating "mammal" as a *rule* rather than a resemblance. The person would simply be reporting the outcome of certain binary questions: (a) does the animal breathe air? [yes]; (b) does it nurse its young? [yes]; (c) does it have warm blood? [yes], etc. So, when "yes" comes up to all of the questions, the matter goes into the "mammal" bucket. Otherwise, it doesn't.[40]

Pinker calls this trait "abstract, combinatorial reasoning."[41] It is frequently imposed upon a whole host of ordinary words—odd number, triangle, geometry, grandmother, etc. Pinker therefore sees two basic cognitive paths available for language meaning. But to use one, he says, you need to dim the other:[42] "When we use a system of rules, we have to turn off the family resemblance system . . ., [so that] a grandmother doesn't have to be grandmotherly nor a president presidential" [SP, 285].

Wittgenstein also noted that it is perfectly within anyone's power to draw a sharp boundary. All that the boundary does is cut off members of the family so that a bright line (temporarily) exists. The key to these boundaries is that they are only drawn for the convenience or objective of the situation. That is, they are drawn solely because they get communicative work done.[43] Wittgenstein writes:

> For I *can* give the concept "number" rigid limits in this way, that is, use the word "number" for a rigidly limited concept, but I can also use it so that the extension of the concept is *not* closed by a frontier. And this is how we do use the word "game" [LW-12, 272, §68].
> . . . To repeat, we can draw a boundary—for a special purpose. Does it take that to make the concept usable? Not at all! (Except for that special purpose). No more than it took the definition: 1 pace = 75 cm. to make the measure of length "one pace" usable [LW-12, 272, §69].

A common mistake is to assume that the occurrence of a sharp boundary *eliminates* family resemblance for that word. This clearly is not the case. The strict definition merely creates a particular *sense* of the idea—usually, an axiomatic or technical one.[44] But the sharply-defined use still shares family resemblance with the uses that are not sharply-defined.[45] This is why the same person can either be pregnant or not, but also be "really pregnant." These two ideas of pregnancy share a family resemblance.

Having explained how the cognition of language works, I now conclude with one last point about technicality.

§ 5. Technicality

Imagine that two people are in a room. One is standing; the other is seated. The one says, "Bring me a chair." The other then looks around, but finds nothing other than a stool, and responds, "I can't—there are no chairs in the room." Imagine a dispute then ensues about whether the stool qualifies as a "chair." One person takes the position that it does, and the other takes the position that it does not. What does this say about language?

Note that what is happening here might be called the *assertion of technicality* ("stools are not chairs"). The issue boils down to this: does the person requesting a chair want the other to fetch something that associates with the chair family (inclusion logic), or something that differentiates from *within* it (inventory logic). One associates things into a family—you might get a living-room bean bag to sit on—but the other fetches the correct chair *entourage*. Fetching the correct entourage, of course, requires that one have certain proficiency in the chair industry. It requires the lexicon of a chair professional. It requires that one speak in a way that catalogues, parses and *differentiates* chairs in the way an expert might.

In a nutshell, this linguistic dispute can exist because people can speak with either a *lay* or an expert vernacular. The view that I espouse throughout this book is Wittgensteinian. It says that that *neither* of the assertions about "chair" is incorrect as far as *language* goes, and that the matter is *not* governed by pulling out the dictionary. Rather, the matter is entirely dependent upon the sense of chair one can claim is "in play" in this language game.

Note that if a person *knows* that another is using a lay sense of "chair" and he or she replies with an expert or technical sense, one could levy the charge of bad manners. Perhaps the person is being a "smartass." But note also that, in some language games—especially lawyering—it may be considered *good* behavior to assert technicalities. (Go watch how lawyers behave toward one another, linguistically, in documents, court papers and so forth.) What this behavior says, in effect, is: "if you can't force my hand, linguistically, you aren't guaranteed it."

And the simple fact is that, even outside of the language games played by lawyers, one frequently asks for something associational in the same way one does something differential. It has the exact same audiology and can even share very similar contexts ("I need a chair"). Because of this, the assertion of technicality operates in language not unlike the assertion of self-defense does in law— it is a reply-behavior that becomes invoked, even though it may be unwelcome.

I move on now to consider how all of this affects the American Constitution.

Notes

1. Numerous conservative law professors have even said that the very name of the new originalism should be, "Original Public Meaning" [RB-2; LS-1, 15]. This is because, as Solum notes, "The core idea . . . is that the original meaning of the Constitution is the original *public* meaning of the constitutional text" [LS-1, 23]. See also [RB-3; KW-3; KW-1].

So popular is this buzzword, in fact, that the history of its usage is now being written. Solum says it was introduced into the lexicon of originalist thinkers "through the work of Gary Lawson[,] with Steve Calabresi as another 'early adopter,'" citing to Lawson's "Proving the Law," *Northwestern University Law Review* 86 (1992): 875 and Calabresi & Prakash, *The President's Power to Execute the Laws*, *Yale Law Journal* 104 (1994): 553 [LS-1, 23]. Solum also directs readers to Vasan Kesavan & Michael Stokes Paulson, "The Interpretive Force of the Constitutions Secret Drafting History," *Georgetown Law Journal 91* (2003): 1127 and Samuel T. Morison, "The Crooked Timber of Liberal Democracy," *Michigan State Law Review* 1 (2005): 465.

2. Imagine someone putting forth the thesis that dictionaries should no longer include anything but public meanings. What would this mean and what would change? It seems only one of two possibilities exist. Either *nothing* would be different, because the

expression "public meaning" would be taken as a poor phrase for the idea of meaning, period. Or, perhaps only the most frequently-used senses of a word would be urged for the book whose task it is, paradoxically, to catalog *all* word sense.

3. One wonders, of course, what relationship these views have to the picture-theory of language Wittgenstein first announced in the Tractatus [LW-3; RM-2, 34-43].

4. The amendment reads: "Excessive bail shall not be required, nor excessive fines imposed, nor cruel and unusual punishments inflicted." U.S. Const. amend. VIII.

5. I contend that this view is problematic even for the framing society itself: its own popular sentiment could never automatically reveal the true meaning of "cruel and unusual," even for cases during that time [11:§2, 12:§1(b)]. Also, this view seems to assume that the framing society is trying to talk to *itself* rather than pass language through time.

6. The claim that no current generation could adopt a judgment about "cruelty" that exceeds the one common to the framing society isn't true. Compare this with two things: (a) what Generation X does in the appendix; and (b) what this book says about law being culturally suitable [6:§2, §4; 12:§1(c)-(d); and Chapter 7].

7. The Commerce Clause reads as follows: "The Congress shall have Power . . . To regulate Commerce with foreign Nations, and among the several States, and with the Indian tribes." At issue is whether the power only concerns the regulation of economic activity, period. Or whether it gives license to regulate more generally, so long as doing so touches upon, or impacts, the economy. If Congress can pass any regulation that merely has an economic impact, its power is much more broad than if it was only allowed to pass "true" commercial regulations, like the Uniform Commercial Code (UCC).

8. Balkin notes that the First Congress passed laws that made it illegal to commit a crime against a peaceful Indian. This shows, he argues, that the Commerce Clause could be used to regulate behavior beyond that of mercantile or trading activities [JB-2, 431-32].

9. In the Constitution, of course, the right to marry is not specifically enacted per se, but is said to exist as a "fundamental right" arising from other sentences that speak more generally about liberty. See *Loving v. Virginia*, 388 U.S. 1 (1967).

10. Although time has not permitted me to elaborate upon the idea of "exotic sense," these passages from Wittgenstein are helpful:

> Given the two ideas "fat" and "lean," would you be rather inclined to say that Wednesday was fat and Tuesday lean, or vice versa? (I incline decisively toward the former). Now have "fat" and "lean" some different meaning here from their usual one?— They have a different use.—So ought I really to have used different words? Certainly not that.—I want to use *these* words (with their familiar meanings) *here*.—Now, I say nothing about the causes of this phenomenon. They *might* be associations from my childhood. But that is a hypothesis. Whatever the explanation,—the inclination is there" [LW-1, 216].
>
> . . . If I say "For me the vowel in e is yellow" I do not mean: "yellow" in a metaphorical sense,—for I could not express what I want to say in any other way than by means of the idea "'yellow" [LW-1, 216].
>
> . . . A new-born child has no teeth."—"A goose has no teeth."—"A rose has no teeth."—This last at any rate—one would like to say—is obviously true! It is even surer than that a goose has none.—And yet it is none so clear. For where should a rose's teeth have been? The goose has none in its beak. Nor, of course, has it any in its wings; but that's not what anyone means when he says it has no teeth.—Why, suppose one were to say: the cow chews its food and then dungs the rose with it, so the rose has teeth in the mouth of a beast. This is not be absurd, because one wouldn't have any idea in advance, where to look for teeth in a rose [LW-13, §117].

11. Solum speaks of originalism being "committed to the idea that constitutional text provides constitutional law a *hard core*" that "should not yield to changing circumstances and values." He continues:

> But some living constitutionalists may deny that there is a hard core. They might believe that even the core of constitutional law is malleable and subject to manipulation. That is, they might assert that the living constitution has a *soft core*. . . . Some living constitution-alists may believe that courts should have the power to amend the Constitution in order to eliminate what Justice Brennan might have called the "anachronistic contours" of the constitutional text. Proponents of this view are not likely to use the word "amendment" to describe this power but that word seems an accurate characterization of the implications of their position [LS-1, 40].

12. Linguists study the phenomenon of favored cases for words. They call it "proto-type theory." See, e.g., Rosch, E., "Principles of Categorization," in *Cognition and Categorization,* ed. E. Rosch and B. B. Loyd (Mahwah, NJ: Erlbaum: 1978); Rosch, E., "Co-herences and Categorization. A Historical View," in *The Development of Language and of Language Researchers: Papers Presented to Roger Brown,* ed. F. Kessel (Mahwah, NJ: Erlbaum: 1988); and Smith, E. E., & Medin, D. L., *Categories and Concepts* (Cambridge MA: Harvard University Press: 1981).

13. If they truly did not understand each other when speaking the word, they would look puzzled and have "a foreign language problem." They would need to ask what the word "religion" meant. It would be like being in another country and not knowing an item on the menu.

14. The clause reads, "No person shall . . . be deprived of life, liberty, or property, without due process of law." U.S. Const. amend. V.

15. It was common in the south among plantation owners to talk of "liberty" as something not only entirely consistent with, but in support of, slavery. The famous quota-tion from Samuel Johnson notes how peculiar this seemed "across the pond." He re-marked, "How is it that we hear the loudest yelps for liberty among the drivers of Ne-groes?" Quoted in George William Van Cleve, *A Slaveholders' Union: Slavery, Politics, and the Constitution in the Early Republic* (University of Chicago Press, 2010), 42. And there is Patrick give-me-liberty-or-give-me-death Henry, who, when leading the opposi-tion against the Constitution at the Virginia ratifying convention, said this:

> Among ten thousand implied powers which they may assume, they may, if we be en-gaged in war, liberate every one of your slaves, if they please. And this must and will be done by men, a majority of whom have not a common interest with you. They will, there-fore, have no feeling for your interest. . . . In this State there are 236,000 blacks, and there are many in several States; but there are few or none in the Northern States. May Con-gress not say that every black man must fight? Did we not see a little of this last war? We were not so hard pushed as to make emancipation general: but acts of Assembly passed, that every slave who would go the Army should be free. Another thing will contribute to bring this event about: slavery is detested—we feel its fatal effects—we deplore it with all the pity of humanity. Let all these considerations, at some future period, press with full force on the minds of Congress. . . . [T]hey will search that paper, and see if they have power of manumission. And have they not, sir? Have they not power to provide for the general defense and welfare? May they not think that these call for the abolition of slavery? May not they pronounce all slaves free, and will they not be warranted by that

power? There is no ambiguous implication or logical deduction. The paper speaks to the point. They have the power, in clear, unequivocal terms, and will clearly and certainly exercise it. (Quoted in Thomas Valentine Cooper and Hector Tyndale Fenton's, *American politics (non-partisan) From the Beginning to Date* (C.R. Brodix, 1884), 11.

16. See, e.g., Bruce J. Winick, "On Autonomy: Legal and Psychological Perspectives," *Vill. L. Rev.* 37 (1992): 1705.

17. The clause reads, ". . . nor shall private property be taken for public use, without just compensation." U.S. Const. amend. V.

18. The clause reads, "No State shall . . . pass any . . . Law impairing the Obligation of Contracts." U.S. Const. Art I, §10, cl. 1. This clause has become controversial in the post–New Deal age. I leave the issue of that controversy, possibly, to another day.

19. Wittgenstein's famous passages:

Consider for example the proceedings that we call "games." I mean board-games, card-games, ball-games, Olympic games, and so on. What is common to them all?—Don't say: "There *must* be something common, or they would not be called 'games'"—but *look and see* whether there is anything common to all.—For if you look at them you will not see something that is common to *all*, but similarities, relationships, and a whole series of them at that. To repeat: don't think, but look!—Look for example at board-games, with their multifarious relationships. Now pass to card-games; here you find many correspondences with the first group, but many common features drop out, and others appear. When we pass next to ball-games, much that is common is retained, but much is lost.—Are they all "amusing?" Compare chess with [tic-tac-toe]. Or is there always winning and losing, or competition between players? Think of [solitaire]. In ball games there is winning and losing; but when a child throws his ball at the wall and catches it again, this feature has disappeared. Look at the parts played by skill and luck; and at the difference between skill in chess and skill in tennis. Think now of games like ring-a-ring-a-roses; here is the element of amusement, but how many other characteristic features have disappeared! And we can go through the many, many other groups of games in the same way; can see how similarities crop up and disappear.

And the result of this examination is: we see a complicated network of similarities overlapping and criss-crossing: sometimes overall similarities, sometimes similarities of detail.

I can think of no better expression to characterize these similarities than "family resemblances;" for the various resemblances between members of a family: build, features, colour of eyes, gait,. temperament, etc., etc. overlap and criss-cross in the same way.—And I shall say: "games" form a family. Ludwig Wittgenstein, "On Family Resemblance and On Seeing As: Selections from Philosophical Investigations," in *Art and Interpretation: An Anthology of Readings in Aesthetics and the Philosophy of Art* (Broadview Press, 1999), 225.

20. This is a simplified cluster; many more members exist. One is advised to Google "chair" to see what qualifies these days. An image search yields all sorts of unimagined things. Also, see this lecture: http://ludwig.squarespace.com/lecture-topics/2012/4/5/035-the-language-game-of-chair.html

21. I've made this set simple. It's for explanatory purposes only.

22. And hence, some kinds of chairs have back support and are sat upon upright, with knees bending a certain way. Others are like stools, with no back support and legs more droopy. Still others, like recliners, allow for a different sort of body position.

23. This is meant as a simplified understanding. A more sophisticated account would

have the brain being able to "make sense" by picking up only *most* (or some) of the traits. This suggests that perhaps some traits are more important than others during the process of understanding.

24. Wittgenstein made it very clear that these were just *examples* of a larger phenomenon applicable to language generally. He mentions all sorts of words and phrases in *Philosophical Investigations*, from proper names like "Moses" [§79] and "Excalibur" [§39-§45], to the word "is" [§38, inserted slip] and "number" [§68-§69], and many others. Also, he specifically tells you that his idea is not limited to "game" and "chair." He says it is a general phenomenon in language. He writes, just before introducing the example of games:

> Here we come up against the great question that lies behind all of these considerations.— For someone might object against me: "You take the easy way out! You talk about all sorts of language-games, but have nowhere said what the essence of a language-game, and hence of language, is: what is common to all these activities, and what makes them into language or parts of language." . . . And this is true.—Instead of producing something common to all that we call language, I am saying that these phenomena have no one thing in common which makes us use the same word for all,—but that they are *related* to one another in many different ways. And it is because of this relationship, or these relationships, that we call them all "language" [LW-12, 271, §65].

So the point is that, what makes something a language game is the fact that meaning is use, which causes "family resemblance" as a general phenomenon.

25. The philosopher who first wrote about word sense is the German mathematician, Gottlob Frege. See his seminal paper in 1892, *Über Sinn und Bedeutung* ("On Sense and Reference"). He described the former as "thought" or "the mode of the presentation," and to the latter, roughly speaking, as being the thing it referred to. From my perspective, the biggest difference between Frege and Wittgenstein is how this dynamic is pictured. Central here is the rejection of the isomorphic (one-to-one correspondence) view of language and of the acceptance that meaning is use. Hence, instead of seeing a two dimensional structure between sense and reference, Wittgenstein sees a rich dynamic between sense and *family*, and the grammar that situates it.

26. This sense of "chair" presents the issue of "polysemy," which I discuss in [6:§3].

27. One should be careful to differentiate senses that are "cognitively polysemous" and senses that are not. As I contend in [6:§3], if this is the issue, the matter is extra-familial rather than intra-familial. This is like arguing over whether people are related. If it gets too distant, the idea has to be cut off at some point, else "relation" becomes another sort of idea.

28. The term "acidosis," of course, *does* have more than one sense, but it is very limited. It could mean having an arterial pH below 7.35 or having "requisite acidity" as indicated by such a measurement. See generally, Barbara L. Bullock, *Pathophysiology* (Lippincott, 1996), 219. The key is whether the measure is allowed to change. It might be that, in the future, the diagnostic value will be adjusted, as with high blood pressure. And so the question is whether the term refers to the measurement reading only or the concept the reading serves. One could speak of it in either sense.

Also, it is argued that indexicals ("give me *this* chair") lack more than one sense, and the same is urged for proper names [SK]. See David Braun, "Indexicals," *The Stanford Encyclopedia of Philosophy*, ed. Edward N. Zalta (Summer 2012 Edition),

http://plato.stanford.edu/archives/sum2012/entries/indexicals/ (accessed June 12, 2012).
It is beyond the scope of my present endeavor to comment upon these issues, save a brief
mention about indexicals elsewhere [6:§1, note 2]. For proper names, see [LW-1, §39-45, §55,
§79], discussing "Excalibur" and "Moses."

29. He quotes from the famous passage from the *Investigations* [SP, 271].

30. He continues, "[M]ost of our everyday categories, and not just games, show
Wittgenstein's family resemblance and crisscrossing features. Many vegetables are green,
but carrots aren't; many are crunchy when raw, but spinach isn't" [SP, 273].

31. Noting that category words have fuzzy borders [SP, 272], he states: "People aren't
quite sure whether garlic, parsley, seaweed or edible flowers should count as vegetables,
and the Reagan administrated created a ruckus when it justified cutbacks in funding for
school lunches by reclassifying ketchup as a vegetable. If a clamp is a tool, why not a ball
of string? Is a scorpion a bug? Is a sport utility vehicle a car or a truck or a car? Is syn-
chronized swimming a sport?" [SP, 273]

32. He writes, "[C]ategories have stereotyped features: traits that everyone associates with the category, even if they have nothing to do with the criteria for membership.
When people think of a grandmother, they think of gray hair and chicken soup, not of a
node in a genealogical tree" [SP, 274].

33. He writes, "[T]he members of a category are not created equal, which is what
one would expect if they were admitted into the category by meeting the definition.
Everyone agrees that a blue jay is somehow a better example of a bird than a chicken or a
penguin, and that an armchair is a better example of furniture than a grandfather clock"
[SP, 272-273].

34. See Michael McCloskey & Sam Glucksberg, "Natural Categories: Well-Defined
or Fuzzy Sets?" *Memory and Cognition*, 6 (1978): 462-472. Study participants agreed
with exemplar cases, but half of the subjects could not agree whether stroke was a "disease," a pumpkin a "fruit" or a leech an "insect." When asked a month later, many had
changed their minds.

35. See S. L. Armstrong, L. R. Gleitman, and H. Gleitman, "What Some Concepts
Might Not Be" *Cognition* 13, no. 3 (May 1983): 263-308. Study participants said "7" was
an excellent example of an odd number, but "447" was not as good. They also thought
that "housewife" was an excellent example of a woman, but "policewoman" was not.

36. One is what he calls "associational memory," and the other has something to do
with "abstract, combinatorial reasoning." [SP, 278-287]. The specific reference to "abstract
combinatorial reasoning" is on 286.

37. He writes:

We cannot bring every object home and put it under a microscope or send tissue samples
out for lab testing. We have to observe a few traits that the object wears on its sleeve and
infer the traits that we cannot see directly. Good categories let us do that. If Tweety has
feathers and a beak, Tweety is a bird; if Tweety is a bird, Tweety is warm-blooded, can
fly, and has hollow bones. Bad categories do not: If we knew only that Tweety's name
begins with a "T," nothing of interest would follow [SP, 281-282].

38. He writes, "We live in a lawful world in which traits tend to hang together in the
same way in many objects. . . . Our mental categories are useful because they reflect the
lawfulness of the world" [SP, 282].

39. Pinker writes:

People can learn categories with clean definitions, crisp edges, and no family resemblance, such as "odd number." They can learn that a dolphin is not a fish, though it has a strong family resemblance to the fishes, and that a seahorse is a fish, though it looks more like a little horse. They can understand that Tina Turner is a grandmother, though she lacks all the usual traits, and that my childless great-aunt Bella was not a grandmother, though she had gray hair and made a mean chicken soup. Though people refer to women in their third trimester as "very pregnant," they also understand what it means when parents say to their daughters, "You can't be just a little bit pregnant" [SP, 274].

40. For elaboration, see this lecture segment: http://ludwig.squarespace.com/lecture-topics/2012/4/5/037-sharp-boundaries.html

41. This seems similar to what philosophers call an "analytic statement" [App: 57, note 15] or what I call "axiomatic grammar." I say this because of the words Pinker uses to describe this idea: "[Sharp-boundary words] are part of a system of interlocking rules that churn out handy deductions or computations[,] . . . the product of their own rule systems" . . . allow you to deduce the unobservable . . . [are] . . . combinatorial and recursive . . . allow us to reason about an unlimited range of cases" [SP, 284-285].

42. He mentions research subjects who saw the same terms as having sharp or fuzzy boundaries. He writes, "So they must have been capable of turning their fuzziness on and off. Family resemblance categories are real, but so are classical categories; they live side by side in people's minds, as two ways of construing the world" [SP, 275].

43. I often use this simile. Imagine an open field. One day, a person erects a net of some sort (e.g., volleyball). The purpose of the net is to facilitate the use of the field for *that* activity. But the net can be removed for other activities in the field. In the simile, the field is the family-resemblance word. Sometimes it is used with nets; other times it is not.

44. For a good account of this, see the following lecture clips on the term "bachelor:" http://ludwig.squarespace.com/lecture-topics/2012/4/5/032-bachelor-and-legos.html; http://ludwig.squarespace.com/lecture-topics/2012/4/5/0321-more-on-bachelor.html; http://ludwig.squarespace.com/lecture-topics/2012/4/5/033-the-grammar-of-bachelor.html.

45. Wittgenstein writes, "If someone were to draw a sharp boundary[,] I could not acknowledge it as the one that I too always wanted to draw, or had drawn in my mind. For I did not want to draw one at all. His concept can then be said to be not the same as mine, but akin to it. . . . The kinship is just as undeniable as the difference" [LW-12, 276, §76].

Chapter 5

The Flexible Constitution

In the last chapter, I examined the way that language works. In this chapter, I answer a simple question: how does this affect the Constitution? As Table 5.1 shows, the document is composed of ordinary words.[1] I now present four consequences that follow from having a plain-language constitution.

Table 5.1: Examples of Ordinary Words in the U.S. Constitution		
• speech	• commerce	• "Equal protection"
• religion	• abridge	• "Privileges and immunities"
• arms	• unreasonable	• "Republican form of government"
• property	• jeopardy	• "Due process of law"
• process	• regulate	• "Probable cause"
• taxes	• punishment	• "Just compensation"
• cruel	• assemble	• "Speedy trial"
• unusual	• redress	• "Impartial jury"
• search	• grievances	• "Excessive bail"
• seizure	• persons	• "Excessive fines"
• press	• houses	• "Rights retained by the people"
• crime	• papers	• "Full faith and credit"
• war	• effects	• "Good behavior"

§ 1. Sense-Shifting

The first consequence is that the Constitution is open to *shifting sense*.[2] This is where a judge changes the sense of an idea in the document as time moves forward.[3] I present three examples of this below.

(a) "The Army"

By what authority does the president (or Congress) have control over the

Air Force? At the time the Constitution was written, there was no such thing as forces in the air (no planes). Is this a problem for the Constitution (or for the Air Force)? I imagine most people would not see it as such. They would simply dismiss the matter as "changed circumstances" or would see the issue pragmatically. But I don't want to do this. I want to approach it as a linguistic exercise. Consider what the idea of "army" means in the following provisions:

- The President shall be Commander in Chief of the Army and Navy of the United States . . . . Art. II, §2.
- Congress shall have Power to . . . raise and support Armies, but no Appropriation of Money to that Use shall be for a longer Term than two Years. Art 1, §8, cl.12.
- Congress shall have Power to . . . provide and maintain a Navy. Art 1, §8, cl.13.
- Congress shall have Power to . . . make Rules for the Government and Regulation of the land and naval Forces. Art 1, §8, cl.14.

Let's suppose a person makes the following argument. "The President does not have authority to command the Air Force because of the language in Article 2. The Air Force is not 'The Army' or 'The Navy'—it's a separate unit." It's separate, he says, not only because we have christened it as such, but because the operations undertaken to wage war by air require their own distinct behavior. In short, the Air Force does its own thing. He goes on to say that any person with proper knowledge of military science would understand the inherent differences between an air force and an army in terms of what each *does*. He even says that the federal government does not have the power to create an air force, because of the plain language of Article I, Section 8 (above). He insists that only the state governments can do that by virtue of the Tenth Amendment.[4]

Note what this argument does, linguistically. It gives the idea of army (and air force) a specialized grammar. The person is speaking as though he's an expert in the area of military science.[5] Not only is he treating the term "army" as a *proper name* for a specific branch in the fighting forces, but he also is treating it as a *natural kind*.[6] This means that, properly conceived, the job that the United States Air Force does is inherently distinct from the job that the Army does—no matter how each is named—and that, as such, these are *behavioral terms*.[7]

If we accept this way of speaking, it has dire implications. If the Constitution gives the federal government the power to create an army, and if this idea is taken to mean a specific branch of the forces that engages in a specific type of war-behavior, it follows that the power given to Congress is only to create something that does *army things*. Therefore, if the experts in military science say that the U.S. Army is not principally concerned with attacking from the air—simply because of what it is (what it does)—then the constitutional view should be that the federal government cannot create *any* military organization that does such a thing, no matter what it names it.

However, one needn't give the idea of "army" an expert vernacular. One could see the idea as being a very general word for "the troops." And if, in fact, General Washington could be visited by a time traveler from the future and told about "the army in the sky," he would completely understand the gist of the idea. It would be intelligible to him. And the gist is simply that armies can now fight in the sky, ever since the creation of machines that allow for such a thing. This way of speaking would consider the U.S. Navy as simply being "the army on the seas." The term army simply comes to mean "the soldiers" (the troops). One might think of this as being a lay vernacular or even a child's sense of the word.[8] It's the same sort of vernacular that allows a bar-stool to be a chair.[9]

And so, the point boils down to this. The sense that we give "army" is the one we find most *appropriate*, not the one that is "truly there"—because there *isn't* one that is truly there. What is "truly there" are all those senses of army that could be understood in the language game. And the only way for legislators to eliminate a sense is to speak more rigidly when enacting text—to set forth legalese, a definition section or concrete language. That is the only way that rival senses can be *legally* removed from legislation—at least in modern legal cultures like America, which is heavily "positivistic."[10]

Note, also, that there is still a third sense of "army" that is possible. Imagine speaking with the grammar of two branches instead of four. It is only in modern times that we speak of four specific branches of the fighting forces. But if we assume a grammar that only has two buckets—land and sea—such a lexicon would *have* to place airplanes *somewhere*, even if waging war with them was a distinct kind of behavior. And so, this way of speaking might say that, if a plane took off from the sea (on a carrier), it would be part of the Navy, but if it took off from the land, it would be part of the Army—at least for purposes of classifying the species. And that's exactly what this vernacular is: it's taxonomical (categorical).[11]

And if this vernacular could be understood in 1789, it would mean that, *even back then*, the existing language game could accommodate a plane being invented. It would not present a "changed circumstance" for the Constitution, and we wouldn't have to hear the cries of pragmatists to "fudge it." The simple fact of the matter is that a plain-language constitution doesn't need fudging precisely because it is so *flexible*.[12] As such, if a war plane had been invented in (say) 1800, the existing language game could accommodate the event even if it was using a dichotomous land/sea lexicon to speak about fighting forces.

But what does this example really show us? It shows us several things. First, it shows us that the reason why the federal government is allowed to have the Air Force and why the president commands the same is because of a *cultural construction* (arrangement) that we have made with the blessing of a plain-language document, which could very well be arranged in *other* ways. We surely could arrange a scenario where the president did *not* command the Air Force. And we could at least think of a *possible* cultural arrangement (a possible world) where only state governments were allowed the power of the U.S. Air Force while using the *same exact constitution.*

And the point is even much stronger than this. Not only could this state of affairs be possibly arranged, but it is very easy to imagine that, within our own history, the sense of "army" in the Constitution shifting over time.[13] It could easily come to mean something different in our future than it does now or has been in our past. But how is this possible? Doesn't it violate "the rule of law?" The answer is that it violates *nothing.* And there are five reasons why:

1. The term "army" is not defined in the Constitution;
2. It can easily carry more than one sense in ordinary language;
3. Each of those senses could be understood if spoken across time, so that Americans in 1787 could get the gist of the idea;
4. Sense-shifts are not uncommon in ordinary language games, even in situations where it amounts to bad manners [4:§5]; and
5. The language games of lawyers regard sense-shifting as acceptable behavior (even a prowess).

And so, if the sense of "army" changes over time, it matters nothing to either language or law that it has shifted. Furthermore, although (1) through (5) are compelling enough, (5) could stand as its own independent reason. When one comes to see what American legal culture does with language and what counts as an acceptable argument, one comes to see that shifting the sense of an idea is part of what is normal behavior. It doesn't matter if the subject is contracts, divorce decrees, property documents, statutory language, court orders or whatnot. This is precisely why positivistic legal culture is so *pedantic* in its draftsmanship—it's trying to anticipate and nail down every contingency so the opponent cannot take unwanted positions (wiggle). Yet, the Constitution sits atop of this very legal culture and exhibits *none* of these dense linguistic characteristics.

And so, this is why a plain-language constitution is legally allowed to shift. And note also that it is *pointless* to try to speak of this entire phenomenon in terms of "the original meaning of 'army.'" This way of speaking creates a convoluted picture. All that needs spoken of are the *senses* of army that can be understood if speaking across time. And even if one of those senses becomes deprecated in *our* language games, it merely becomes spoken of as an *archaic sense,*[14] not "the original meaning." And so, rather than speaking of "the original meaning of 'army,'" we should instead speak of army: (a) in the lay or child sense (troops); (b) as a proper name for one of four specific fighting divisions; (c) as the entity that engages in a distinct kind of fighting behavior (an expert sense); or (d) as a crude axiomatic category (with navy) involving sea/not-sea.

And therefore, the only possible thing that is left to talk about when one speaks of "the original meaning" is merely the particular social arrangement that the framing generation made for the terms "army" and "navy" in the Constitution —how they arranged military society around these words. But even here, it is better to be clear and say: "the first construction" or *arrangement*. Hence, there is no point in using the phrase "original meaning"—it causes nothing but confusion in jurisprudence.

Having just considered how sense-shifting works with the term "army," I now move on to consider another example.

(b) "Citizen"

Another good example of sense-shift in the Constitution concerns the word "citizen." In the late 1700s, the idea of citizenship was in flux in America. Even in England after the Glorious Revolution, people were still considered "subjects." Thinking of one another as "citizens" represented a new way of thinking about the state and society—one that had experienced the transition from the medieval world of monarch-and-subject to the Enlightenment's new ideas about classical liberalism.[15]

Because of this, however, a strange grammar emerges in the language culture of 1787. It is a grammar with *ranks*. There are four social ranks that can be spoken of: citizen, "denizen," "alien" and slave. A *denizen*, we are told, is the equivalent today of a second-class citizen.[16] It is someone who is "officially admitted"—as in, not a temporary visitor—but who lacks certain prerogatives, such as voting rights. An "alien," of course, is a foreigner who is staying in the country for a limited time under the permission of a visa. Hence, a "denizen" is higher in rank between a slave and alien, but is lower than a citizen. Illustration 5.1 shows the system.

Illustration 5.1: American Social Ranks in the late 1700s

Of course, the more popular sense of "citizen" today eliminates the idea of ranks. There are no official second-class citizens in America today—"denizen" has left our citizenship grammar. This makes being a "citizen" a simple either/or—either you are officially admitted ("citizen") or not ("alien"). And everyone who is officially admitted *today* has the rights of "citizens" even under the *other* way of speaking.

To understand how citizen can shift sense, consider the following hypothetical. Imagine there is a country that discriminates against women by not automatically giving them citizenship at birth. They must do good deeds to earn the status. And imagine that there is a female, x, who is running for president, while also claiming to be a citizen. Imagine the Constitution of this country has the following provision: "No person except a natural born Citizen, or a Citizen of the United States, at the time of the Adoption of this Constitution, shall be eligible to the Office of President."[17]

At issue is whether x is qualified to be president. The issue is not whether she is "naturally-born," but whether her good deeds in the polity are sufficient to allow her to vote and run for office.[18] Imagine there is a dispute on this issue: one side claims she is a citizen, another that she is only a denizen. Our concern is not whether x has escaped the trappings of being a denizen—whether she has done the requisite good deeds—it is whether, when reading the word "citizen" in the Constitution, future generations are required to use denizen-logic. At issue, in short, is whether citizenship must always be spoken of with a grammar of ranks.

And the answer is quite clearly "no." The idea of "citizen" can shift sense in the Constitution the same way that "army" did. And the reason for this is simply because people speaking to one another across time, using the term "citizen," could understand each other perfectly well, no matter if they spoke with a grammar of ranks or not. If people from different epochs could successfully argue with one another about whether x was a "citizen," they each would understand the other's use of the basic idea. It would be intelligible. All that would be happening is that they would prefer different social arrangements.

To see this, imagine two Christians arguing over whether x, after death, will go to heaven. One believes in purgatory and the other does not. Purgatory is, of course, a kind of intermediate rank. So long as each understands who x is and what she has done, the argument is not over the facts. And nor is it about what "heaven" is, as a general idea. For heaven is simply the desired, perfect everlasting place Christians hope to be.[19] And so, the difference in the argument is simply whether each approves of arranging the system of heaven with a middle rank for the border cases.[20]

It would be the same as if two people argued over whether x was "married," where the situation involved a same-sex marriage. One might say, "She's not married; it's a civil union—God doesn't recognize same-sex marriages." And the other might reply, "Of course she's 'married' you fool." The argument here is not over any *facts*—each understands who x is and what she is doing in her life. And it is also not an argument over the meaning of "marriage." Instead, it is simply a question of whether one prefers to speak of the idea with the grammar of ranks that discriminates against some unions, versus a grammar that does not.

So the point is this: whether x is a "citizen" is ultimately determined by what *arrangement* we want to *give* the idea. If we *want* to use denizen-logic (ranks), our inquiry might come to focus upon whether x remains, in fact, in a second-class position. This is just what the justices in the hypothetical are assumed to be focused upon. But if we don't want to speak of "citizenship" with ranks, we can simply avoid that inquiry altogether. There is nothing in the quoted language of the hypothetical Constitution (above) that prevents this.

The only issue, therefore, is what cultural arrangement to make for the idea. If the country in the hypothetical stops discriminating against women later in its development, then it would be quite rational for justices to begin speaking of "citizen" without a grammar of ranks—the way some speak of "heaven" without a system of purgatory, and others of "marriage" without regard to "civil union."

And note that it does absolutely *no good* to say that any sense from the past must be "the original meaning of 'citizen.'" Instead, the meaning for any historical period is simply the same *basic idea* that anyone could choose to speak of, no matter whether they adorned it with rank. And again: if any generation wants to codify a particular *sense* of citizen—if it wants everyone to speak of this idea (constitutionally) with ranks in mind—it must do so with appropriate specific language. A good way to do this would be to include a definition section in the law, the way that statutory codes frequently do. Otherwise, different senses of the idea could be put in play, so long as they could be successfully spoken about in the language game.

And this is why, in fact, the Civil War generation decided to make the matter much more clear for its progeny when passing this language: "All persons born or naturalized in the United States, and subject to the jurisdiction thereof, are citizens of the United States and of the State wherein they reside." U.S. Const. amend. XIV, §1.

Having just shown how sense-shifting works with the idea of "citizen," I now consider my final example of the phenomenon.

(c) "Age"

When law professors discuss whether any constitutional provision has a clear or fixed meaning, it is not uncommon to hear someone bring up the Presidential Age Clause. Because this clause is often put forth as a determinate sentence that has a perfectly clear answer, I want to briefly consider it. The clause reads as follows: "[No] person [shall] be eligible to that Office who shall not have attained the Age of thirty-five Years, and been fourteen Years a Resident within the United States." U.S. Const. art. II, §1, cl. 5

In truth, this clause is no different from any other in the Constitution in this critical respect: family-resemblance still rules. This means that border cases do, in fact, exist. Consider the following senses of "age:" calendar, biological. The issue is what is being counted. The former counts, in theory, the number of revolutions the earth makes around the sun;[21] the latter counts biomarkers in the aging process.[22] As such, the latter idea would allow one who had aged more quickly to qualify to be president before their 35th revolution around the sun (birthday). The same would be true for one who hadn't aged enough by the day of their 35th revolution.

Also, note that there can be different senses of the *metric*. Is it 35 years relative to the 1789 life span, which needs adjusted for inflation the way dollars are?

Looming behind all of this is the wisdom of the central idea: does our culture need leaders with a certain amount of life experience—and isn't 35 too young these days? If so, one could easily read "35 years" as being "35 equivalent years." This is the same sort of logic that allows a dog to get an extra six years for each revolution around the sun that it lives. Because "dog years" is a perfectly functional way of speaking for that sort of issue, one could easily see this issue spoken of as "socially-equivalent years."[23] The question is whether the number 35 counts absolute revolutions around the sun or sets forth a standard for life achievement in 1787 society which is reflected in such a count.[24]

Here's the point. Because the Constitution does not address these issues, the provision in question theoretically has *border cases* that are not disposed of. The border is not closed because the idea of "age" has many intelligible senses in the language culture.[25] If you walked into a tavern in 1789 and commented that x was "younger than his age," you would be completely understood. It would not be a foreign expression. Because of this, the meaning of the legal text could be given one of those senses, if doing so became regarded as appropriate or compelling in a given case—i.e., the best act of judgment one could provide for the matter.

And if any generation would find it unsettling that the Presidential Age Clause has open borders, it is incumbent upon them to close the borders with appropriate nomenclature, lest the matter of presidential age remain a function of the casuistry judges wish to deploy concerning it.

I have just shown three examples of how sense-shift can occur in a plain-language constitution. I now move on to consider the next consequence of having a flexible constitution.

§ 2. Many Ways to Follow

The second consequence of having a flexible charter is straightforward: there are many ways to follow it. And each example of "the following" is just as obedient to the next, provided there is family resemblance in the usages.

Importantly, whenever a legal rule is composed entirely of ordinary words, the people who purport to comply with it have no alternative but to *elect* or *construct* a state of compliance. You have to pick something. Among all the various options that could be selected, any one of them is merely an *arrangement*. The biggest mistake that conservative originalists make is that they confuse the arrangements of the founding generation with the meaning of the language that required such choices in the first place. They think, in short, that the law means how the first generation elected to behave (or think).

But in fact, when a framing generation puts in place a social arrangement, all that it does is give subsequent generations an example or *illustration* of how to follow the Constitution. All that it does is say to the future, "Here's the way I did it." "This is the arrangement I made." The subsequent generation is then free to either follow the examples and practices handed to them or to select alternative arrangements that are also obedient to the document's general words. In short, they are free to say, "Well, I elected to do it this other way."

What this means is that different generations with different cultures—say, agrarian versus industrial—can each follow the law differently, yet both be obedient to its original meaning. And that is exactly the point: there really is no such thing as "the original meaning." Instead, there are only the various things that are linguistically possible. Referring to all of these possibilities (the array) is different from referring to any one instance chosen in the past.

Importantly, originalists do not understand how language meaning and generational arrangements interact over time. When a generation culturally arranges its constitutional idea, it may not see that choice as being merely an *example* of how the law could be followed. This is because the choice occurs from *within* that culture. It is only when culture changes that one sees that other examples could be put in play, because they are also linguistically possible.

Hence, American culture in 1787 surely agreed that hanging was not "cruel or unusual punishment." But what it most likely did not see (as a generation) was that this was as a mere *cultural arrangement* of the Eighth Amendment. Instead, it saw it as "the law" (itself). But if someone from today could speak to someone from 1787 and explain why we regard death by hanging to be cruel and unusual, the two could perfectly understand each other from the standpoint of what the phrase "cruel and unusual" says in *language*. In other words, there would be no foreign language problem: each would understand the English phrase. They might disagree about their respective judgments for the idea—they even might adopt preferences for word sense—but they would not misunderstand the basic gist of what "cruel and unusual" meant. I call this the *intelligibility thesis*. It says that different generations who live in different cultural periods of development can *both* comply with the linguistic meaning of the same constitution *differently*, so long as each can still understand how the other is using the same words [2:§3].

And what this also says is that an act of legislation never truly codifies a generation's specific cultural arrangement (or sense of an idea) unless the text of the law says so, with appropriate nomenclature. Instead, what the Constitution enacts is only the requirement that generations culturally arrange flexible ideas. The Constitution tells us, for instance, to put in place some sort of program against "unreasonable searches." It tells us to come up with a program for "free speech." It tells us to select a program that allows for religious worship without "respecting an establishment." So long as the programs we select can be defended as merely being social arrangements of the document's flexible ideas, the "following of law" has taken place.

It's the same as if a mother had said to two of her children going off to school, "Pick a good major, eat well, take health supplements, and don't waste your money." If two children end up with different majors, different diets (e.g.,

Atkins versus Zone), different supplement regimens and different ideas about what constituted monetary "waste"—it is entirely possible that *both* have followed mother's directions rather well. And that neither has violated "the original meaning." And it is of course completely *foolish* to say that, if one child went first (was older), that his choices constituted the true or original meaning of mother's rules.[26]

§ 3. Interpretation v. Construction

A third consequence of setting forth a constitution in ordinary words is that it exposes a common falsehood in conservative thought. There are many originalists who speak of this curious distinction: interpreting the Constitution as opposed to construing it [RB-3; KW-3; KW-1]. Presumably, interpretation is a behavior that is more faithful to the document, while construction is more akin to "making it up."

However, given what I have presented, this distinction is now upside-down. It is originalism that offers a constructed account of "the real Constitution," because of the way that ordinary language works and the fact that the document is *not* written in legalese. It does this, simply, by mugging all of the other meanings or senses that plain words might legitimately take on. It ropes off and hogties plain text using contrived rules that have nothing to do with the way language really works and also fly in the face of the norms used by lawyers to assert what legal language can mean.[27]

And what is odd about this is that conservatives frequently are the ones who preach the idea that the Constitution is a *legal document* rather than a symbolic social statement, like the Declaration of Independence. But what they appear not to remember is that legal documents carry with them drafting norms, which require such things as definition sections, detail, exceptions clauses, construction and severability statements, specified contingencies, "small print" and otherwise pedantic linguistic behavior. And that, absent these things, lawyers are permitted to take positions in court that legitimately say that such things have not been properly addressed.

One wants to say it this way. For statutes and administrative law, originalists are part-and-parcel of positivistic culture—they want a *legal* system. But for constitutions, they become religious with the document: they want the meaning to come from some sort of expositor in the past as though what is handed down is a kind of gesture or sacrament to that entity.

So, again, originalists seem to have the whole thing backward. They seem to espouse a kind of constitutional religiosity for something that, if it were a legal document, would simply let the text speak for itself [13:§1-§2]. And that means our choices for what the Constitution can mean are hardly blemished in the way originalists often suggest.

§ 4. Cooperative Talking

A fourth consequence of setting forth the Constitution in ordinary words concerns the baptismal thesis that was discussed in Chapter 3. Recall Larry Solum's thesis, which proclaims that the Constitution acquired a fixed and determined meaning at the time it was enacted [3:§1]. But what, exactly, was "christened" (approved)?

Obviously, one could never take the position that the ordinary words in the Constitution fail to develop sense in the language culture—that they, in essence, act like Kripkean sorts of words. And as a result, one could not deny that more than one example can be imagined for how to follow any provision. Given this, what, exactly, is the fixed meaning? On one hand, it can't be that *nothing* is fixed, because that would mean the same as if nothing was *spoken*—as if no written document existed. Or it would mean that senseless, meaningless scribbles were being handed to each generation. Surely, then, *something* is "fixed." But what is it?

The only thing that is fixed is the basic *gist* or general idea that always accompanies ordinary-language—the thing, in short, that allows family resemblance itself to exist. One might describe this as a pre-existing cognitive framework or a "pattern associator," as Pinker did. It is the thing that allows language to be intelligible across multiple senses and contexts. It is what allows us to speak of different senses of the same idea without becoming confused about the core or basic notion. In a manner of speaking, what is fixed is what Pinker called "the language instinct"—which is the whole reason that language can exist as a given, yet also be adaptive.

And, if all of this is true, it leads to a rather bold conclusion. It suggests that judges are not mind-readers, religious expositors or the keepers of the sacred covenants—and they are not given over to anthropological quests to discover Law's Noah. That is, they do not exist to *fight* or *deny* the problems of a plain-language constitution; they exist to *accept* them. Their proper role, in short, is to fill in "law's blanks"—that's why they are the "judges." And once this role is accepted, it means that judges take on the responsibility of helping to *speak* the language of the Constitution—to give it voice and sense—as opposed to trying to pretend that it can be read without such behavior.

I call this view *cooperative talking*. It says that judges are charged with speaking the words of the Constitution back to the framing culture, at minimum, in a way that could be understood in those language games (the intelligibility thesis). Therefore, it is our generation who is talking to "them," not vice versa. The past isn't directing our lives; we are only being handed a plain-language document with prior examples of how it was carried forth (arranged). What the past is saying to us is, "It's your turn now." We can accept the framing generation's arrangements—or some other generation's—or we can carry forth the flexible ideas with our *own* way. And if we do decide to socially arrange the document in a different way, it doesn't matter if our sense of a constitutional phrase is not *exactly* the same as theirs, so long as the language culture could understand the senses as having family resemblance.

Imagine a game where turns are taken. Each time a person takes a turn, he or she follows the rules while exercising choice. When the Constitution is handed from one generation to the next, all that is happening is a kind of turn-taking. Perhaps we regard the very first turn as a special one—we look up to it. But there is nothing in the activity of passing a plain-language document to one another that requires us to follow the past turns (to mimic prior choices). That would be a different game entirely [7:§3]. Instead, we look to the past only for helpful advice as to how we might go about our turn at the play.

But if all this is true, where does it stop? Where can it be said that ordinary language *ends,* and why doesn't this account create a willy-nilly constitution? And what is it that judges of a plain-language document are forbidden from doing when claiming to follow it? All of this I answer next.

Notes

1. The table is illustrative; it does not attempt a comprehensive list.

2. But for now, let's assume that the shift doesn't create a polysemy problem [6:§3].

3. Chris Green is a conservative American law professor who is partial to analytic philosophy and who believes that the sense of a constitutional idea is not permitted to change. Deploying the sense-reference distinction from Frege, he believes the reference of a constitutional word can change, but not its sense. For the reasons I state in my book, I obviously could not agree with his outlook. But do see his scholarship: "Originalism and the Sense-Reference Distinction," *St. Louis University Law Journal* vol. 50 (2006): 555; available at SSRN: http://ssrn.com/abstract=798466 (accessed June 12, 2012); "The Original Sense of the (Equal) Protection Clause: Subsequent Interpretation and Application," *George Mason University Civil Rights Law Journal*, vol. 19 (2009): 197; available at SSRN: http://ssrn.com/abstract=1100121 (accessed June 12, 2012); and "'This Constitution:' Constitutional Indexicals as a Basis for Textualist Semi-Originalism," *Notre Dame Law Review*, vol. 84 (August 14, 2008), 1607; available at SSRN: http://ssrn.com/abstract=1227162 (accessed June 12, 2012).

4. The Tenth Amendment reads as follows. "The powers not delegated to the United States by the Constitution, nor prohibited by it to the States, are reserved to the States respectively, or to the people." U.S. Const. Amend. X.

5. Note how similar this argument is to the example in [4:§5] where the person claimed that a bar stool wasn't a "chair." In that example, the person was acting as a chair professional, speaking with the vernacular of an expert. I had called this sort of maneuver an *assertion of technicality.*

6. See, e.g., Alexander Bird and Emma Tobin, "Natural Kinds," *The Stanford Encyclopedia of Philosophy*, ed. Edward N. Zalta (Summer 2010 Edition), http://plato.stanford.edu/archives/sum2010/entries/natural-kinds/ (accessed June 12,

2012).

7. Here's some realistic background. Before 1947, what we might call the "Air Force" was officially part of the U.S. Army, called the "Army Air Force"—but it was also made an autonomous group, distinct from the "Army Ground Forces," by virtue of an executive order in 1942. So it seems that not long after its birth, the Air Force did acquire its own behavioral routine (organization), for whatever that is worth. See Gordon L. Rottman, *U.S. Army Air Force (1)* (Osprey, 1993), 3.

8. Imagine a child playing with toy soldiers or playing the game of Risk. "The army" is simply the people who fight.

9. But what about the capital "A" in Article II—does that matter? Doesn't that show that "Army" is a proper name? The answer is *no*. Aside from the fact that capitalization norms in the Constitution are "special," a plural form of army with a capital "A" is spoken of in Article I (Art 1, §8, cl.12). Because the document therefore speaks of "Armies," one could easily imagine a decision written in the Sherlock Holmes style of John Marshall, wherein it is deduced that the capital "A" is a style convention only. The capitalization could be taken to denote general importance or emphasis, not a proper name.

10. When I use the word "positivistic" in this sense, it is similar to what other people mean when they say "hyperlexis" [3:§3, note 9]. It means that the lawyering culture in America requires that everything be spelled out. It is characterized by comprehensive codes, "statutification" [3:§3, note 10], dense administrative regulations, definition sections, elaborate and thick contractual clauses, fine print, exceptions, wherefores and whatnot. Lawyering in legal cultures like America is simply linguistically *pedantic*. That is the way that the language games are played.

11. This seems very much like saying that a dolphin belongs to the category, "mammal," because of the way the test works. It meets the axiomatic yes/no rule that is set up [4:§4]. The only difference, of course, is that the classification system for mammals is put forth by science. The one here is put forth by, presumably, bureaucrats (administrators). And so, the grammar is akin to someone who, when completing her taxes, could not classify dry cleaning as a "business expense," even if it really (naturally) was. Whatever the rules are for classifying, they are.

12. Ian Bartrum discusses a similar idea using the concept of metonymy. See [IB-2].

13. Would anyone actually doubt that the sense of "army" in 1787 is different in some way from the sense of the idea today? Cf. how the sense of "war" has evolved with its behavior ("police action"). This is true of anything. Isn't the sense of "football" different in some respects from the leather-helmet days compared to what is happening now? Why is it that people say of the same exact game (e.g., professional tennis), "The game has changed in the last twenty years—it's a different game." Of course, in one sense, it is not a different game: it's the *exact same* game. But yet, in another sense, it is much different (racket technology, pace of the ball, athleticism).

14. *Merriam-Webster's Collegiate Dictionary*, 11th ed. (2004): 18a, Explanatory Notes, Usage labels: "The temporal label archaic means that a word or sense once in common use is found today only sporadically or in special contexts."

15. Consider the following from Joseph Ellis:

Finally, who were these American people being bonded together? If Washington wished the national government to be regarded as "us" rather than "them," how did he define the "us?" He addressed his remarks in the Farewell Address to his "Friends, and Fellow Citizens." While he undoubtedly thought this description cast a wide and inclusive net that pulled in residents from all the regions or sections of the United States, it did not include all inhabitants. The core of the audience he saw in his mind's eye consisted of those adult white males who owned sufficient property to qualify for the vote. Strictly speaking, such men were the only citizens. He told Hamilton that his Farewell Address was aimed especially at "the Yoemanry of the country," which meant ordinary farmers working small plots of land and living in households" [JE-1, 157].

16. William Blackstone, *Commentaries on the Laws of England, Book 1*, 374 (Chapter 10): "A denizen is a kind of middle state, between an alien and a natural-born subject, and partakes of both of them."

17. I've made the discussion hypothetical for simplicity's sake. The parallel is to Section 1, Article II, Clause 5 of the U.S. Constitution.

18. I read the text of the Constitution this way: it doesn't say that only the birth-automatic citizens can be president; it says that only naturally-born ones can be. I've taken this to mean that x can qualify because she was born in the polity, so long as she otherwise meets the supplementary criteria. An alternative read would say that the provision only allows a person to be president if he has the *kind* of citizenship that is automatic with birth (males). This reads "natural-born citizen" as "birth-automatic citizens." Of course, there are other ways to read the middle clause as well. For purposes of the hypothetical, let's just stick with the first read I mentioned.

19. And even if they *did* have differences in what they thought heaven to be, they are likely only to be differences in how to construct the heaven *system*, not something that has a completely different *grammar*.

20. And even if the dispute was not about whether purgatory should exist in the heaven system, but was simply about how tough the entrance criteria is, this, too, would merely be a dispute about which *system* of heaven one favored, not what "heaven" is as a general idea.

21. This is admittedly an interesting question. If one could imagine a scenario where the earth took longer to revolve around the sun, would the same calendar be used? This raises the question of what is a "year." Is it a cyclical idea: the earth having come back to the same point in the rotation (the seasons starting all over again)? Or is it the fixed unit of length of 365.25 days. Astronomy speaks of the "Julian year" (365.25) while others speak of a "calendar year" (the time it takes for a planetary body to make a complete rotation).

22. For the sake of discussion, let's assume this includes mental-health aging or maturation. One could easily imagine a bio-indicator for cognitive maturation that is discovered.

23. C.f., isn't it true that, in some respects, today's 50-year-old is yesterday's 40? Is there not a social equivalency of some sort? Isn't the speaking of time-adjusted age similar in some respects to the way we speak of "constant dollars?"

24. This is the same issue that concerned the meaning of "acidosis" in [4:§2, note 28]. Is the numeric measurement unto itself or in the service of another idea? Is it a mindless 35, or 35 in the service of requisite perspective in life?

25. Balkin seems to miss this point. He writes, "Changes in circumstances cannot alter the minimum age for the President . . . because the text states a clear and determinate rule." He also writes, "[T]he underlying goal of maturity in a president does not mean that we can dispense with the 35 year age requirement" [JB-2, 481; JB-1, 305]. But of course,

the requirement of 35 years of age is *not* being ignored when a biological sense of age or flexible metric is used. In both cases, you are still counting to 35. The issue is *what* you are counting. Also, the provision doesn't say that a president has to be 35, it says that *not* being 35 rules you out. Perhaps other things are needed to "rule you in." Maybe an immature 36-year-old wouldn't make it.

26. Indeed, this would even apply to the mother herself. For if she had self-imposed those same rules when going to college, her way of following would not be what she passed along to her kids. If, however, she wants to command those specific things, she needs to say them.

27. So-called liberal originalists, like Balkin, are also susceptible to this criticism when taking positions like the following: (a) "commerce" has to mean something broad because of the way the Federalists in the First Congress behaved when passing Indian statutes; and (b) the word "age" in the Constitution cannot take on another sense unless something in history suggests the Presidential Age Clause was meant as a standard when passed [JB-2, 431-32, 481; and JB-1, 305].

Chapter 6

Structuralism and Polysemy

In this chapter, I confront the common misunderstanding that I harbor an "anything goes" approach to language. Or that I treat ordinary-language constitutions as "willy-nilly." Nothing could be further from the truth. I also address the question of what judges from different historical eras who encounter the same plain-language document are *not* allowed to do when claiming to follow its language. In other words, when does ordinary language go out of bounds?

§ 1. Structuralism

When people are first presented with the idea of family resemblance, they often react insecurely. They often confuse something being general, vague or even arbitrary on the one hand with it being a cluster or a family on the other. The two ideas are not the same. Family resemblance only means that, of the things that "count," an array or cluster exists instead of a singularity. It doesn't mean that the concern becomes arbitrary or even general.

Consider this example. It would be general or vague to say, "Bring me something I can use." But it would not be general or vague in the same way to say, "Bring me a chair." For more precision, one could say, "Bring me a recliner." Finally, one could say "Bring me *that* chair" (an indexical), or "Bring me a Wenzhou Times Company Guest Chair Model with Cushion Backrest, Model WJ277572" (a rigid designator).[1] The last two examples try to make it so that only a single item can be fetched.[2]

The simple fact is that the text of the Constitution does not have the precision of either indexicals or rigid designators. It refers with arrays or clusters. This doesn't make the document arbitrary, willy-nilly or even too general; it simply makes it *flexible*.[3] This only means that more than one way exists to follow any provision.

Besides, the beauty of family resemblance is that it solves more problems for language than it creates. As Pinker quite rightly notes, linguistic flexibility is a natural cognitive adaptation that is central to our form of life. It makes communication *better*. One of Wittgenstein's important revelations, in fact, is the idea that people can effectively communicate even though they do not have exact details or definite parameters to their ideas.[4] Wittgenstein writes: "But is it senseless to say: 'Stand roughly there?' Suppose that I were standing with someone in a city square and said that. As I say it I do not draw any kind of boundary, but perhaps point with my hand—as if I were indicating a particular *spot*. And this is just how one might explain to someone what a game is" [LW-12, 273, §71].[5]

And so, when the Constitution tells us, in effect, to put in place a program for "unreasonable searches," or a plan for "equal protection," it is not unlike the person in the passage above saying, "Stand roughly here"—which is a perfectly useful thing to tell another.[6] This hardly makes the Constitution willy-nilly.

The term that I use to describe the way that constitutional language can be both inexact, yet sufficiently efficacious, is *linguistic structuralism*.[7] This idea is very similar to one that John Brigham appealed to in his important 1978 publication, *Constitutional Language*.[8] Law professors also use the word "structuralism," but in another context.[9] In the context I mean, the term refers to a person's hand being guided even though one specific answer is not dictated. Structures help narrow our choices (set the agenda), even though they leave us free to make the final selection. So, one could read Wittgenstein as agreeing with linguistic structuralism, because of passages like this one:[10]

> For I *can* give the concept . . . rigid limits . . . but I can also use it so that the . . . concept is *not* closed by a frontier. . . . "But then the use of the word is unregulated, the 'game' we play with it is unregulated." — It is not everywhere circumscribed by rules; but no more are there any rules for how high one throws the ball in tennis, or how hard; yet tennis is a game for all that and has rules too [LW-12, 272, §68].

Having just shown that language can be perfectly efficacious when it leaves borders open (flex-talking), I move on to the next reason why a plain-language constitution is not willy-nilly.

§ 2. Culturally Appropriate

Ordinary-language constitutions are capable of being *intelligent* across time. They allow subsequent epochs in history to follow general ideas in different ways. This allows law to achieve its most central virtue: fitting society. Only a constitution with general words and broad dictates would have the best chance of surviving hundreds of years into the future. Given what we know of how culture develops, it is very important indeed that generations speak to one other, over time, through the vehicle of family resemblance.

Therefore, so long as constitutional judgments are culturally appropriate for their time [7:§3(b); 12:§1(c)-(d)], it matters absolutely *nothing* to either language or law that the sense of an idea will adjust itself or that its social arrangement will change. So long as a judge has a *cultural vindication* for what he or she does—so long as law fits society—the least of our worries would ever be that a new voicing of a constitutional idea became inaugurated in the judicial law-books.

§ 3. Polysemy

So far, I've said a great deal about family resemblance. But throughout this book, I have also dropped several endnotes about something I have been calling "polysemy." What I am going to do now is draw a very important line: I'm going to try to answer the question of when certain uses of ordinary language *necessarily* go "out of bounds." I draw the line around a theory of *polysemy* that I will now announce. But it's going to take a moment to explain, because my definition may not be the same as others.

(a) Definition

The concepts of "polysemy" and "homonym" are sometimes difficult to differentiate. In a simple sense, polysemy is said to be a word that has more than one meaning.[11] Homonym, by contrast, is said to be two words that share the same pronunciation—*sometimes* the same spelling—which also have different meanings.[12] The crux of the problem seems to be that polysemy wants to count meanings whereas homonym wants to count words.

Unfortunately, this distinction becomes rather curious. We are told, for example, that "crane," as in a bird or construction equipment, is polysemy.[13] But this, we are told, is homonym: (a) "bank," as in riverbank or financial institution;[14] or (b) "tire" as in fatigue or a car wheel.[15] And consider words like "bear," where it means either an animal or an act of carrying; or "porter," as in a weak beer or a man who carries luggage.

I want to suggest a way to clarify this. Philosophers talk of words having "sense." If a word has only one sense, it is rigid. But if it has more than one sense, each can be understood by how *familial* they are. In other words, once multiple senses are found, the next step is to determine whether multiple *families* are also present.

For example, see Illustration 6.1. It shows two family clusters. One is for the word "chair;" the other is for the word "executive." Imagine someone in a room asking for a chair, meaning a seating device, but receiving a chair of an academic department (a live person). The problem is that the live person isn't a member of the family of seating devices. Therefore, one has accessed the wrong family (cluster). And so there are two potential issues here: one that is *cross-familial* and one that is *intra-familial*.[16]

Illustration 6.1: Intra- and Extra-Familial

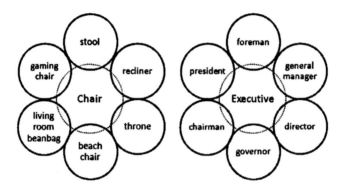

In Table 6.1, I speak of this as being two types of errors. Type-1 is where a speaker wants a "regular chair" but gets a barstool. This is a classic family-membership problem. Type-2 is where a person wants a seating item but gets a chair of a department. I prefer to call this type of error "polysemy."[17] Some may want to call it a kind of homonym, but I cannot bring myself to use that word. To me, "homonym" is best left for examples like boar and bore. And I think polysemy is best for trying to differentiate across cognitive families rather than within them. Therefore, throughout this book, my use of the term polysemy has meant what I have just indicated. If linguists object to this, perhaps *cognitive polysemy* would be a better term.[18]

Table 6.1: Polysemy and Cluster Errors

Problem	Symptom	Given Name
Type-1	Person asks for a chair in the sense of a seating item and receives a throne or a living-room beanbag.	Family Resemblance (Cluster Problem)
Type-2	Person asks for a chair in the sense of a seating item and receives a chair of an academic department.	Polysemy

(b) Significance

What, exactly, is the significance of this maneuver? I want to suggest that this is a way that ordinary language might "close the border" or mark a boundary of sorts, on its own, rather than relying upon the temporary boundaries and stipulations that speakers arrange in their individual language games. Polysemy, it seems, is naturally out of bounds.

But how can I say that? Is this an a priori account? My answer is "no." If one were to watch communication norms across various sorts of contexts, I believe one would discover something interesting. Type-1 problems are treated as being a matter of courtesy between speakers, but Type-2 problems can be returned for a full exchange of their value. That is, if I choose *not* to get you a bar stool when you ask for a "chair"—asserting a technicality and depriving you of a seat—I might be called a dirty name for doing this. But I don't get accused of cheating language. In fact, it is language that has *allowed* me to be devilish. This is why lawyers are allowed to behave the way they do. But if you ask for a chair and I bring you an executive, the norms are such that you can successfully claim *not* to have asked for *"that."* In other words, you can't be charged in the sale: there was no true exchange made in the linguistic marketplace. In a manner of speaking, all of your "language money" is returned.

If this view is accepted, any polysemous interpretation rendered by a judge is not obedient to language. To further clarify, Table 6.2 provides several examples of the issue I am raising. The implication is clear: for a judge to interpret any word in the table correctly, he or she must find the correct family resemblance.

Table 6.2: Examples of Cognitive Polysemy

Term	Options	Term	Options
Gay	Happy or homosexual	Crane	Construction equipment or bird
Chair	Seating device or an executive	Pupil	A student or the eye
Banks	Financial houses or river banks	Present	A gift or "being at the event"
Bays	Horses or bodies of water	Mole	Growth or small burrowing animal
Tire	Fatigue or car wheel	Match	Ignites or paired together

(c) Legal Examples

Here is what I have said so far: all constitutional sentences spoken with ordinary words across time carry with them a language warranty that they be understood free from polysemy. An example is whether the term "arms" in the Second Amendment refers to guns or limbs.[19] Another popular example is the Constitution's protection against "domestic violence."[20] If one reads that term as referring to spousal abuse rather than insurrection, there would be a Type-2 error. This is because "wife-beating" and armed riots are polysemous accounts of the term, as I have defined that.

Finally, consider the Constitution's Corruption of Blood Clause. It reads as follows: "The Congress shall have power to declare the Punishment of Treason, but no Attainder of Treason shall work Corruption of Blood, or Forfeiture except during the Life of the Person attainted" *U.S. Const. art. III, §3, cl. 2.*

If one isn't familiar with the history of the phrase "corruption of blood," one is in danger of misunderstanding it. Imagine someone taking the idea to mean an act of torture or death by poison ("corrupting the blood"). The idea would be that, upon conviction for treason, a person couldn't be administered toxins or chemicals by the state.[21] So, in essence, the provision would be read as an anti-torture or anti-death measure.

Why is this interpretation problematic? The answer is that it fails to catch the basic *gist* of the idea. The expression "corruption of blood" is, today, an historical idiom stemming from the English common law. It's a colorful expression that refers to a criminal being unable to bequeath property to descendants because of a serious crime. The property cannot pass at death, and nor can descendants inherit from other relatives passing through the criminal's estate. In a matter of speaking, the bloodline is now "corrupted." Hence, it is polysemous to say that the legal phrase refers to either chemical poisons or a testamentary disability. One of these is the wrong family resemblance.

(d) Not Originalism!

One of the unfortunate confusions that American law professors have shown all throughout their re-invention of originalism is that they fail to see the difference between Type-1 and Type-2 problems. Over and over again, the law professors have appealed to the problems of constitutional polysemy as the reason why originalism needed to be re-invented (imposed).[22] But a very quick and simple point must now be made: *polysemy has nothing to do with originalism.*

To see this, imagine a teacher asking a class what Plato had meant by the expression "the Forms." One would never say that the correct answer is "originalist" while the wrong ones are the "living account." Rather, the correct students simply understand Plato's expression while the others do not. This means they have an *accurate* read, not an "originalist" one.

Originalism doesn't mean "getting an accurate read." Otherwise, having good reading comprehension would mean being a good originalist. Imagine having a student who was quite good at grasping the professor's point. One would never say to her upon hearing a perfect class comment, "Caroline, you are such a great originalist; you've understood everything I've said."[23] Likewise, one wouldn't say of an archeologist who had learnt to translate hieroglyphics or of a student learning a foreign language, that both had become "originalist."

Later in this book I take up the issue of what originalism actually is [13:§1]. I direct the reader there for further discussion.

§ 4. Assertability Conditions

I opened this chapter by showing why a plain-language constitution is not a willy-nilly idea. But I also promised to show what judges from different historical eras who read the same document are *forbidden* from doing if they want to be obedient to its language. The answer is now ripe for announcing.

So long as a judge's treatment of text is intelligible to the past and avoids polysemy, the *minimum* has occurred to say that "the language has been followed." However, for the judge to follow the language *well*, he or she also needs to give the ideas in the text the best assertability conditions (grammar) possible, and reach a result that is culturally appropriate to the circumstances.[24] All of these standards help the judge not only be language-obedient, but a good casuist as well [7:§3(a)-(b)].

But what do I mean by having good assertability conditions (grammar)?[25] I simply mean that the things judges assert, either about the law or matters external to it, be free from shallow thinking and reveal a sufficiently informed, refined framework. The judge's opinion should be more than just intellectually defensible, it should reflect the best that the intellectual culture can provide for whatever subjects it addresses. I speak more about this in the next chapter and in Chapter 12 [12:§1(c)-(d)].

Of course, there have been many legal scholars who have advanced similar ideas, but they have stressed morality as being the key feature. Lon Fuller, for example, believed judges must rule in a way that avoided making the law a sham or a mockery.[26] And other scholars (along with Fuller) have espoused the need for judges to use only considerate and thoughtful means when making the law the best it could be.[27] But, the most important in this respect is Ronald Dworkin, who introduced us to the idea that legal systems involve more than just rules—they involve (in his way of speaking) esteemed judicial principles, weighty moral standards and the need for integrity in decisions.[28] Of particular note is Dworkin's idea that justices must be sufficiently attentive to their linguistic choices, something he calls "textual integrity."[29]

What is the difference between my account and scholars who follow Dworkin's path? The difference lies in two things. First, unlike Dworkin and scholars such as Sotirios Barber, James Fleming and Michel A. Moore, I do not speak of the problems of constitutional law as intrinsically belonging to moral reasoning. Rather, I speak of them as being something Wittgenstein described as *aesthetical* judgments—i.e., judgments that a connoisseur would make.[30] The second difference is that my view stresses *culture* much more than morality for its own sake.

In the next chapter, I elaborate upon these ideas.

Notes

1. Wenzhou Times Co., Ltd., is a specialty manufacturer and marketer of quality wooden toy, furnitures and promotion gifts. Model WJ277572 is one of its chairs.

2. But reducing to one is always a difficult problem. For the indexical, "Give me *that* chair" might result in a perfect replica being given. The question is whether you want

that *type* or that exact one. And for the rigid designator, the issue is reversed: although the type (model) is quite clear, many specific cases of it could be fetched. To individuate any one of them with a rigid designator, I suppose, one would need a serial number of some kind, like automobiles have (VIN). The point is only to show the challenges that exist when truly trying to "reduce to one" with uses of language alone.

3. Ian Bartrum discusses a similar idea using the concept of metonymy [IB-2].

4. When communicating in ordinary words and short sentences—e.g., "Bring me the chair"—we would like to think that our language specifically directs. Or that we "speak our intentions." But in truth, what we really say to one another is, "Through this behavior, guess what I really want in this circumstance, and help me." In other words, people who speak to one another don't often send completed, fixed messages; they send *incomplete* messages that require the other person fill in the missing parts [2:§3]. So much of what the language game really is, is agreement to help one another. If we are handed something with two of three blanks already filled in, we simply become good at filling in the third ourselves. This is how we communicate (we are used to it). As we get to know people personally, we can even communicate with two blanks missing. A mother sometimes knows what a child wants merely by seeing the child's eyes [RM-2, 99-106].

5. Other relevant passages:

How should we explain to someone what a game is? I imagine that we should describe *games* to him, and we might add: "This *and similar things* are called 'games.'" . . . But this is not ignorance. We do not know the boundaries because none have been drawn [LW-12, 272, §69].

. . . One might say that the concept "game" is a concept with blurred edges.—"But is a blurred concept a concept at all?"—Is an indistinct photograph a picture of a person at all? Is it even always an advantage to replace an indistinct picture by a sharp one? Isn't the indistinct one often exactly what we need? [LW-12, 273, §71]

. . . I use [names] without a *fixed* meaning. (But that detracts as little from its usefulness, as it detracts from that of a table that it stands on four legs instead of three and so sometimes wobbles) [LW-1, §79].

6. See the example I gave of the mother who, when sending a child to college, gave inexact, but meaningful, commands [5:§2, at end].

7. For more on "structuralism," see [SW, 28-30].

8. Brigham mentions structuralism in several places. He writes:

A model of the judicial decision based on language rather than on rules or attitudes best portrays how students of politics may characterize the place of law in this situation. . . . This view is responsive to concerns expressed by critics of contemporary social science. It is the meaning and structure of language that sets "the frame within which political thought and action proceed" [JBr, 159].

. . . Thus, the language of the law both facilitates political action and limits it. It is perhaps this paradoxical quality of language that makes it so difficult to examine in political terms. Yet, with law, it is the conceptual structure which, along with the individual capacities of attorneys, is the power of the law [JBr, 122].

. . . But "discretion," when exercised within a conceptual tradition, may be characterized as "legal" if the effective cognitive limits on choice are products of that tradition. This broadened view of the legal part of judicial decision suggests that attitudinal considerations operate along with, rather than in opposition to, the meaning and structure evident in constitutional language [JBr, 50].

9. There is a tradition in legal scholarship that uses the term "structural" to refer to arguments that are predicated upon design features in the Constitution [B&E, 117-33]. See also, Charles Black, *Structure and Relationship in Constitutional Law* (Ox Bow Press, 1969). I discussed this in note 28 in Chapter 3 (arguments for grounding separation of powers). When I use the word "structuralism," I have in mind is something more like epistemic or cognitive structuralism. I mean something more in the nature of a pre-existing cognitive framework that judicial minds work within. See John Brigham [JBr, 159].

10. Wittgenstein also writes, "If I tell someone 'stand roughly here'—may not this explanation work perfectly? And cannot every other one fail too? . . . But isn't it an inexact explanation?—Yes; why shouldn't we call it 'inexact?' Only let us understand what 'inexact' means. For it does not mean 'unusable'" [LW-1, §88].

11. See *The American Heritage Dictionary of the English Language*, 4th ed. (Houghton Mifflin Company; 2000), Polysemous: "Having or characterized by many meanings: highly polysemous words such as play and table." See also, *Collins English Dictionary—Complete and Unabridged*, 6th ed. (HarperCollins, 2003), Polysemy: "the existence of several meanings in a single word."

12. *Webster's New World College Dictionary* (Wiley Publishing, Inc., 2009), Homonym: "a word with the same pronunciation as another but with a different meaning, origin, and, usually, spelling (Ex.: bore and boar)." C.f. *American New Heritage Dictionary of the English Language*, 4th ed. (Houghton Mifflin Company, 2009), Homonym: "One of two or more words that have the same sound and often the same spelling but differ in meaning, such as bank (embankment) and bank (place where money is kept)."

13. Wikipedia: http://en.wikipedia.org/wiki/Polysemy (accessed June 12, 2012).

14. *The American Heritage Dictionary of the English Language*, 4th ed. (Houghton Mifflin Company, 2009).

15. Wikipedia: http://en.wikipedia.org/wiki/Homonyms (accessed June 12, 2012).

16. Note that one can also talk about *extended families*. A departmental chairperson might bear some linguistic relationship to a chair that you sit on, if, e.g., the historic use of "chairman" can be traced to one who sat at the head of the table in the largest chair. My point here is that, even things that are not actually in the same "cognitive family," could, nonetheless, be thought of as being long-term cousins or distant relatives. The same sort of thing exists for talking about real families. How many branches are you talking about—do you mean so many hundreds of years, or thousands upon thousands? We could all be relatives in some sense of talking (cf., space aliens). So, when I talk of "family resemblance" in the context of polysemy, I am not talking about evolutionary or distant relations. I mean "ordinary families."

17. It isn't rare for philosophers to have peculiar senses of words. To a Wittgensteinian, for example, "grammar" is much more than it is to an English professor. Polysemy is the same sort of thing. There are some technical uses of the word in linguistics that don't mean exactly what I mean. I'm concerned with cross-familial word meaning, where "families" come not from etymology, but from cognitive associations.

18. In an e-mail discussion group, a fellow by the name of Larry Tapper suggested that I call this problem "disambiguation." Wikis use this term when more than one entry exists for the same word. For example, when searching for "Mercury," one must choose between an element in chemistry, a planet or a Roman god. The reason I shunned this advice is because "disambiguation" is the process of *resolving* this problem, not the

problem itself. I needed a word for this particular *kind* of ambiguity. For more on "dis-ambiguation," see: http://en.wikipedia.org/wiki/Wikipedia:Disambiguation (accessed June 12, 2012).

19. The provision reads: "A well regulated militia being necessary to the security of a free state, the right of the people to keep and bear arms shall not be infringed" U.S. Const. Amend. II.

20. The provision reads: "The United States shall guarantee to every State in this Union a Republican Form of Government, and shall protect each of them against Inva-sion; and on Application of the Legislature, or of the Executive (when the Legislature cannot be convened) against domestic Violence." U.S. Const. art. IV, §.4.

21. This reading probably requires that the clause about forfeiture be read inde-pendently. Hence, forfeiture is only allowed during the life of the defendant, while chem-ical injections and other poisons can never be administered as punishment for the crime.

22. Jack Balkin argued that "domestic violence" could not mean spousal abuse, or else "original meaning" was violated [JB-3, 552]. When arguing this a second time, he also said that "Republican Form of Government" cannot mean a government controlled by the Republican party [JB, 430-31]. And Larry Solum—who, by the way, makes the same point about "domestic violence"—also notes the archaic sense of "deer," meaning, essentially, "beast" in Middle English [LS-2, 3-4, 64-65 and 172].

23. It's not that one couldn't speak this way. It's that, if they did, it would inaugurate a new grammar for the idea, and it would be speaking of something different.

24. I referred to judging being "culturally appropriate" in §2. I discuss this in [12:§1(c)-(d)]. The reason that judging must be culturally appropriate has to do with juris-prudence, not with language. If judicial interpretations do not fit society, the institutions of law have trouble functioning properly. And this is why, paradoxically, some theories of jurisprudence even hold that the text of a constitution may need to be violated by judges in extreme circumstances—e.g., during the Civil War or times of extreme danger. Again, I express no direct preference about such issues. My only point is to stress that what language requires and what jurisprudence requires are not always identical.

25. To understand the term "grammar," see Chapter 1, note 1.

26. See Lon Fuller's eight ways to make law a failure. *The Morality of the Law*, rev. ed. (Yale University Press, 1964), 38-39.

27. See Lon Fuller. *The Morality of the Law*, rev. ed. (Yale University Press, 1964); Henry M. Hart Jr. and Albert Sacks, *The Legal Process: Basic Problems in the Making and Application of Law*, tentative edition (Harvard University Press, 1958); and [RD-5, 140].

28. [RD-1, 355-399; RD-2, 119-177; RD-4, 118-147; and RD-6].

29. [RD-1, 338], section titled "Textual Integrity" argues that judges should do the fol-lowing: "Integrity requires [the judge] to construct, for each statute he is asked to enforce, some justification that fits and flows through that statute and is, if possible, consistent with other legislation in force. This means he must ask himself which combination of which principles and policies . . . provides the best case for what the plain words of the statute plainly require."

30. Wittgenstein uses the term "aesthetics" in a somewhat peculiar sense. He doesn't limit the idea to paintings, poems or literature. Being a tailor or seamstress is included. It could even include reading an X-ray. It applies to anything where an "eye" or "taste" for the thing in question develops. The idea is therefore about judgments by *connoisseurs* of something [7:§1; LW-2, 1-40; RM-2, 99-106; RM-1, 403-07, 529-33, 536-38, 544-50].

Chapter 7

Law as Connoisseur Judgment

In the summer of 1938, Ludwig Wittgenstein offered a course about "aesthetics" to about ten students, who were, in effect, quietly recruited by three of Wittgenstein's colleagues.[1] The lectures were informal: they were held in one of the students' private rooms.[2] All that history knows regarding these Cambridge performances can be found in the reconstructed notes from three students,[3] published forty years later.[4] The students have very similar, but differing, notes.[5] The lecture content was spontaneous, even for Wittgenstein.[6]

During the class, Wittgenstein used the term "aesthetics" with a somewhat peculiar sense. He didn't mean something limited only to art appreciation. He meant, more generally, the kind of understanding for which appreciation of paintings, poems, etc., is only an *example*. Other examples include knowing how to be a good tailor or seamstress. It applies to anything where an "eye" or "taste" for the thing in question develops.[7] In fact, Wittgenstein's approach to aesthetics really has nothing to do with art *per se*, but rather with the grammar and activity undertaken by connoisseurs of something. As such, the lectures are about artisan or *connoisseur judgment*.

In this chapter, I briefly sketch my position that constitutional judging[8] is an aesthetic in a Wittgensteinian sense. As such, saying that *x* is constitutional (or not) is ultimately an *artisan* judgment. It isn't a statement of fact or even a moral issue (for its own sake). And nor is it a science, a self-contained system of reasoning, an historical question—or even the expression of political attitudes or ideology (as a *behavior*). Rather, to properly say what the Constitution means requires that one engage in the behavior of a connoisseur, some of whom can be good or bad at their craft. I now venture to explain this idea.

§ 1. Connoisseur Judgment

Imagine that three people are asked to listen to a piece of classical music. The first, *x*, is a young person who mainly listens to popular (top 40) music. The second, y, is a guitar instructor at a music store. He knows music theory and can play various popular styles—country, pop, rock and blues. The third, z, has specific training in classical music. She is accomplished and has played in classical ensembles before. She knows both the old and newer performances occurring in the genre. She is as studiously adept with the subject (book knowledge) as she is a performer. Now, suppose that, after the three have heard the piece, each has the following reaction: x dislikes it; y loves it and z finds it unforgivably flawed. What is the nature of these respective judgments? What, philosophically, is different about them? [9]

Wittgenstein has some very helpful input on this subject. For him, simply feeling awe or disgust—or any sort of sensation—is not what connoisseur judgment is. It isn't simply an attitude or a gut reaction. It isn't being a "knee-jerk." And it certainly isn't the possession of a mere opinion or attitude about something. Instead, it's an ability that one learns to *aspect see*—that is, to see the thing in question from a certain vantage point. [10]

The key is that the cultivation of the vantage point is *transformative*. One who doesn't know about classical music, but then learns about both it and the "connections" others have who deeply appreciate it, will have attained a certain perspective. Not only will the person himself admit to the transformation, but it will arrive through a "wow moment"[11]—he will be able say, "Oh I get it now (I see it)." This doesn't mean that he will necessarily agree with the other experts; it simply means that he now has the ability to see what they do. A connoisseur, therefore, is a person who has attained the position to see the relevant aspect, which cannot be seen without learning an orientation. [12]

What Wittgenstein is really investigating here is what it means, philosophically, for a person to be *insightful*. He notes that, in aesthetics, a person of *judgment* has to emerge. [13] This can only happen after the person receives the requisite social training and experience. [14] Only then can he or she acquire the appropriate "eye" for the thing in question and talk about standards of correctness. [15]

But the idea of learned insight isn't something limited only to art. When a mother knows what her child wants merely by seeing his eyes—this, too, is a kind of connoisseur judgment. This is because she has learned to aspect-see in a way that many others have not. So, a parent who correctly interprets a child's facial expression can be insightful in the same sort of way that an art critic is when interpreting the expression of a painting.

But note that seeing the aspect is one thing; creating specimens for it is another. In the case of painting, for example, the art critic's judgment is an activity different from the actual "hand labor" needed to paint. [16] So, although it is possible for both critics and painters to share the same aspect (vantage point), the appreciation of painting constitutes a behavior distinct from the labor needed to create actual specimens. One wants to say it this way: for art, you have craft looking at a craft. This isn't so with reading faces. The person who makes a facial expression isn't (normally) engaged in a craft or technique[17]—only the person who learns to read them well is.[18]

Importantly, connoisseurs only have the ability to *show* their judgment to others—to teach its orientation[19]—not to create a science out of it ("showing versus saying").[20] That is, describing it calls for a narrative.[21] This is because, when asked to show why a judgment is "correct," the only option is to reveal how to see the aspect. This, itself, involves a kind of teaching or telling (story-like). Also, if the aesthetic is described fully, one has no choice but to disclose a cultural orientation.[22] This is because a full understanding of how the connoisseur is oriented requires the telling of things that reveal the packaging or influence of a culture.

Note also that the recipient of the story can only be in a position to make sense of the connoisseur's judgment if the aspect is properly seen.[23] This is why connoisseurs who share the same aspect immediately understand the basis of each other's judgments. Lay people, by contrast, need an orientation. Wittgenstein notes: "A connoisseur couldn't make himself understood to a jury, for instance. That is, they would understand his statements, but not his reasons. [But] he can give intimations to another connoisseur, and the latter will understand them." [RM-2, 104].

But that doesn't mean lay people cannot learn from connoisseurs. To the contrary, once the frame of reference (orientation) is understood, this insight can instruct people just as much as the field of science or any discipline. Wittgenstein says: "People nowadays think that scientists exist to instruct them, poets, musicians, etc., to give them pleasure. The idea *that these have something to teach them*—that does not occur to them" [LW-5, 36].

But still, this doesn't mean that connoisseurs are always "right." There are two different kinds of problems that can occur here. First, not all connoisseurs are equal in ability (some are poor). Just as you can have a poor tailor, seamstress, haircutter, painter, etc.—so too can you also have a poor art critic or judge of a constitution. They are poor either because they have trouble seeing the relevant aspect in question (aspect-blindness) or simply have poor skills at creating specimens. As Ray Monk says with respect to the former concern: "[T]he value of the evidence varies with the experience and the knowledge of the person providing it, and this is more or less the *only* way of weighing such evidence, since . . . it cannot be evaluated, weighted, *pondered*, by appeal to any system of general principles or universal laws" [RM-2, 104].

The second problem concerns "alternative aspects." This is where something can be seen from the vantage point of two different aesthetics. The word for this is "genre." Wittgenstein again is helpful: each genre, he says, has its own behavior-orientation that governs what is "correct."[24] This means that correctness is always only genre-centric. As such, if one were to discuss correctness *across* genres—a kind of universal correctness—only confusion would result. People would talk past themselves. Wittgenstein writes: "Suppose Lewy has what is called a cultured taste in painting. This is something entirely different to what we called a cultured taste in the fifteenth century. An entirely different game was played. He does something entirely different with it to what a man did then" [LW-2, 9, remark 29].[25]

Finally, Ray Monk notes that the idea of aspect-seeing plays an important role in Wittgenstein's overall thought. You can see it in his views about art and culture,[26] his views about "imponderable evidence,"[27] his famous duck-rabbit ("seeing as") [LW-1, 193-229], and in the positions he takes on rule following and mathematics. As Monk notes specifically about the lectures on aesthetics, "Wittgenstein brings to his discussion of these subjects many of the same examples that he used in other contexts—Cantor's Diagonal proof, Freud's confusion between cause and reason and so on—so that his discussion of aesthetics, for example, looks not so very different from his discussions of the philosophy of mathematics or philosophy of psychology" [RM-1, 403-404].

Having just finished describing what it means for someone to have a connoisseur judgment, I now discuss how this idea implicates constitutions.

§ 2. The Relationship of Law to Art

I contend that the judgments lawyers and judges make about constitutionality are aesthetical judgments in a Wittgensteinian sense. They have all of the right features: (a) a learned way to appreciate correctness; (b) the showing of "correctness" through a narrative or orientation (not a science); and (c) the revealing of culture in the showing. Good constitutional judgment requires one to see an aspect. And, understanding constitutional judgment from a prior era requires one to adopt a refinement of that aspect ("genre").

And like art, legal judging has developed "a craft looking at a craft"—for there are now bona fide critics in the field who claim to speak for the behavior in an authoritative manner.[28] So, like painting, it is one thing to talk about the skills needed to create a specimen in the field and another to talk of how to appreciate those specimens. The former concerns technical things like writing skills, absorbing all the pertinent facts and issues, etc. But the latter involves something larger. It asks how the jurist fares at making constitutional judgments, given all the possibilities. That is, how well does he or she choose among all of the things that the Constitution could be said to require? Importantly, just as there are bad movies and bad acting, there are horrendous decisions. But there are also Academy Award performances.

But what is it that really separates one from the other? It appears that a key element has something to do with *aspect seeing*. To see this, compare Dworkin's views on good legal judgment with Wittgenstein's views on good aesthetical judgment. It's striking how similar the two are. To be a good judge (in either case), you should not mechanically follow a rule as a blind servant might; you must, instead, have a higher sensibility.[29] Wittgenstein, of course, was speaking almost 50 years earlier. But compare these two passages and note how similar they are:

Dworkin:
> Imagine a community that follows] a set of rules, which they call, "rules of
> courtesy" . . . . They say, "Courtesy requires that peasants take off their hats to
> nobility," for example . . . . For a time this practice has the character of taboo:
> the rules are just there and are neither questioned nor varied. But then, perhaps
> slowly, all this changes. Everyone develops a complex "interpretive" attitude
> toward the rules of courtesy, an attitude that has two components. The first is
> the assumption that the practice of courtesy does not simply exist but has value,
> that it serves some interest or purpose or enforces some principle—in short,
> that it has some point—that can be stated independently of just describing the
> rules that make up the practice. The second is the further assumption that the
> requirements of courtesy—the behavior it calls for or the judgments it war-
> rants—are not necessarily or exclusively what they have always been taken to
> be but are instead sensitive to its point, so that the strict rules must be under-
> stood . . . by that point. Once this interpretive attitude takes hold, the institution
> of courtesy ceases to be mechanical; it is no longer unstudied deference to a ru-
> nic order. People now try to impose meaning on the institution—to see it in its
> best light—and then to restructure it in the light of that meaning [RD-1, 47].

Wittgenstein:
> In the case of the word "correct" you have a variety of related cases. There is
> first the case in which you learn the rules. The cutter learns how long a coat is
> to be, how wide the sleeve must be, etc. He learns rules—he is drilled—as in
> music you are drilled in harmony and counterpoint. Suppose I went in for tai-
> loring and I first learnt all the rules, I might have, on the whole, two sorts of at-
> titude. (1) Lewy says: "This is too short." I say: "No. It is right. It is according
> to the rules." (2) I develop a feeling for the rules. I interpret the rules. . . . Here
> I would be making an aesthetic judgment about the thing which is according to
> the rules in sense (1). On the other hand, if I hadn't learnt the rules, I wouldn't
> be able to make the aesthetic judgment. In learning the rules you get a more and
> more refined judgment. Learning the rules actually changes your judgment. [LW-
> 2, 5, §15].

Ronald Dworkin, of course, is the most important legal scholar to compare
legal judging to art. He argues that constitutional interpretation is not unlike how
learned professors of literature make interpretations of poems, novels or other
creative acts [9:§2(d)]. In this way, Dworkin is trying to define the parameters for
making sense of constitutional judging as a *behavior* (what it is).

But if judgments about constitutionality are ultimately connoisseur judgments, what is the exact behavior that is being appreciated? In dance, we know
what the behavior is (for each genre). The same is true for music. If constitutional judging is an art in which connoisseurs are in charge, how does a judge
have to behave to create the right kind of *specimen*—and how to you "score it?"
I address these issues next.

§ 3. The Appreciable Behavior

In this section, I consider two questions. The first is taxonomical. In all cases of aesthetics, connoisseurs know which things *qualify* as specimens in their field or genre and which do not. Presumably, the ones that do not qualify belong to some other field or genre.[30] The second question I address is qualitative: what makes one specimen better than another?

(a) Taxonomical Question

If a judge is bribed, has he or she actually "judged?" The point, of course, is not whether one could *say* yes or no to the question *linguistically*, because this only asks in what *sense* the statement could be true or false. Rather, the issue is whether bribed judging is the kind of behavior that connoisseurs who appreciate constitutional judgment would recognize as a true specimen of the craft. It would be the same sort of thing as asking whether lip synching belonged in a singing contest.[31]

Note that the answer to the taxonomical question is not something aspirational or a priori. What separates one aesthetic from another has nothing to do with whether a given behavior is frowned upon. So, bribed judging and lip synching are "out" not because they are atrocious, they are out because they simply are not the kind of behavior that one undertakes to carry out the craft in question—"to do the job," as it were. Just as holding a gun to the head of a judge would not be a way to "practice law."[32]

And so, what must a person do, *behaviorally*, when making a constitutional judgment, to be said by connoisseurs of the craft to have undertaken a specimen of their aesthetic? What bodily behavior must transpire and what mental or cognitive tasks must occur? It seems to me that four basic elements exist, which I depict in Illustration 7.1.

Illustration 7.1: The Elements of Constitutional Judging

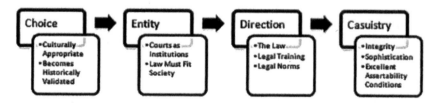

I claim that the absence of any one of these elements renders any attempt to judge the Constitution the wrong sort of thing, the way that one can engage in a form of dance inappropriate for a given genre. It would be like playing jazz when asked to play classical music. And so, if any of the elements are missing, the person is performing the *wrong* aesthetic. The four elements are: (a) a choice; (b) on behalf of another entity; (c) with supplied direction (d) using casuistry.

Consider the following scenario. Imagine a person who, each year, must pick a charity to receive a donation. Perhaps she feels obliged to give 10% of her annual disposable income to worthy causes. And so, she is forced to decide who receives the annual gift. This is a choice that involves numerous possibilities.[33]

Now assume that the person must justify or explain her choices, each year, so that each act of giving seems to cohere with one another. This is called *casuistry*.[34] Every time a choice is made, it must be said to cohere in some way with the prior choices. This makes the choices appear as though they are not random—unless, of course, randomness is being used as the official principle of distribution (fairness).[35] And if a choice in the past should ever seem *not* to cohere, this problem either needs fixed or admitted, so that something gets overruled. This is because the point is always to provide a standing explanation for *all* of the choices, so that we know how the *philosophy* of choice is said to occur.[36]

Now imagine another requirement. The person isn't allowed to make this annual choice on behalf of herself; she must make it on behalf of another entity. Perhaps she is charged with distributing the monies of a trust. She must give 10% of the annual growth in the fund to worthy causes, using casuistry. Finally, imagine that she is given *directions* or guidance as to how the choices should cohere. Better yet, she is even given *training*.

This, it seems, is what constitutional judging is as a *behavior*. It is a choice that is made on behalf of another entity (the Court), with directions and training being supplied (law), using casuistry for the explanation.[37] The point of the behavior is to make the choices cohere not only with each other, but also with the supplied directions—and only after being exposed to the stimulus of the training.

(b) Qualitative Issues

If I am right on the taxonomical issue, what makes any given specimen of constitutional judgment better than another? Another way of saying it: why is Dworkin such a good art critic?

Illustration 7.1 provides criteria for celebrating each taxonomical element. The choices judges make are said to be "good" when they are culturally appropriate and when history validates them (in retrospect). The choices must know something about courts as institutions (Hamilton) and of the need for law to fit society. This isn't a value judgment; it's a statement about how American courts as institutions function *empirically*—they don't seem to work well when divorced from society.[38] Finally, to have especially good casuistry, the way that the decisions are said to cohere must have integrity (Dworkin) and should show the best sophistication that intellectual culture can muster.[39] In short, the assertability conditions should be the best possible.

Notice that certain things are outside of the judge's control. You cannot single-handedly control the culture or the way history will break. Indeed, the best you can do is carefully ride a wave that you believe is already breaking (sexual orientation).[40] And you also must mind the institutional limits of the office, because part of the behavior involves preserving the Court as you distribute its constitutional product.

Finally, the judgments you render must show the best that intellectual culture has on the issue at hand. This becomes most tricky, no doubt, if culture is failing or is in flux (transforming). Much of what the political scientists call "ideology" or "politics" in judging, no doubt, is really just poor casuistry. It's simply a case of the jurist adopting an unrefined framework and unconvincing rationalizations. The premises are poor. The insight is hideous. And the same decision seems like it could come from the mouth of the A.M. talk radio host.[41]

Indeed, much of what I say about originalism in this book is how its assertability conditions are poor. I show that originalists are confused over how to regard a plain language document that is functioning as a "super statute" in a modern (positivistic) legal system. But it is too lazy to dismiss originalism as "ideology" without first understanding its inherent confusions. And once the confusions are understood, "ideology" becomes a mere conclusion for what originalism is, not the indictment of it.

One wants to say it this way: we should not care whether any decision is left or right. That is not the issue. The issue is whether constitutional choices are: (a) culturally appropriate and become historically validated (in retrospect); (b) exhibit a sufficient understanding for how courts as institutions function in American government; (c) offer the best that intellectual culture has for the issue at hand; and (d) cohere with the supplied directions in an integrous way. When all of the elements are undertaken well, you have what can only be regarded as exemplary constitutional judgment.[42]

(c) Conservatives and Beyond

One of the problems that conservatives have is that, in constitutional judging, they frequently appreciate the *wrong* aesthetic (behavior). To see this, imagine the following scenario. There is a constitution founded at time *x* that includes the word "liberty." The judges from this time rule that a given practice, *P*, is not protected by the liberty provision. Perhaps *P* is gay sex. Now imagine that, 200 years later, a conservative judge rules that the word "liberty" is forced to have this same exact meaning, because this is what history handed us. What is the fallacy here? It's that judges from time *x* performed *casuistry;* the conservative did not. All that the conservative did was celebrate or mimic the prior era's choice.[43] As such, he or she did not do what a judge of a constitution is required to do.

Although we can speak of this behavior as an extremely poor specimen of the craft, an expert must regard it as *the wrong craft* (aesthetic). Constitutional judging isn't the activity of mimicking or celebrating ancient judgment; it's the activity of judgment itself. That's what the ancients themselves were doing in their own time [12:§1(d)]. The only way a conservative can properly validate the past, therefore, is if there are valid *contemporaneous* reasons to show that the same judgment still remains the best choice for the trained casuist to make, today, on behalf of the Court, using the supplied directions—as if the matter was being decided fresh [13:§1(c)]. In short, conservatives must use their own noggins, not someone else's.

This is a point that Wittgenstein himself can support. He speaks about the effect of time on connoisseur judgment. He uses the example of a coronation robe during medieval times. His point is that, to interpret the robe originally, you must adopt the psychology of the culture and time with respect to it. He says:

> You talk in entirely different terms of the Coronation Robe of Edward II[44] and of a dress suit. What did *they* do and say about Coronation robes? Was the Coronation robe made by a tailor? Perhaps it was designed by Italian artists who had their own traditions; never seen by Edward II until he put it on. Questions like "What standards were there?," etc. are all relevant to the question "Could you criticize the robe as they criticized it?" You appreciate it in an entirely different way; your attitude to it is entirely different to that of a person living at the time it was designed. On the other hand, "This is a fine Coronation robe!" might have been said by a man at the time in exactly the same way as a man says it now [LW-2, 9, §31].

My point here is very simple. The interpretation of a constitution in the manner in which Wittgenstein speaks would be strange because it would be the *wrong* kind of *behavior* for the aesthetic. Compare developing an eye for a colonial dress versus developing a colonial eye for "cruel and unusual punishment." Where do people generally need these sorts of "eyes?" In both cases, you need them for things like theater, drama, and cultural studies. But this is not what the behavior of judging *is*—it's not the right aesthetic. A Supreme Court jurist is not an appreciator of past culture; he or she is a casuist, with directions and training, on behalf of a third party. In short, the very same thought process that allowed an "eye" to develop for "cruel and unusual punishment" in the late 1700s must be used by thinkers today to develop their *own* eye for the period in which they live. You learn to perform *this* aesthetic (craft), not to appreciate the prior era's picks. Learning the appreciation of the prior picks is a completely different *kind* of appreciation. It's a completely different genre or perhaps a different form of art.

I have now finished my brief argument as to how constitutional judgments are an aesthetic in a Wittgensteinian sense. The implication is clear: what the Constitution "really means" is something that is an artisan judgment. That doesn't mean that all opinions about the subject are equal—quite to the contrary, only those that properly see the relevant aspect and appreciable behavior are the ones that matter most. As such, poor opinions about constitutionality reduce to only one of two things. They either exhibit aspect blindness (total or in degree), or they reflect a poor ability to create specimens of the craft. And so, you have people who either do not understand constitutional judgment and/or people who simply make for poor deciders.

Therefore, we must get away from this idea that some decisions of the Court "follow the Constitution," while others do not. In truth, every opinion given by any justice *attempts* to "follow law." Instead, we must ask ourselves which of these followings are better than the others. The question is never whether a judge is following a constitution; it is always whether he or she is following it *well*.

This, I think, solves all of the problems.

Notes

1. The course wasn't publicized in the official course listing, because Wittgenstein was trying to keep his enrollment down. He only liked to lecture to a small group of students. The three colleagues who recruited the students were fellow philosophers John Wisdom, G. E. Moore, and Richard Braithwaite [RM-1, 402]. Wittgenstein also offered a course on religious belief "about the same time," which I assume means later in the summer [LW-2, Preface—no pagination].

2. The preface to *Lectures and Conversations* indicates that the lectures were given in "private rooms." Monk says they were held in one of James Taylor's rooms, a Canadian graduate student taking the course [RM-1, 402].

3. The students were Yorick Smythies, Rush Rhees and James Taylor.

4. The notes are neither a verbatim nor a complete account of the material. The preface indicates that the authors "do not vouch for their accuracy in every detail: they do not claim to give a verbatim report of what Wittgenstein said." It continues, "[A] word about the choice of material. This is only a selection from the extant students' notes of Wittgenstein's lectures. Yet, in spite of appearances, it is not a random selection" [LW-2, Preface—no pagination].

5. The preface indicates that the most complete specimen of notes was chosen for the text of the book, with variations appearing in footnotes. When quoting the book in these endnotes, I'm showing all the versions. I have excavated the footnoted material so that it appears as little notes below the body of the quoted item. The variations are indicated by superscript "A" or "B," followed by the student's last name.

6. Wittgenstein himself cautioned, "If you write these spontaneous remarks down, some day someone may publish them as my considered opinions. I don't want that done. For I am talking now freely as my ideas come, but all this will need a lot more thought and better expression" [RM-1, 403].

7. Wittgenstein writes, "Ask yourself: How does a man learn to get a 'nose' for

something? And how can this nose be used?" [RM-2, 100].

8. One could apply this idea to any appellate judging, not just constitutional issues. Because the concern of the book is with constitutionality, however, I don't feel the need to venture down other roads at the moment. I want to stay with a focused concern.

9. I've left nothing but images here. One could insert all sorts of details that could affect the conclusion. Perhaps z has become so much of a snob that others with similar credentials would never share her reaction. Perhaps y only likes the music because it sounds like a movement in a rock opera that he knows. I've left it to the reader to mix and substitute additional facts in various ways. I only want the idea to be contemplated.

10. Wittgenstein is taken as saying:

> If a man goes through an endless number of patterns in a tailor's, [and] says: "No. This is slightly too dark. This is slightly too loud," etc., he is what we call an appreciator of material. That he is an appreciator is not shown by the interjections he uses, but by the way he chooses, selects, etc. Similarly in music: "Does this harmonize? No. The bass is not quite loud enough. Here I just want something different . . . ." This is what we call an appreciation [LW-2, 7].

11. Wittgenstein is taken as saying:

> A man says it ought to be read *this* way and reads it out to you. You say: "Oh yes. Now it makes sense." . . . I had an experience with the 18th century poet Klopstock.[A] I found that the way to read him was to stress his metre abnormally. . . . When I read his poems in this new way, I said: "Ah-ha, now I know why he did this." What had happened? I had read this kind of stuff and had been moderately bored, but when I read it in this particular way, intensely, I smiled, said: "This is *grand*," etc. But I might not have said anything. The important fact was that I read it again and again. When I read these poems I made gestures and facial expressions which were what would be called gestures of approval. But the important thing was that I read the poems entirely differently, more intensely, and said to others: "Look! This is how they should be read."[B] Aesthetic adjectives played hardly any role [LW-2, 4-5].
>
> [A] Friedrich Gottlieb Klopstock (1724-1803). Wittgenstein is referring to the Odes. (*Gesammelte Werke*, Stuttgart, 1886-7). Klopstock believed that poetic diction was distinct from popular language. He rejected rhyme as vulgar and introduced instead the metres of ancient literature.—Ed.
>
> [B] If we speak of the right way to read a piece of poetry—approval enters, but it plays a fairly small role in the situation.—Rhees.

12. It's not that lay people do not see their own sort of aspect. An uninformed view might see *some* kind of aspect in classical music when criticizing (or praising) it. However, the picture of account stems only from things that are self-evident. As such, to *knowingly* criticize (or praise) the music requires that one first be able to see the aspect that is hidden—the one that connoisseurs have. Only after this is seen can a person knowingly render a judgment about the matter. Without indulging both kinds of perspectives, the person cannot properly make sense of the two.

13. Wittgenstein is taken as saying:

> In what we call the arts a person who has judgment develops. (A person who has a judgment doesn't mean a person who says "Marvellous!" at certain things.).[A] . . . When we

make an aesthetic judgment about a thing, we do not just gape at it and say: "Oh! How marvelous!" We distinguish between a person who knows what he is talking about and a person who doesn't"[B] [LW-2, 6, §17].

[A] In what we call the arts there developed what we call a "judge"—i.e., one who has judgment. This does not mean just someone who admires or does not admire. We have an entirely new element.—Rhees

[B] He must react in a consistent way over a long period. Must know all sorts of things.— Taylor.

14. Wittgenstein writes:

An important fact here is that we learn certain things only through long experience and not from a course in school. How, for instance, does one develop the eye of a connoisseur? Someone says, for example, "This picture was not painted by such-and-such a master"—the statement he makes is thus not an aesthetic judgment, but one that can be proved by documentation. He may not be able to give any good reasons for his verdict.— How did he learn it? Could someone have taught him? Yes—Not in the same way as one learns to calculate. A great deal of experience was necessary. That is, the learner probably had to look at and compare a large number of pictures by various masters again and again. In doing this he could have been given hints. Well, that was the process of learning. But then he looked at a picture and made a judgment about it. In most cases he was able to list his reasons for his judgment, but generally it wasn't they that were convincing [LW-6, §925].

15. Wittgenstein is taken as saying:

If a person is to admire English poetry, he must know English. Suppose that a Russian who doesn't know English is overwhelmed by a sonnet admitted to be good. We would say that he does not know what is in it at all. Similarly, of a person who doesn't know meters but who is overwhelmed, we would say that he doesn't know what's in it. In music this is more pronounced. Suppose there is a person who admires and enjoys what is admitted to be good but can't remember the simplest tunes, doesn't know when the bass comes in, etc. We say he hasn't seen what's in it. We use the phrase "A man is musical" not so as to call a man musical if he says "Ah!" when a piece of music is played, any more than we call a dog musical if it wags its tail when music is played.[A] [LW-2, 6, §17].

[A] C.f. the person who likes hearing music but cannot talk about it at all, and is quite unintelligent on the subject. "He is musical." We do not say this if he is just happy when he hears music and the other things aren't present.—Taylor

16. Indeed, perhaps the painter is a student who is poor at the craft, and the critic is a teacher who knows well a poor specimen—but who, himself, cannot paint especially well. In this situation, the teacher performs the job of connoisseur admirably so that the student learns to see the deficiencies from the standpoint of the aspect. But in both cases, neither performs the actual labor of painting very well.

17. This assumes that the person isn't, e.g., a clown in a circus (or a mime), in which case "making faces" *could* be regarded as its own aesthetic.

18. And another point must be made. This whole area of concern is about "expert judgments," not about metaphysics. No one is talking about things like tarot cards or horoscopes. So when Wittgenstein describes people who come to learn what their children are thinking by a look they see in their eyes, it is not anything related to what a

person does when they attempt to read a palm. The issue is about learned insightfulness, not the indulgence of mystical arts.

19. Wittgenstein is taken as saying:

> In order to get clear about aesthetic words you have to describe ways of living. We think we have to talk about aesthetic judgments like "This is beautiful,"[A] but we find that if we have to talk about aesthetic judgments we don't find these words at all, but a word used something like a gesture, accompanying a complicated activity[B] [LW-2, 11, §35].
>
> [A] Cf. "This is a fine dress."—Rhees.
>
> [B] The judgment is a gesture accompanying a vast structure of actions not expressed by one judgment.—Rhees.

20. [RM-1, 405]. Wittgenstein is taken as saying, "It is not only difficult to describe what appreciation consists in, but impossible. To describe what it consists in we would have to describe the whole environment" [LW-2, 7, §20]. He continues:

> You can get a picture of what you may call a very high culture, e.g., German music in the last century and the century before, and what happens when this deteriorates. A picture of what happens in architecture when you get imitations—or when thousands of people are interested in the minutest details. A picture of what happens when a dining-room table is chosen more or less at random, when no one knows where it came from[A,B] [LW-2, 7, §22].
>
> [A] Explain what happens when a craft deteriorates. A period in which everything is fixed and extraordinary care is lavished on certain details; and a period in which everything is copied and nothing is thought about—Taylor
>
> [B] A great number of people are highly interested in detail of a dining-room chair. And then there is a period when a dining-room chair is in the drawing-room and no one knows where this came from or that people had once given enormous thought in order to know how to design it.—Rhees

21. As Ray Monk writes, "[I]t can be seen as evidence for a particular judgment, but usually it cannot be described other than as evidence for that judgment (e.g., 'How do you know your father dislikes your boyfriend?' 'I could tell by the way he looked at him' 'And how did he look at him?' 'Well, . . . as if he didn't like him')" [RM-2, 104].

22. Wittgenstein is taken as saying:

> The words we call expressions of aesthetic judgment play a very complicated role, but a very definite role, in what we call a culture of a period. To describe their use or to describe what you mean by a cultured taste, you have to describe a culture.[A] What we now call a cultured taste perhaps didn't exist in the Middle Ages. An entirely different game is played in different ages [LW-2, 8, §25].
>
> [A] To describe a set of aesthetic rules fully means really to describe the culture of a period.—Taylor

23. I can't resist: this is precisely what a good college professor should do in a classroom. He or she should try to get students to see an aspect in something that cannot be readily seen. We tend to think knowledge is about information or data. Though this is part of it, what really matters is how well a person can see the aspects of the matter. Being insightful is more important than simply knowing information.

24. Wittgenstein is taken as saying:

We talked of correctness. A good cutter won't use any words except works like "Too long," "All right." When we talk of a symphony of Beethoven we don't talk of correctness. Entirely different things enter. . . . In certain styles of architecture a door is correct, and the thing is you appreciate it. But in the case of a Gothic cathedral what we do is not at all to find it correct—it plays an entirely different role with us.[A] The entire *game* is different. [LW-2, 7-8, §23].

[A] Here there is no question of *degree*.— Rhees.

25. Note the implication of this passage for originalism. We couldn't mimic an 18th century understanding of the Constitution because it would be engaging in a different kind of game (behavior) [7:§3(c)].

26. One should remember that Wittgenstein had never considered the subject of aesthetics to be divorced, esoteric or deserted in any way from his "normal" philosophic concerns. Indeed, the Preface to *Lectures and Conversations* states, "The notes printed here reflect Wittgenstein's opinions on and attitude to life, to religious, psychological and artistic questions. That Wittgenstein himself did not keep these questions separate is clear, for example, from G.E. Moore's account of the 1930-33 lectures (*Mind* 1955)." The reference is to Moore's article, "Wittgenstein's Lectures in 1930-33," which is reprinted in, *Ludwig Wittgenstein, Philosophical Occasions, 1912-1951*, ed. James Klagge and Alfred Nordmann (Hackett Publishing Co., 1993), 46. Also, the general sentiment of the point is well supported in Monk's *Duty of Genius*.

27. For a brief but good account of "imponderable evidence," see [RM-2, 99-106].

28. I would argue that Ronald Dworkin is the best art critic that the craft of judging has seen in the last century.

29. More support from Wittgenstein can be seen in this remark, concerning when the rules of the same game can be changed. He writes:

But, after all, the game is supposed to be defined by the rules! So, if a rule of the game prescribes that kings are to be used for drawing lots before a game of chess, then that is an essential part of the game. What objection might one make to this? That one does not see the point of this prescription. Perhaps as one wouldn't see the point either of a rule by which each piece had to be turned round three times before one moved it. If we found this rule in a board-game we should be surprised and should speculate about the purpose of the rule. ("Was this prescription meant to prevent one from moving without due consideration?") [LW-1, §567]

30. I'm not saying there will be a sharp boundary here. Surely there are border cases. And also, new genres could develop within any field. Nonetheless, there will always be plenty of examples that get *legitimately* excluded from membership. Part of what the connoisseur is doing in this instance is protecting artistic integrity. The aesthetic would be destroyed if it did not have some boundaries—unless, of course, it was an aesthetic predicated precisely upon that (e.g., modern pop dance). Besides, when connoisseurs erect walls, they don't do anything other than relegate the excluded to their own sort of fortress (their own respective genres).

31. We could imagine, of course, there being a lip synching contest, but this would be a different kind of contest (a different aesthetic) than one where contestants actually sang. And it's also possible, I imagine, for one to have a contest where both singers and "lip synchers" entered, in the same way that a fight contest might enroll wrestlers and

kick-boxers. But even here, the question is whether your point is to appreciate a fracas (donnybrook), versus whether it is to appreciate wrestling or kick-boxing respectively. In the latter situation, it would seem odd for them to be together.

32. Note what's being said here: holding a gun to the head of a judge isn't practicing law poorly, it's not "practicing law" at all. Yet, if one said of another who did such a thing that he had "practiced poorly," the expression could surely be understood (humorously). This is because we could imagine the practice of law in another world where the robbing of a decision would be part of the behavior. Perhaps this is the way the courts of the Devil work. But, even so, this is a totally different aesthetic—we are speaking of a totally different kind of system going on.

33. It seems to involve the skills of comparison-and-contrast, except that one could surely create a logic for it. For example, the person could be a "cause-donator," giving all the money each year to a pet peeve (e.g., breast cancer) or favorite charity. But the point is, even this creation began with the need to make a *choice*.

34. I don't use this term with a negative connotation, the way it was understood centuries ago. Dictionaries still list both. Casuistry is: "1. in the positive sense, (a) the art (science, ideology, doctrine) that deals with questions of right or wrong conduct, or (b) the actual application of moral principles to particular conduct. 2. In the negative sense, sophistical, equivocal, false, or misleading reasoning or teaching about one's moral conduct, duties, and principles. *The Harper Collins Dictionary of Philosophy,* 2nd ed., ed. Peter A. Angles (HarperPerennial, 1992), 37.

35. And if they do appear random when they are not supposed to, they look "ditsy" or specious. One would say of such a thing that the casuistry being used was extremely poor.

36. And again, any problem that may exist in the stated philosophy only indicates that the casuistry is poor.

37. There might be another element here. You aren't the only one doing this: a bunch of people throughout history are. People are taking turns. So, it is not that one person has to make all the choices on behalf of another entity—each cohering with the directions, after training—it's that one person has to take a few *turns* doing this. You have to fit your contribution in with all the other people who have already done it. And if you are good, you probably also should think how people who come after you will be able to work with your choices (foresight). This is quite similar to Dworkin's "chain novel."

38. Gerald R. Rosenberg, *The Hollow Hope: Can Courts Bring About Social Change?* (University of Chicago Press, 1991).

39. This isn't a contradiction. If intellectual culture believed in *x*, it must bear *some* relationship to that society, though it may not be popular. When I say law should fit society, I do not mean that it should fit majority sentiment (preference). I mean it should fit its cultural behavior and orientation—its form of life, so to speak [13:§3, note 33].

40. This seems to have a kind of Machiavellian flavor to it, except it isn't concerned with being devious and maximizing your own gain. Rather, it simply says that, before a judge can do anything, he or she must know the cultural environment in which the judgment occurs.

41. For an analysis of what I mean here, see the following lecture clip on the Rehnquist flag burning opinion: http://ludwig.squarespace.com/supremes/2008/5/5/24h-the-rehnquist-dissent-in-texas-v-johnson-a-pathological.html

42. We've got to stop this idea that judging has to be liberal or Rawlsian to be "good." Such a thing would only be true in a liberal or Rawlsian political culture. But we do have to demand that, whether a decision is left or right, that it also exhibit a refined and insightful framework—that it be, as I say, the best that intellectual culture has to offer on the issue at hand.

43. The idea that I present here is similar, but still somewhat different, from Philip Bobbitt's views about "conscience." Bobbitt argues that, if you surrender your mind to a calculus or mantra, you are no longer making a choice of conscience, which is what judging requires. Note that he targets liberals as well as conservatives: "[D]eciding to rely upon Rawls is not deciding a case" and, "[D]oing justice requires a mastery of the art of deciding and not the principles of a theory of justice" [PBt-2, 174, 170]. Bobbitt is against any kind of a priori approach or formal analysis (calculation). You, yourself, must choose, and not pretend something can do it for you. My difference with Bobbitt is only slight here. I am against *mindless* calculation, not calculation per se. So long as the calculation can be defended on its own merits—so long as its proponent *believes* rather than submits—it matters nothing that the choice adopts the style of arithmetic. Analyticity is fine for us to wield so long as it doesn't wield us.

44. This should read Edward the Confessor, according to another student (James Taylor). See notes 3 and 5.

Part II:

Understanding Originalism

Chapter 8

The Philosophy of Framers' Intent

The best place to begin a discussion of originalism is to start with the past. Suppose someone took the position that the Constitution can only mean what its framers intended.[1] This view is called *Original-Intention*,[2] and, for efficiency, I abbreviate it OI.

§ 1. The Role of Text

There are two basic ways that OI can be structured. One, which is uncommon, is called *text-free*. It says that the Framers' intentions are more important than the text of the Constitution itself. This view wouldn't care what is written; it would only care what the document's *creator* desired. It would make the Constitution similar to a biblical text, in that one must discover the mind of the lawgiver to properly speak about the scriptures. In fact, in this view, the lawgiver's mind *is* the law. Therefore, a text-free version of OI would disregard any constitutional provision that seems contrary to the wishes of "the Framers,"[3] to the extent that such a view could be defensible.[4]

This is not what most OI-theorists believe. Most are *text-centered*. For this idea, intent is discussed only in the context of what *sentences* mean. The difference is that one view treats the minds of the Framers as autonomous; the other requires them to serve (in some way) the words of the document.

I contend that text-centered OI requires *covenant-training*. It requires one to learn the master's preferences for his or her commands—to learn the favored arrangement—so that those desires can be enforced when reading the Constitution. This view treats the text of the document as a sort of *covenant* bestowed by the Framers to their progeny, requiring training to understand the things that would have pleased the grantor in carrying forth the behest.[5]

§ 2. Temporal Issues

Aside from the question of what the Framers wanted for the Constitution, another challenge is *when* they are allowed to have held such beliefs. There are two perspectives to consider. One says that the desires of Framers must be gauged at the time the legal provision(s) in question are enacted (formalistic).[6] The other says that the views are allowed to arrive *after* the passage (devotional).

In formalistic versions of OI, the search for Framers' intent ends after the law in question is passed: any desires arising post-passage are irrelevant.[7] This view implicitly says that Framers themselves are only relevant for the event they participated in ("the framing"), not for reasons of their supposed general greatness or prowess. It is helpful to think of this view as *event-centric*.

The opposite position is *devotional*. It believes that Framers' wishes are the most paramount legal truth, period—no matter when those beliefs are formed.[8] Being formalistic or devotional is something separate from being text-free or text-centered. This means that these distinctions form a matrix, which is presented in Table 8.1. Text-centered, formalistic OI is the version that most legal conservatives actually espoused throughout American history, at least prior to the 1990s.[9]

Table 8.1: Original Intention Matrix

	Text-Free	Text-Centered
Formalistic	Whether the Framers think that flag-burning should have been protected by the Constitution at the time the document is passed. ——— Whether the Framers think that abortion should have been protected by the Constitution at the time the document is passed.	Whether the Framers think flag burning counts as "speech" under the First Amendment at the time the Constitution is passed. ——— Whether the Framers think abortion counts as a protected liberty under the Ninth or Fifth Amendment at the time the Constitution is passed.
Devotional	Whether the Framers think flag-burning should have been protected by the Constitution at any point in their lives. ——— Whether the Framers think abortion should have been protected by the Constitution at any point in their lives.	Whether the Framers think flag burning counts as "speech" under the First Amendment, at any point in their lives. ——— Whether the Framers think abortion counts as a protected liberty under the Ninth or Fifth Amendment, at any point in their lives.

Note how the cells in Table 8.1 implicate distinct roles in American government. For text-centered/devotional OI, the only truly perfect (or righteous) judges who could ever sit on the Supreme Court would be the Framers themselves. This is because "ultimate law" in this belief system is what Framers would come to espouse for the meaning of the provisions in the Constitution during their lives, no matter if such thoughts occur after passage and even amount to a reversal of their original beliefs. The formalistic version of this school says same thing, except that the beliefs must be frozen in time specifically during the point of passage.

The other two approaches, however, don't treat the Framers as judges; they treat them as *legislators*. For example, text-free/devotional OI believes that Framers have the right, in theory, to re-author or re-issue the fundamental law throughout the tenure of their lives. So if they get it wrong the first time, they could, later on, cabal the corrections from their collective temple—at least according to this theory of constitutional righteousness. The formalistic version also treats Framers as legislators, but only for all of those things they would have agreed to pass initially, had they *perfectly* considered them. The idea is thus: if the Framers had produced a *perfect* or *comprehensive* Constitution—one that would have addressed all of the problems according to their exact wishes— what would the "fundamental law" have said? If this differs from what was actually written, this is what the "true law" is.

Having just considered the issue of *when* Framers can believe things, I now consider *what* they are allowed to believe.

§ 3. What Kind of Beliefs Matter?

Imagine that one could talk to the Framers today. What sorts of questions would an OI theorist ask to gain better information about what the Constitution means? Essentially, the issue reduces to this: are Framers allowed to expound upon the Constitution with *prescriptive beliefs*, or must they be confined to *event-testimony*?

By "prescriptive beliefs," I mean all of those beliefs that allow one to endorse a *framework* about the world. For example, Framers in the late 1700s might have opinions on: (a) how best to orchestrate social utility or general welfare; (b) philosophical understandings (e.g., Montesquieu); (c) the latest scientific news or Enlightenment thought; (d) world views, cultural orientations, religious and political convictions, and so forth. Note that if Framers are allowed to rely upon these things when stating (or clarifying) "fundamental law," their occupancy becomes similar to that of a sage or wise man. All versions of devotional or text-free OI seem to flirt with this idea to some extent.

However, if Framers are confined only to giving *event-testimony*, their occupancy changes remarkably. They would more resemble those who give lay testimony in court. Imagine a world where Framers were summoned to answer questions about the Constitution, but could only field two basic inquiries: (a) "what happened when *x* was passed into law"; and (b) "what were your complete thoughts about it during the event?" To explore this view in more detail, I present the Memory Pensieve.

(a) The Memory Pensieve

Let's imagine a possible world where one could know perfectly and completely the thoughts of Framers during the passage of law, using Dumbledore's *Memory Pensieve* (from the Harry Potter series). The Pensieve is the liquid-filled stone basin that Dumbledore uses to see the memories of other people.[10]

Imagine that we have the Pensieve, but can only use it to gather event testimony from each Framer. Therefore, we are able to know, with complete certainty, the state of mind of each person who participated in the adoption of the Constitution. Table 8.2 summarizes the possible statements that we could gather from this information,[11] with the very last column indicating what the law is, according text-centered/formalistic OI.

Table 8.2: The Framers' Possible Memories

Type	Degree	Explanation	End Result
Intention	3rd 2nd 1st	We mean the text to say this concept We mean this concept to have these criteria We mean these instantiations	Concept is the law Criteria are the law Instantiations are the law
Confusion	– 3rd 2nd 1st	Confusion or mistake produced this text Confusion existed for this concept Confusion existed for these criteria Confusion existed for these instantiations	Fix text (backup plan?) Fix concept (backup plan?) Fix criteria (backup plan?) Fix instantiation (backup plan?)
Assumption	3rd 2nd 1st	We assume the text means this concept We assume the concept has these criteria We assume these instantiations	Concept is the law Criteria are the law Instantiations are the law
Projection	3rd 2nd 1st	We insist the text says this concept We insist the concept has these criteria We insist these instantiations are covered	Concept is the law Criteria are the law Instantiations are the law
Demurral	3rd 2nd 1st	We never considered this concept We never considered criteria We never considered an instantiation	Reconstruct or consult a back-up plan?

Several points must now be made about the table. First, note that only five basic kinds of statements are possible. They are: intention, confusion, assumption, projection[12] and demurral. Each of these statements is *provision-centric*.[13] They each take constitutional text as a *given*.

(b) Specificity of Belief

Note how the table handles *specificity* in belief. The table mentions three different levels of analysis: concepts, criteria and instantiations.[14] This terminology was explained in Chapter 2. Note that the table does not discriminate against levels of meaning. Framers are allowed to make instantial judgments about the Constitution (e.g., that it does not protect abortion) as much as they are allowed to make conceptual judgments (that it protects privacy). This is different from what some American law professors argue. They don't like history to make instantial judgments.[15] I discussed this view elsewhere in the book [2:§2(a); 3:§4, note 35].

(c) Confusion?

The second point that must be made concerns the problem of confusion and demurral. Both of these mental states effectively leave constitutional text *without meaning* at one or more levels of analysis. This is because the "true meaning" of the provision lies in the memories of the Pensieve, not in the text itself (for this school). What would text-centered/formalistic OI do in such a situation?

My answer is that, if the confusion is *understandable*,[16] the school would fix it, because doing so is still in the service of the Framers' desires (as validated by the Pensieve). But if the confusion is not understandable—it's much worse than a simple mistake—it seems that this school of thought not only runs out of any orthodox answer, but finds itself in quite a pickle. On the one hand, "ultimate law" is the will of "the Framers." Yet, complete information has shown that this supposedly exalted authority is intellectually deficient *within its own mind* (on its own terms). Hence, if the lawgiver *himself* admits this, what do the believers do next? It seems they either become the constitutional gods themselves (living constitutionalism?) or they impose some sort of backup plan— such as what Framers would have thought had they *not* been confused. Both of these, of course, venture outside of the boundaries of OI, strictly speaking, because they start the process of *correcting* Framers.[17]

The same holds for demurral. You must either say what the Framers would have done had they *not* demurred (reconstructing that event), or you must, yourself, become "the Framers" (drafting anew). And both of these options, it seems, *add to* or create fundamental law in ways incongruent with the central premises of the school.[18]

§ 4. Imaginary Personification

From all that I have said above, it should be quite clear what all versions of OI have in common. They all invent a personification or chain of thought—the will of "the Framers"—that is used as the core feature in the belief system. Reading the Constitution, therefore, requires you, in essence, to serve the wishes of someone else's mind (in theory). A good term for this is *boss logic*.

But most importantly, note that the personification is *imaginary*. It isn't imaginary in the sense of fictional literature—the Framers, of course, were real people. But it is imaginary in the sense that various lives are pretended to be a single mind—one amalgamated persona or chain of thought that can provide (imagined) direction. That is the central feature of all OI belief systems. The idea is that "ultimate law" is the proper servitude owed to this conceptualized persona.

In summary, then, OI asks two things of its adherents. First, one must offer an idea of what history allows for the imagined (collective) judgment of "the Framers." And second, one must claim that this imagined mindset constitutes fundamental law in one way or another (text-free, text-centered, devotional, formalistic).

Note

1. Keith Whittington notes an interesting colloquy between conservative Senator Sam Ervin and former liberal Supreme Court Justice Thurgood Marshall during the latter's confirmation hearings. The exchange reveals the thinking of its time:

> As the Warren Court's rights revolution became increasingly controversial in the late 1960s, critics of the Court frequently recurred to original intent to ground their disagreement with the Court's innovative rulings. The tension is evident in an exchange between Sam Ervin and Thurgood Marshall during the latter's confirmation hearings in 1967. Unsatisfied with Marshall's initial response, Ervin repeated the question: "Is not the role of the Supreme Court simply to ascertain and give effect to the intent of the framers of this Constitution and the people who ratified the Constitution?" Marshall answered, "Yes, Senator, with the understanding that the Constitution was meant to be a living document" [KW-2, 599]. See also, Gregory Bassham, *Original Intent and the Constitution* (Rowman & Littlefield, 1992), 12.

2. [RB-2, 620; KW-2]. See also the following on original intent: Robert H. Bork, "Neutral Principles and Some First Amendment Problems," *Ind. L.J.* 47 (1971):1; and Raoul Berger, *Government by Judiciary*, 2nd ed. (Liberty Fund, 1997). See also [OV, 1248], which reads: "Prominent from the 1960s to the mid-1980's, intentionalism sought to interpret the Constitution by determining the subjective intentions and expectations of its drafters. . . . [T]he framers expected that their intent would govern how their posterity interpreted the Constitution," citing Raoul Berger, Government by Judiciary (1977), 365-66;

3. I place this word in quotes regularly. The reason is because the grammar of the expression often forces us to think of an institutional process (drafting and passing law) as though it was a *personification* [8:§5 and 9:§1]. Because the belief system requires this picture, I cannot resist the quotes.

4. Properly translated, this idea asks a simple question: what would the Constitution look like if it were *re-written* to perfectly match Framers' desires? That is, what would the document have said in a state of perfection wherein every relevant wish of "the Framers" was clearly expressed? Whatever revisions one might make to the document's language in this respect is considered "the true law."

5. It's the same sort of logic a child uses when running to his or her parents. "Can I do this?" The telling of "yes" or "no" teaches the system of belief, so that the child learns

how to follow. This is another way of saying that an aesthetic is being taught. Wittgenstein's idea of "showing versus saying" is helpful here. You don't teach the idea by "proof" or appealing to something a priori; you teach it by showing in real life how it works (social training). Once the child is a master in the father's tutelage, he or she has graduated from the covenant training.

6. See, e.g., Richard A. Primus, "When Should Original Meanings Matter?" *Mich. L. Rev.* 107 (November, 2008): 186-87, who writes: "Originalism is a family of ideas and practices that locate the authoritative content of legal provisions in meanings that prevailed, actually or constructively, at the time when the provisions were enacted." See also, Keith Whittington, who writes: "Originalism regards the discoverable meaning of the Constitution at the time of its initial adoption as authoritative for purposes of constitutional interpretation in the present" [KW-2, 599]; and "The guiding principle is that the judge should be seeking to make plain the 'meaning understood at the time of the law's enactment'" [KW-1, 3].

7. Of course, the idea of "passage" may need defined. If a framer votes upon the law at the Constitutional Convention, but is not part of the ratifying convention, can he change his mind before passage ends—or does it end for him when he votes? If it ends when he votes, this is an *orthodox view of passage.* Another view would allow all of those thoughts that occurred throughout the entire process—from May of 1787 through June 21st of 1788.

8. What if one tried to imagine the desires of Framers, if they could still be living today? If we imagine beliefs being bound in cultural time—e.g., beliefs about abortion—it might be possible to ask how they would have evolved, had the person lived through major transformations in culture. Although speculative, it isn't beyond contemplation. Illustration 8.1 attempts to conceptualize this.

Illustration 8.1: Original v. Dynamic Intention

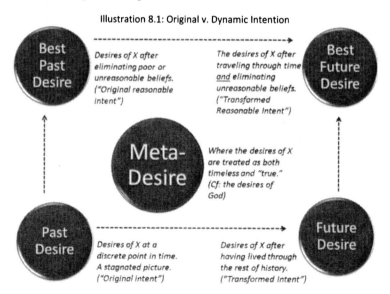

But this is no longer "originalism." It should more properly be thought of as belonging to the "living constitution" paradigm, which has as its central feature the belief that constitutional meaning is dynamic and changes over time. See, e.g., David Strauss, *The Living Constitution* (Oxford, 2010).

Finally, note that framing beliefs can further be subdivided by their *reasonableness*. The idea would be that, hypothetically, if Framer x held views that Framers in general would consider beyond the pale, those views could not be "canonized" (as it were). Or, imagine a hypothetical country that had a poor group of framers, compared to framing standards across similar cultures and/or time. If a country has "poor framers," perhaps a version of *Reasonable-Belief OI* would throw out some of those views. I consider this sort of issue elsewhere [9:§1(b) and 11:§1(b)].

9. "The text of the document and the original intention of those who framed it would be the judicial standard in giving effect to the Constitution," Edwin Meese III, Speech Before the American Bar Association (July 9, 1985), reprinted in *Originalism: A Quarter-Century of Debate,* ed. Steven G. Calabresi, Regnery (Publishing, Inc. 2007), 47. Online: http://www.ruleoflawus.info/Constitutional%20Interpretation/Federalist%20Soc.-Great%20Debate-Interpreting%20Our%20Constitution.pdf (accessed June 12, 2012):

10. One assumes there is only one of these things. A wizard can extract a thought from someone and plop it into the Pensieve to "see it." When I ascribe ownership to this idea—e.g., Alexander Hamilton's Memory Pensieve—I mean the Pensieve in the movie as though it was filled with Hamilton's memories about the law at the time of passage. Likewise, if I say "the Framers' Pensieve," I mean the Pensieve filled with all of the memories of Framers at the time of passage.

11. The table reports the state of mind of the Framers as though such things were uniform across membership. Of course, the reality would be much more complex and messy. But I need to postpone discussing this sort of problem until the next chapter [9:§1(a)-(c)]. So, for now, I'll pretend as though uniform mental states exist.

12. Care should be taken to differentiate statements labeled "assumption" in Table 8.2 versus those labeled "projection." Both involve situations where the language of a provision can be taken as being flexible. The difference is that "assumption" admits the flexibility, whereas "projection" does not. Hence, if the Framers admit that the text can be read in different ways, but resolve this dilemma by showing how they *assumed* it would be read, this is called assumption. But if they insist the language *does* cover something specific—denying it can be read another way—this is called projection.

Here is a good example of projection. Imagine the Constitution had not used the word "property" in the Due Process Clause of the Fifth Amendment. And imagine a contemporary scholar taking the position that the idea of "liberty" in that amendment need not cover property rights, because a meaningful system of liberty could be arranged that excluded such rights. If the Framers themselves responded by saying, "Oh yes, the word 'liberty' surely does include property"—denying it could be read in any other way—this is projection. For all that it says is, "This is how we speak." The key issue is whether they admit that the term could have a different sense or not. The failure to admit is what makes it a projection.

13. Also, no statement can be *revisionist*. Framers couldn't say, e.g., "We were mistaken about this provision," because this would only make sense after the mistake is known. Instead, during the event, it is better to characterize such a thing as *confusion*, because it stresses how the matter occurs in real time. Although it might be possible in

some sense to consciously intend a mistake—as when one wants to be silly, devious or contumacious—this sense of mistake is not what I have in mind. I mean the kinds of mistakes that are not known to the person when they transpire, which is exactly what makes them "mistakes."

14. I labeled beliefs about concepts as being in the 3rd degree, criteria the 2nd and instantiations the 1st. I borrowed this from criminal law. When a criminal commits a first-degree murder, he or she intends something more specific than a killing in the second or third degree. So, if Framers have a mental state about a constitutional provision that is in the 1st degree, they have in mind a very specific outcome.

15. Included in this group are Jack Balkin, Randy Barnett and Keith Whittington [LS-1, 25]. Even conservatives have argued this. But, as Larry Solum notes, that doesn't mean it isn't a defensible idea to others. Solum writes, "Of course, some originalists may . . . argue that original expectation . . . is viable" [LS-1, 25]. For a so called liberal originalist who is against the use of history to make instantial judgments, see my discussion of Jack Balkin [2:§2(a); 3:§4, note 35].

16. One can speak of confusion in two ways. One is where the text itself is confused on its face, as in the case of gibberish. The other is where *Framers* are confused, as with the extreme cases of (say) schizophrenia or dementia—or of the more common problem of simply having a poor grasp of something. A mind that would enact a gibberish provision could only have one of two kinds of excuses. Either there is an innocent mistake by an otherwise rational actor—e.g., not paying attention during the drafting/approving of sentences—or there is some deeper flaw in the person's mental capacity. In short, even in the case of enacting a gibberish law, the confusion will either be *understandable* (excusable), or it will not.

And all of this raises a rather interesting conundrum for text-centered/formalistic OI. What does it do when Framers make "innocent" (understandable) blunders versus those involving poor or deficient intellectual capacity? It is one thing, after all, if the memories of Framers reveal a mistake in the way a clause was written, because, e.g., "The process just tripped us up." But it is another if the memories show, "My God, we just didn't know what we were doing when we passed that—our thoughts didn't approach anything coherent."

17. See note 8, above.

18. It's not that you couldn't construct a school that would have a backup plan. It's that whatever you use for "ultimate law" in this respect will be different from what OI says is fundamental law. So I'm just emphasizing that the school has no choice but to fudge its main principles, because they have "run out," so to speak.

Chapter 9

Why Framers' Intent Is Flawed

In this chapter, I criticize "Framers' intent" or original intention, abbreviated as OI. The most important critics in this area have been Ronald Dworkin [RD-2, 33-57] and Paul Brest [PB]. I explain their criticisms, and others, but not by author. Instead, I present the *ideas*, dropping citations and quotations where appropriate.

§ 1. An Unattainable Idea

The first set of criticisms address factual matters. They claim that the idea of "Framers' intent" is empirically problematic, unattainable in practice or even mythical (reified). This differs from criticisms in §2, which claim that, even if OI could be successfully obtained, it is still irrelevant.

(a) Who are "the Framers?"

Imagine the following process for passing the fundamental law, which, for convenience, I call *Process Q*. There are eight steps[1] that cause different groups of people to play some role in the process, depicted in Illustration 9.1.

First, 13 sovereign states select 55 delegates to a constitution-drafting convention, which uses a "revolving door process," where some members come and go throughout the entire session (step-1). The convention uses a committee system wherein several small workgroups formulate the specific articles assigned to their jurisdiction (step-2). The articles, once complete, are sent for approval before the entire convention of the whole—noting, of course, that not all of the members are always present (nor always the same) (step-3). Then, a final committee called *Style and Arrangement* reduces all of the approved articles to a short and condensed document called "the Constitution," but which, in doing so, adds to and changes some of the language (step-4). Then, 39 of the 42 delegates present on the final day place their mark of approval upon the document, with 14 others not in attendance (step-5). Next, upon receipt of the approved document, the sovereign states authorize respective ratification conventions (step-6). The delegates to the said convention are then selected by popular vote of the adult males who happened to be enfranchised (step-7). Lastly, the Constitution is debated and ratified (step-8).

Illustration 9.1: Process-Q: Creating the Constitution

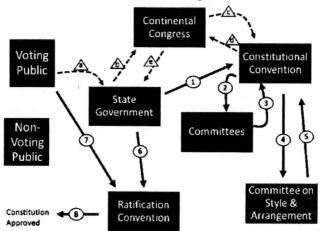

Each line represents a different set of actors who take some action to create a constitution. Dotted lines are informal or indirect actions.[2]

In each of eight steps described above, different participants have their hand in what might be called the "sausage-making process." So, the question must be posed: who, exactly, are "the Framers?" Which of the participants in Process-Q are given the license to say what the Constitution means, and why? Consider the following problems:

- Do those who drafted the language have preference over those who merely voted to accept it (*drafter-centric*)? Or is it the other way around (*approver-centric*)?
- Do committees have preference over the convention as a whole (*committee-centric*)? Or is it the other way around (*floor-centric*)?
- What about the Committee on Style and Arrangement—is it considered a super-committee or something providing only gloss? Did it make substantive changes or only cosmetic ones?
- Do the ratifying conventions have preference over the authorship convention (*ratifying-centric*)?[3] Or is it the other way around (*authorship-centric*)?
- Do the intentions of the public that selected the ratifying delegates count (*public-inclusive*)?
- Do the intentions of the disenfranchised public count, especially if such exclu-

sions result in morally unacceptable laws (*fully-public-inclusive*) [PB, 230]?
- What about the existing sovereign states—do the views of the governments that authorized the convention count in any way (*state-inclusive*)? (And what about the views of the public that elected the government that authorized the convention?)

The central issue here is straightforward. The more fractious and decimated the democratic ritual—the more piecemeal it is—the more difficult it is to say who "the Framers" are.[4] In fact, to actually set forth any people called the Framers seems to require that one first adopt a *theory* of Framers.[5] And this, it seems, could always be reasonably disagreeable on its face. Rarely, however, does one see people setting forth disciplined criteria for who qualifies—or, more importantly, who does not. Rather, in many cases membership is either assumed to be the adored historic figures[6] or is simply not inspected deeply at all.[7]

The fact of the matter is that the framing of the Constitution can really only be understood as an *institutional* process involving all sorts of people doing different labor at multiple access points. It isn't the will of a single testator unto its heirs. It's a political process that doesn't lend itself to the biblical caricature of the law being handed to followers by a single, super persona. As such, OI will experience great difficulty when trying to personify (reify) a bureaucratic and legislative institutional process.

(b) Which Mental States?

Aside from the question of who gets counted, there is also the issue of what mental states to consider. In any collective endeavor to pass the law, there will always be a wide variety of thoughts among the participants. To begin to make any kind of philosophic sense this, one must distinguish between two very different kinds of questions. The first is why a lawmaker votes to approve or disapprove the provision in question (voting beliefs). The second is what he or she understands the provision to "say" (substantive beliefs). The former is a *bodily intention*—i.e., the thoughts that persuaded the person to cast the vote (move the body). The latter is merely a *cognitive phenomenon*—what he or she thought something meant.[8] This distinction is captured in Table 9.1.

Table 9.1: Basic Objects of Legislative Belief	
Name	**Description**
Voting Beliefs:	The reason that X votes to approve a specific law, Q. (Bodily Intention)
Substantive Beliefs:	What X believes Q enacts (does). How it changes the law, what it provides for, etc. (Cognitive Phenomenon)

The first question for OI is: what does it do with voting beliefs? Consider the problem of ulterior motive. This concerns situations where lawmakers vote for reasons of ulterior payoff. Table 9.2 provides three kinds of payoffs. In each case, the intention of the lawgiver is devious. What if Framers had voted for a provision only to protect southern political power, slavery, or northern financial interests[9]—or, perhaps, only in exchange for the capital of the United States being located inside southern borders?[10] Is this an acceptable "Framers' intent?"

Table 9.2: Ulterior Mental States

Name	Legislative Behavior
"Horse Trading"	I'll vote for your favorite provision if you vote for my favorite provision.
Parochial	As long as I receive a certain amount of funding for my district, I'll vote for this constitutional amendment
Strategic	I'm against the provision, but I'll vote for it to receive more campaign contributions or a better committee seat.

Perhaps one of the most important issues is whether to picture "the framing" as *declaratory* or *competitive*. One who sees it as declaratory will have no choice but to picture a group of people trying to say something, through the document, to present and future generations. This is called "speaker's meaning," discussed shortly [9:§2(d); 10:§3]. However, if one sees it as competitive, the picture is not unlike a sporting event: there are *rival* mental states, along with winners and losers. In this situation, what does OI do?

For example, are the mental states of those who opposed the Constitution, and lost, simply discarded?[11] And what about the mental states of those who, when approving the Constitution, actually wanted a third alternative (middle ground)? They couldn't get this because they were forced into an all-or-nothing vote.[12] Should these "captured" beliefs reflect what the participants *really* wanted? Finally, do the intentions of fence-sitters and tie-breakers matter more or less than those who are wholeheartedly committed? What if these intentions are not like the others, but were needed to pass the law?[13]

And what happens when a lawmaker's substantive beliefs are poor? Should poor beliefs about what the law means be cast aside—and what if a majority no longer exists for passage?[14]

The point of all of this is simply to show that, not only are there *people* who must be identified as "Framers," but, within that group, there are *mental states* that must be selected as well. And this seems to require a theory of some sort, which would at least be reasonably disagreeable from the very outset. This, in fact, is what Dworkin's basic point is [RD-2, 43-57].

(c) Skepticism

There are several arguments made against OI that directly advocate certain forms of philosophic *skepticism*.[15] These arguments either deny that there is such a thing called "Framers' intent," or they deny that it can ever be acceptably known.

First, there is *information-skepticism*. This view holds that the records of the constitutional convention and of the ratification process are simply not good enough, historically, to tell us what each participant properly believed [RB-1, 105; KW-2, 605]. The authorship convention, in particular, was held in secret, and only Madison's notes reveal anything substantive about it—and those were published some 50 years later.[16] There is even speculation that the notes may have been "sanitized."[17]

Secondly, there is *commensuration-skepticism*. This claims that, even with perfect information, one could not honestly commensurate the views of *any* group or public into a single coherent mind.[18] If one attempts to treat multiple entities as one entity (or form), merely by combining pieces of them, I call that an *amalgamation*.[19] All claims about "Framers' intent" are inherently amalgamating. They require that one gather *selected* behaviors or mental states, and throw them together, piecemeal.[20] It's an inherently Frankensteinian concept.[21]

If one were to peer honestly and completely into *all* of the participants who framed the Constitution, one would simply find thoughts that were diverse, opposed, unequal, and unlike. It would be a collection of thoughts that were insightful, unaware, helpful, uncertain, informed, prejudiced, hopeful, limited, thoughtful, self-interested, pedestrian, good-natured, confused, far-sighted and short-sighted.[22] Out of this mix, it is simply not possible to have a coherent mindset. Instead, what you would have is a kind of "Sybil."[23] The only possible choice is to construct the orientation that you like the best—picking and choosing among participant attitudes that would fit your sewing desires ("the Frankenstein").

Still another view is skeptical of what can be derived from voting behavior generally. For example, *Arrow's Impossibility Theorem* says that, when any group of people—including legislators—have three or more preferences, a simple vote of the majority does not allow for a result that truly maximizes overall preference.[24] Also, the very phrase, "the will of the legislators," is misleading: it belies the fact that policy preference is often negotiated, fragile, messy and even constructed "on the fly."[25]

Finally, there are those who argue that the true "will of the Framers" was only to set forth a general structure for governance, within which future policy struggles must be waged.[26] As such, it is pointless to consult framing intent for any of our controversies today, because the true intent is to make each new generation decide these struggles themselves, within the complicated processes that make up American government. One might call this *policy skepticism.*[27]

§ 2. A Misguided Idea

One of the more interesting criticisms of OI is centered not upon whether we can ascertain Framers' intent, but rather whether we should even *want* to. This line of argument claims that "Framers" are irrelevant. I present this view below.

(a) Knotted Grammar

Consider the following hypothetical. Imagine a medieval society where there existed a Chamber of Elders that both handed down and kept the meaning of the fundamental law.[28] One might think of the Chamber as being the Law Lords. In such a world, there seems to be no need to use what I had called Process-Q to enact the unquestionable law [9:§1(a)]. Indeed, this process would seem to be pedestrian or demeaning to a world that believes the Elders are the rightful expositors of the great truths. And so, when a society does show that it believes in Process-Q, it seems also to show that it is culturally beyond the age of sages and "wise men," in that it no longer has use for this sort of legal metaphysics. One wants to say: the grammar of "law" has now become something different.

And so, if, indeed, "the Framers" in our system lack the power of Elders by virtue of the behavior-framework that is set forth in Process-Q—if this is the way we are supposed to make a constitution—how is it that they are said to retain the power over what the document "truly means?" How do they retain the right to be the expositor of the concepts, criteria or instantiations[29] needed for the document's text? After all, they are not listed as Article II or III judges, and nowhere are they mentioned as possessing any kind of legal power.[30] It seems, therefore, that the idea of appealing to "the Framers" in a modern legal system is something incongruent or out of place with the basic kinds of behaviors that encompass that system. In short, the idea has poor assertability conditions.[31]

(b) Textualism

Having just set forth a very different kind of indictment against OI, I now present one of the most important prosecutors—a view that American law professors sometimes call *textualism*.[32] The argument goes like this: the law in modern legal systems is not, and never was, the intentions of its draftsmen or approvers—it is only the textual sentences passed during the democratic process. Therefore, if any lawgiver wants his or her intentions to be the law, they have to be stated sufficiently in words that become approved when receiving the majority of "ayes" on the floor of the legislative assembly. Only then will those intentions become *codified*. Absent this, intentions are treated much like aspirations—something that merely *could* be. Simply, the enacted law is only ever its language, and nothing more.

The American Supreme Court justice who is best-known for championing the mantra of textualism in current times is conservative Antonin Scalia. He believes the law is not what lawmakers intended to write, it is only what is written.[33] He once said the following in a popular book authored specifically to address his legal theories:[34]

It is simply incompatible with democratic government, or indeed, even with fair government, to have the meaning of a law determined by what the lawgiver meant, rather than by what the lawgiver promulgated. . . . Government by un-expressed intent is . . . tyrannical. It is the law that governs, not the intention of the lawmaker. . . . Men may intend what they will; but it is only the laws that they enact which bind us [AS-1, 17].[35]

But what is most peculiar about Scalia's beliefs is that they are focused only upon *statutory* law. He is against the idea that a statute can be understood by appealing to legislative-intent documents—i.e., committee reports and floor speeches. He believes that these documents cannot supplant the law itself (the text) and that lawmakers strategically slant their content anyway [AS-1, 29-36]. But my point is clear: if textualism provides a fair reason to dispose of the quiet intentions of Congressmen, it surely can dispose of the intentions of Framers. Not only is there nothing in the philosophy of textualism that prevents it from being applied to constitutional law, but it would seem like a contrivance *not* to (if one were smitten by it).[36]

(c) The New Unit of Analysis

By far, the most important thing that textualism does as a philosophy is alter the unit of analysis in jurisprudence. It not only places the text of the Constitu-tion above the wishes of its creators—but, in a way, it *divorces* it from them. One wants to say: it cuts off the document from its placenta. No longer is the Constitution a ward of its caretaker. It treats the provisions as though they are *independent* of the proclivities of any historical group of people—even when it comes to saying what the words of the text mean.

Therefore, in this model of law, there is neither covenant-training nor direct servitude [8:§1]. There is no need to ask someone (in theory) what the special meaning or preferred case is for something. Rather, the idea is that the document stands independently upon its own sentences and the inferences or ideas given thereby. Therefore, the servitude that is owed goes to the text itself, not to those who created it. This forces the reader to select the best *candidate* for meaning that could possibly exist for any provision—no matter whether that comes from a contemporary philosopher, an academic from the 1950s, or a 1787 framer. It doesn't matter whether it comes from Thomas Jefferson or Martin Luther King Jr. The focus is simply upon who has the better ideas for the provisions—who can give them the best account—drawing upon any intelligent resource whatso-ever.

And if this means that we end up with different or competing ideas about what "equal protection" or "due process" means, so be it. The only thing that counts as fundamental law in this (new) model is simply what is believed to be the best social arrangement for the given text [7:§3(a)-(c)]. Hence, the meaning of the Constitution can change over time and is beholden to the overall forces that come to define the general era in history [11:§2(d); Chapter 12].

Therefore, the central indictment of OI is that it deploys a *flawed criterion* for what law fundamentally is in the American legal system. Its labors are centered upon a false object. The minds of the Framers do not constitute "fundamental law" in the American legal system. Instead, from now on, the judges have to cater to the quality of their *own* minds—i.e., how considerately they think about constitutional ideas—rather than pretending to cater to someone else from the past [7:§3(c)].

(d) Beyond Speaker's Meaning

Note that both textualism and OI posit different *behaviors* for legal judging. If one takes Framers as being the central point of concern, one has no choice but to pretend that judging is *conversational*. The psychology works like this: you pretend that the Framers are speaking to you through the document—that they are passing along orders or commands that you have to obey (boss logic). To follow the communication properly, you have to follow what scholars call "speaker's meaning," which is simply what you imagine the speaker to have in mind.[37]

However, once the central focus changes from what "the Framers" have in mind to what the provision can be *taken* to mean, the act of judging becomes something different. It becomes the business of comparing and contrasting possible states of affairs (pictures of account). You must try to make the possible ideas for the Constitution be the most coherent, relevant and purposeful they can be[38]—something that can change as intellectual culture advances and as society becomes rearranged [Chapter 12]. In short, the judges are asked to be a caretaker for a competing body of ideas, rather than servants for historic persons (bosses) said to hold some special stewardship over the matter.

This, of course, causes judging as a behavior to become something different. It no longer is conversational. Ronald Dworkin is the central scholar who has argued for a juristic model that is non-conversational. Dworkin argues that constitutional interpretation is not unlike the way that learned professors of literature make interpretations of poems, novels or other creative acts. Dworkin writes,

> [Constitutional interpretation] . . . is like artistic interpretation in this way: both aim to interpret something created by people as an entity distinct from them, rather than what people say, as in conversational interpretation, or events not created by people, as in scientific interpretation [RD-1, 50].
>
> I propose that we can improve our understanding of law by comparing legal interpretation with interpretation in other fields of knowledge, particularly literature [RD-2, 146].
>
> We can usefully compare the judge deciding what the law is on some issue

. . . with the literary critic teasing out the various dimensions of value in a complex play or poem [RD-1, 228].

In this book, I offer a unique contribution to this discussion. I propose that there are actually *four* models of judging that can be arrayed in a two-by-two matrix, presented in Table 9.3. The rows are concerned with whether constitutional interpretation is pictured as a conversation or as something Wittgenstein called an "aesthetic" [7:§1]. The columns are concerned with whether this picture focuses upon the actor (author) or reactor (reader).

Table 9.3: Interpretation Matrix

	Actor	**Reactor**
Conversational	1. *Speaker's Meaning*: What is the speaker saying to me in this document? How do I follow his will?	2. *Wittgensteinian*: How can I participate in this language game? What is a proper use I can make of these words?
Aesthetical	3. *Celebratory*: What did the gesture or speech act stand for from the perspective of the actor's life, his generation and/or the times?	4. *Philosophic*: How can I provide the best and most coherent account of the ideas handed to me in this document?

Approaches based upon conversation are depicted in the first row. Box 1 represents "speaker's meaning." In this scenario, you simply imagine that the author of a writing is speaking to you, and you must tend to his or her wishes. Box 2 represents the Wittgensteinian approach [Chapter 5]. It is concerned with how the reader can acceptably participate in the language game given over by the words in the document. That is, how can you speak the words back to the authorial culture successfully, with the use of the terms being understood?

Aesthetical approaches are depicted in the second row. Box 3 is concerned with how the Framers or their historical time can be celebrated as an epoch in history. The concern is for the things that made the Framers or their generation relevant—what their lives represented, the ideals of the time, etc. This approach is *celebratory*; it appreciates the era or epoch.[39] I cover celebratory approaches elsewhere [App: 12-32].

Box 4 is Dworkin's view [3:§4(a)]. It concerns how the ideas in the Constitution can be given their best and most coherent account. This is a philosophic enterprise. I explained in Chapter 7 why I consider approaches like this to be aesthetical. My views are based upon Wittgenstein.

My ultimate view is that the only way to properly judge the Constitution in a modern legal culture like America's is to use a combination of Boxes 2 and 4. I contend judging is conversational in only one limited sense: each generation takes turns *speaking* the language of the Constitution backward through time, rather than pretending to be spoken to. In essence, each must give voice to the text in a way that is at least intelligible to the past—in a way that could be understood in those language games.[40] I call this view *cooperative talking* [5:§4].

But the act of speaking the Constitution *well* is, as Dworkin suggests, a task not unlike an art or aesthetic. As such, constitutional interpretation involves the use of *artisan judgment*—the kind of judgment made by an connoisseur of something—about the best way to socially arrange the document's words and ideals [7:§1-2]. How well judges do this is defined by connoisseurs in charge of properly appreciating this activity. In Chapter 7, I elaborated upon what this idea meant.

Notes

1. The real process has more than eight, if you consider the informal and indirect parts. They are depicted in broken lines in Illustration 9.1.

2. State government representatives are elected (step-a); delegates are sent to Congress (step-b); the Congress approves of undertaking reform (step-c); the Constitution, once drafted, is informally sent to the Congress (step-d), which informally sends it to the States (step-e). "Informally" is done by cover of letter to certain officials in the respective institutions.

3. For those who have argued that ratifiers should be included, see: Charles A. Miller, *The Supreme Court and the Uses of History* (Belknap Press 1969), 157-88; Richard H. Fallon, Jr., "Judicially Manageable Standards and Constitutional Meaning," *Har. L. Rev.* 119 (1996): 1317; and Charles A. Lofgren, "The Original Understanding of Original Intent," *Constitutional. Commentary* 5 (1988): 113. See also [LS-1, 19-20].

4. [PB, 214-15]. See also [RD-2, 43, 47-48], asking "who counts" and what combination of individual intentions matter.

5. One could imagine several different OI-theories being added to Chapter 8 based upon the theory adopted. Cf. drafter-centric OI, convention-centric OI, ratification-included OI, etc.

Note also that "the framing" never really ends, so long as substantial amendments can be made. What does one do with constitutional amendments that are massive in scope and structurally re-defining? The only solution appears to be picking between the two. Imagine a belief system that required all subsequent framings to be obedient to the major ideas of the initial one. This would mean, for example, that the Civil War amendments had to be obedient to the meta-desires of the original Framers. If the first framing has priority, one might call it *First-In-Time OI*.

But note that the ranking could go the other way. One might take the position, for example, that the Civil War amendments fundamentally restructured the 1787 plan of governance, making it a "second framing" of sorts. This view would hold that Framers of 1865-1870 intended for the states to be subjugated to the national will, an event that forever changed the Constitution. One might call this view *Last-In-Time OI*.

6. One of the criticisms that one could levy against OI is that it indulges idolatry. To the extent that versions of it depend upon a "great man thesis" that artificially elevates the status (or prowess) of popular historical figures, the criticism seems fair.

7. It is not uncommon, in fact, to see Thomas Jefferson being included as a "fram-

er," even though he was not even in the country when the Constitution was passed. See, e.g., Jethro Koller Lieberman, *A Practical Companion to the Constitution: How The Supreme Court Has Ruled on Issues From Abortion to Zoning* (University of California Press, 1999), 9 (discussing framer intention and including Jefferson); and John R. Vile, *The Constitutional Convention of 1788: A Comprehensive Encyclopedia of America's Founding*, vol. 2 (ABC-CLIO, Inc., 2005), 668 (discussing Jefferson as a framer).

8. See Table 8.2 for a good account of what I mean here.

9. Charles Beard, *An Economic Interpretation of the Constitution* (Macmillan Co., 1913).

10. The Hamilton assumption bill, which was attacked by opponents for its constitutionality, was apparently parlayed that way in the First Congress [JE-1, 48-80].

11. I take up an issue like this in Chapter 11. See my discussion of how constitutional meaning could be constituency-centered [11:§1(a)].

12. [JE-2, 115]. See also [JE-3, 33, 43], where he speaks of ratification in the following terms: "In the end, it was an all-or-nothing choice, which caused most states to go with the Constitution."

13. Note that these problems apply not just to voting beliefs, but substantive beliefs as well. If a provision has more than one possible meaning, surely it could be seen as saying something more liberal (sweeping) by those more generously disposed to its passage, and vice versa. So, the issue of winners and losers is not just confined to voting behavior.

14. Would criteria that discriminated along these lines not also degenerate into a theory of most-knowledgeable Framer? And wouldn't this introduce *tiers* of Framers for any given provision, so that fundamental law becomes the mental states of the most enlightened (informed) cadre or individual? One wonders if this wouldn't turn into a kind of Great-Men Thesis.

15. See Chapter 1, note 17, for an explanation of the term "skepticism."

16. Madison is frequently said to have refused to publish the notes until after all the Framers had died. See Adrienne Koch's introduction in Madison's *Notes of Debates in the Federal Convention* (W.W. Norton, 1987), viii. The notes were not published until fifty years after the Convention.

17. Famous historian Joe Ellis gave a series of recorded lectures, covering 8 CDs, for Barnes and Noble titled, "Patriots: Brotherhood of the Revolution." In Lecture 9, he comments that Madison's notes were probably "sanitized." The lectures are available online: http://www.barnesandnoble.com/w/patriots-joseph-j-ellis/1005959969 (accessed June 12, 2012).

18. [RB-1, 105], noting that Framers' intentions "could and indeed were likely to be in conflict." See also, Gregory Bassham, *Original Intent and the Constitution* (Rowman & Littlefield, 1992), 83, cited by [KW-2, 605].

19. Other words expressing similar ideas might be anthropomorphism, mereological fallacy and reification. *Anthropomorphism* is an interpretation of what is not human or personal in terms of human or personal characteristics (humanization). See, e.g., *Thinking With Animals: New Perspectives on Anthropomorphism*, ed. Datson & Mitman (Columbia Press University, 2006), 3. *Mereological Fallacy* is, roughly, attributing to parts the attribute of the whole. See, e.g., M. R. Bennett, Peter Michael Stephan Hacker, *History of Cognitive Neuroscience* (Wiley-Blackwell, 2008), 241. And *Reification* is treating something, usually an abstraction, as though it were real. See, e.g., Etienne Wenger, *Communi-*

ties of Practice: Learning, Meaning, and Identity (Cambridge University Press, 1998), 58.

20. [RD-2, 39]. Before discussing the different psychological states and other ways that approaches to intention can differ, Dworkin writes, "[T]here is no such thing as the intention of the Framers waiting to be discovered, even in principle. There is only some such thing waiting to be invented."

21. There are two concerns here. One is that you have to pick and choose certain beliefs held by only some participants; the other is that you must *elevate* the status of these items (somehow). So, you might pick the stated position of person *x* in this or that committee, along with a speech of person *y* on this or that date. Perhaps you throw in a letter written by *z* to someone. Let's call these items, collectively, *x-y-z*.

The problem is that you have to elevate the status of *x-y-z* so that they can become "the will of the Framers," or else they cannot be appealed to by the belief system. And there are only two ways to do this. You must either take *x-y-z* to be speaking *representationally* for all the others in the sausage-making process, as if *x-y-z* constitute their agents or mouthpieces (unlikely). Or, you must offer a theory that bestows *rank* upon *x-y-z* (e.g., "the views of the giants"). Without positing either of these, *x-y-z* simply remains the respective outlooks of *x*, *y* and *z* individually.

22. For a discussion about differing psychological states that could belong to even the authorial intention of one person, see [RD-2, 38-57], discussing Framers' intent.

23. This is a reference to the 1976 film, staring Sally Field, who played a psychiatrist treating a patient with multiple personalities. The movie was based on a 1973 book by Flora Rheta Schreiber.

24. See Kenneth Arrow, *Social Change and Individual Values*, 2nd ed. (Yale University Press, 1963).

25. Scalia's dissent in the following case makes this point well:

[A] particular legislator need not have voted for the act either because he wanted to foster religion or because he wanted to improve education. He may have thought the bill would provide jobs for his district, or may have wanted to make amends with a faction of his party he had alienated on another vote, or he may have been a close friend of the bill's sponsor, or he may have been repaying favor he owed the majority leader, or he may have hoped the governor would appreciate his vote and make a fundraising appearance for him, or he may have been pressured to vote for the bill he disliked by a wealthy contributor or by a flood of constituent mail, or he may have been seeking favorable publicity, or he may have been reluctant to hurt the feelings of a loyal staff member who worked on the bill, or he may have been settling an old score with a legislator who opposed the bill, or he may have been mad at his wife who opposed the bill, or he may have been intoxicated and utterly unmotivated when the vote was called, or he may have accidentally voted "yes" instead of "no," or, of course, he may have had (and very likely did have) a combination of some of the above and many other motivations. To look for the sole purpose of even a single legislator is probably to look for something that does not exist. Edwards v. Aguillard, 482 U.S. 578, 636 (1987).

26. See H. Jefferson Powell, "The Original Understanding of Original Intent," *Harv. L. Rev.* 98 (1985): 885. See also [KW-2, 605].

27. Of course, a theoretical problem with this view is that it, too, must overcome all of the other objections that apply to claims like this. To say that the true intent of the Framers was not to pass judgment upon any of our specific policy programs requires that

one first say who "the Framers" are, what mental states count, how they become amalgamated, and why this feigned persona requires our obedience.

28. For purposes of imagery, one could think of the Council of Elrond in J.R.R. Tolkien's, *Lord of the Rings*.

29. "Concept, criteria and instantiation" are explained in Chapter 2.

30. Imagine if the Constitution had set forth its 39 signatories as being "the Supreme interpreters of the document during their lives in being." It would be as if the society had asked its parentage whether it was still in conformity with the great wishes, before the expiry of the said fathers. It would almost resemble something out of the story of Moses—seeking out the Great Expositor to check the virtue of government. Cf., Islamic regimes that use clerics to say whether fundamental law is followed.

31. Wittgenstein writes, "Philosophy unties knots in our thinking; hence its result must be simple, but philosophizing has to be as complicated as the knots it unites [LW-4, §452]. Elsewhere, "Philosophy unties the knots in our thinking, which we have tangled up in an absurd way; but to do that, it must make movements which are just as complicated as the knots. Although the *result* of philosophy is simple, its methods for arriving there cannot be so. . . . The complexity of philosophy is not in its matter, but in our tangled understanding" [LW-10, 52].

32. Unfortunately, the term "textualism," like the term "originalism," appears to be drifting into confusion. John Perry, for example, uses the term to mean "the original meaning of the text," a phrase which is a synonym for "the new originalism." John Perry in *Philosophical Foundations of Language in the Law*, ed. Andrei Marmor & Scott Soames (Oxford 2011), 105.

Because I contend that the new originalism is itself confused, I cannot adopt this way of speaking. To me, textualism means something similar to what Whittington means when he talks (unfavorably) of the Constitution being read "autonomously" [3:§3]. The idea, quite simply, is that the provisions of the document should speak solely for themselves and do not carry with them, like a halo, the personal wishes of any person(s) who enacted them—even if those wishes merely constitute assumptions about "what the law means" [8:§4(a)]. But it's not that those assumptions couldn't be adopted by a judge, of course—it's that, before they are, they must compete against other recommendations for the best account of the ideas in the document. This is because it is the text itself that is owed all of our intellectual attention and devotion, not an entity that wants to act in the legal system as an official caretaker for it ("Framers") [13:§1-§2].

33. Scalia says, "My view [is] that the objective indication of the words, rather than the intent of the legislature, is what constitutes the law . . ." [AS-1, 29].

34. Scalia also characterized judges who believe they are bound to an "unexpressed legislative intent" as potentially being in "self-delusion" [AS-1, 17], noting, "with respect to 99.99 issues of construction reaching the Court, there *is* no legislative intent" [AS-1, 32]. He also quotes approvingly from a Justice who once characterized the use of legislative history as being the "psychoanalysis of Congress" [AS-1, 30].

35. He means "tyrannical" in the sense of posting edicts up high where people cannot easily read them. I edited his reference to Nero out of the passage.

36. Indeed, there have been justices of the Supreme Court who have taken textualist approaches to particular provisions. The most famous may be Hugo Black, who took a supposedly "absolutist" position on the First Amendment, saying it protected things not imagined by Framers, because of the way the legal sentence was phrased ("Congress

shall pass no law . . ."). See, e.g., Howard Ball. *Hugo L. Black: Cold Steel Warrior* (Oxford University Press, 2006).

37. Whittington argues in favor of speaker's meaning in the following remark:

> We can distinguish between three common forms of "meaning": literal meaning, reader's meaning, and speaker's meaning. Focus on the reader's meaning ("What does it mean to me?") is inconsistent with the interpretive enterprise itself. Literal meaning (the "plain meaning") can only be regarded as an interpretive halfway house to the discovery of the speaker's meaning ("What did the speaker mean by this?") [KW-1, 177-78].

38. See the discussion involving Dworkinains [3:§4(a)].

39. It could also apply to individuals as well, if they are being celebrated. For example, one might speak of "Jefferson's Constitution"—i.e., the constitution that embodies Jeffersonian thought—versus "Hamilton's Constitution," the one that captured Hamilton's imagination. Of course, in both examples, one speaks of the same document; it is just that it is given the coloration of the person(s) or era being adored.

40. This is exactly what I contend the first generation did. The first cases interpreted by the Supreme Court were not "special" in that they avoided the very activity that subsequent generations engage in when interpreting the document.

Chapter 10

The New Originalism

Because of the numerous problems confronting "Framers' intent," the belief system largely became discredited in the American legal academy.[1] Or as Randy Barnett once said, "The received wisdom among law professors is that originalism is dead, having been defeated in intellectual combat sometime in the Eighties" [RB-2]. Even many conservative scholars abandoned it.[2]

But instead of giving up, conservatives over the last fifteen years have tried to repair and resurrect their orthodoxy. I refer to this new, born-again creature as the "new originalism." I now venture to explain it.

§ 1. No "Boss Logic"

Perhaps the most basic reform in the new thinking is to deny that it has anything to do with "boss logic" [8:§4]. New originalists want nothing to do with the notion that they have personified the sausage-making process that passed the Constitution. They are not, as Whittington notes, "penetrat[ing] into some alien mind" [KW-1, 59]. And they also vehemently deny that the new orthodoxy requires any kind of homage to an amalgamated personality that is imagined to have given over the Constitution, not unlike the way that Moses handed down the Ten Commandments.

Just as important, however, is what the new originalism does *not* reject. Consider once again the two basic objects of legislative belief that I listed in the last chapter in Table 9.1 [9:§1(b)]. The new thinking quite clearly wants to keep one of them: substantive beliefs. The beliefs that lawmakers hold about what the law *says* is still an extremely important aspect of the new thinking. However, following Scalia's lead, gone is the idea that the law should have anything to do with the ulterior motives for why legislators cast their votes (bodily intentions). It matters nothing, therefore, if Framers voted for reasons of self-interest, strategy, parochial gain, psychology—or even because they sincerely believed in the provisions.[3]

Perhaps the best advocate for the new thinking is Whittington. He makes the point that, although one should disavow the Framers' bodily intentions and other distant aspirations, one must, at the same time, scrupulously follow their *authorial* intention and its general social context,[4] a point I now examine more closely.

(a) Authorial Intent?

Many new originalists are fond of making this proclamation: "There is no meaning without an author," because the text and the authorial intent are one and the same. Whittington writes:

> Each theory . . . assumes that the text can be logically separated from the context of its writing and from the intent of the author, that the text is somehow autonomous. This assumption is flawed. The written text is identical to the author's intent; there can be no logical separation between them and thus no space for an autonomous text capable of adopting new contexts. [A] . . . writing presupposes an intentional agent who can give it meaning. The text is not inherently meaningful but requires active intelligence to breathe life into barren marks. . . . A "text" that is completely autonomous of its writer ceases to be a text at all: that is, it can no longer be interpreted as a meaningful sign [KW-1, 94].

Many scholars, of course, disagree with this edict. Dennis Goldford has confronted it using literary theory [DG, 208-234].[5] And in this passage, Dennis Patterson offers what can only be called the other view: "It is a truism, of course, that the author of a book enjoys no privileged status when it comes to discerning the meaning of his own words. Of course, the author can speak about what he wanted to say, or thought he said, but those intentional states do not in any way affect the meaning of what he has said. The text, one might say, 'speaks for itself'" [DP-3, 1567].

My view on this issue is Wittgensteinian, which means it is the same as Patterson's (above). Because language is based upon public criteria, authors do not have a monopoly upon meaning—only the language culture does. This is the reason why the game of Mad Libs "works."[6] Language is efficacious. Whittington apparently thinks that the author is the one who "gives meaning to barren marks." This is not true: the *culture* provides the meaning.[7] The author merely tries to use the public criteria to make his or her communication successful.

This is an activity no different from tossing a ball back and forth or playing a card in a game. This is why Wittgenstein called it a "language game" [RM-2, 69-82]. The only way Whittington's view could be correct is if there were such a thing as a private language [RM-2, 83-93]. This remark from Wittgenstein is helpful: "But if you say: 'How am I to know what he means, when I see nothing but the signs he gives?' then I say: 'How is *he* to know what he means, when he has nothing but the signs either?'" [LW-1, §504]

There is significant confusion among some originalists about whether Wittgenstein supports their position [KW-1, 59, 99]. The confusion stems from two issues: (a) whether communication occurs absent an author; and (b) whether a person's intention involves an ethereal or mystical sort of substance. You can enlist Wittgenstein against the latter, but not in support of the former.[8]

Therefore, it is Wittgensteinian to say that an act of speech, itself, gains its meaning because of a shared *culture*, rather than an intention.[9] And the ability to "peer into someone's mind" wouldn't alter this general phenomenon. Nothing is hidden from us. Everything we say is done with publicly-accessible criteria. If we use the public criteria successfully, we are understood. If not, it is only like a basketball player missing a shot—it isn't something alien. Therefore, Wittgenstein could *never* be enlisted for the proposition that acts of speech have no meaning—even as communication—without someone intending something (special?) for them.[10]

Unfortunately, there are some originalists who *explicitly* adopt a private language thesis.[11] Frankly, these views can become quite strange.[12] They suggest that a person's meaning is secretly balled up inside the head before he or she speaks, and that the act of speech inculcates language with this special mystery, like a ganache going into the center of a confectionary. This view endorses folk psychology (the idea of a little man inside the head). Wittgenstein quite rightly counsels against this picture of account:

> Thinking is not an incorporeal process which lends life and sense to speaking, and which it would be possible to detach from speaking, rather as the Devil took the shadow of Schlemiehl from the ground [LW-14, 124-125, §339].
>   . . . An intention is embedded in its situation, in human customs and institutions. If . . . chess did not exist, I could not intend to play a game of chess. In so far as I do intend the construction of a sentence in advance, that is made possible by the fact that I can speak the language in question [LW-14, 124, §337].[13]

So, there isn't any curious mystery within a speaker that makes language efficacious. I would also add that a person's intention can often be incomplete [1:§3], and that language is always cooperative to some extent. We often need each other to complete our very own messages [6:§1, note 4].

The issue, therefore, isn't whether a text has meaning without an author; it is which of the possible meanings we should recognize [Chapter 5]. And that depends upon whether the particular language game—in this case, interpreting constitutions—calls for one to guess the person's unstated or understated desire, as the games of ordinary communication frequently do [4:§5; 6:§1, note 4]. Or, whether the game calls for contesting something that has been said with insufficient clarity, as the language games of lawyers routinely do [13:§2].

A good example of this latter point can be seen in Keith Whittington's "poodle hypothetical." He asks us to imagine a text with the command, "Buy a dog." He goes on to say, "Additional information beyond the conventions of the English language would allow the interpreter to exclude more possibilities and further specify the command's meaning. Perhaps in the social context of the sentence, only poodles are available for sale. Perhaps it occurs in a conversation about whether to purchase one of the neighbor's puppies" [KW-1, 7, note 10].

Although this may be true of that particular language game, the question is whether the language games of modern legal culture would treat the text or the social context as being "the law." My position is quite clear. If we want legislation to *forever* require that only poodles can be purchased, the legislation must say so [13:§2]. Otherwise, poodles amount only to things that can be judicially arranged for the choice, which depends upon whether doing so still makes for a good behavioral response (a good judgment) [6:§2, §4; 7:§3(b)].[14]

But despite all of this, the battle cry for a constitution that always (silently) enacts its authorial meaning and social context, without regard to its authors' ulterior motives, lives on in originalist circles. It seems to be exactly what Scalia has in mind when making frequent pronouncements like this: "What I look for in the Constitution is . . . the original meaning of the text, not what the original draftsmen intended" [AS-1, 38].

§ 2. Bystander-Textualism

Perhaps the most important claim of the new originalism arises from this mantra: "the Constitution is fundamentally about its text." Proponents place great stress upon the fact that the Constitution is both a written and a legal document—making it, in effect, an act of legislation (a "super-statute").[15] As such, the new thinking seems to stress a separation of the text from its Framers. However, when making this claim, proponents also do something curious. They *reject* the idea that the text is, in Keith Whittington's terms, "autonomous." This is a common assertion among conservative originalists today: they want textualism, but they don't want it to go "all the way."

So what, exactly, allows constitutional text to only be "kind of independent" of Framers? How does this idea even work? The answer given by new originalists is rather clever. They claim that the text must be understood using a third-party (bystander) perspective that was present during the time of its enactment.

But who or what is this bystander? In practice, it comes in one of two forms. If one listens to Keith Whittington, the bystander is the understanding that the ratifying conventions held when receiving, reading and passing the Constitution into law.[16] Other scholars, however, such as Larry Solum, argue that the bystander is the "public meaning" of the provisions at the time of their enactment.[17] This idea, it seems, asks us to imagine what prudent observers of the process living during its time, would, in theory, have taken the provisions to mean.[18] Both of these ideas are captured in Illustration 10.1.

As a preliminary matter, one might note that the delegates at the ratifying conventions were not, of course, "bystanders." They were key participants. But for those who appeal to them as such, perhaps the idea treats them as a kind of "internal bystander." The argument is thus: when the Constitution was handed to ratifying delegates, they had to read and review it. This means that a successful (internal) communication occurred between authors and approvers. This so called "meeting of the minds" is therefore what constitutes the objective meaning of the text.

Illustration 10.1: Bystander Theory of Meaning

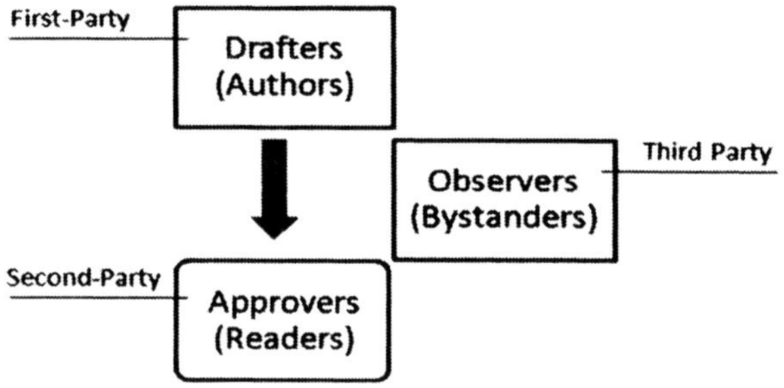

In contrast, those who favor the so-called "public meaning" of the document prefer to rely upon *real* bystanders who were truly external to the process (spectators). Whatever they, in theory, would have understood about the provisions constitutes the "objective read." A good way to differentiate the two: one uses a second-party account of the text; the other uses a third-party account.

The most important thing, however, is not necessarily who or what the historic bystander is—at least not yet. Rather, it is the *effect* that this maneuver is said to have upon the meaning of text. The new originalists believe that an appeal to bystanders can fix or pin down the text, so specific meaning occurs at some level of analysis (concept, criteria or instantiation).[19] The new originalists therefore believe they are capturing an objective reading of the document, which they call "the original meaning of the Constitution."[20] Ozan Varol quite nicely says it this way:

> As Whittington has observed, the primary goal of the new originalism is not to "open up the head of the author and see what is inside" or to determine what Madison would do if he were a Justice on the Supreme Court. Rather, the goal is to ascertain the objective meaning of the text, which is the medium through which the drafters conveyed their intentions to their audience [OV, 1249-50].[21]

It is for this reason that, as early as June 14, 1986, Antonin Scalia encouraged conservatives to start using the term "original meaning" to describe their central concern.[22] It is now common knowledge, of course, that numerous conservative scholars have followed this clarion call.[23]

§ 3. Speaker's Meaning?

There are two simple questions that must be answered before one can properly understand the new originalism: (a) how is it different from text-centered, formalistic OI [8:§3]; and (b) does it abandon speaker's meaning? The answers to these questions vary based upon what entity is posited for the "bystander" and what role it plays in the belief system. I discuss each of these variables next.

To begin, let's pick a specific legal issue. Let's assume that the people who framed the Equal Protection Clause[24] have the following memory of the event: "We didn't intend for it to cover women." And let's assume that those who framed the Due Process Clauses[25] and Ninth Amendment[26] have the following memory: "Neither was meant to apply to abortion" [12:§1]. Statements such as these were already conceptualized in Chapter 8, Table 8.2 [8:§3(a)-(c)]. Because this table is of *crucial* importance to the points I shall offer, I must reproduce it (below). It contains all possible substantive beliefs that "the Framers" could have held for any provision, along with the effect that the same would have upon a judge who adheres to text-centered, formalistic OI.

Table 8.2: The Framers' Possible Memory

Type	Degree	Explanation	End Result
	3rd	We mean the text to say this concept	Concept is the law
Intention	2nd	We mean this concept to have these criteria	Criteria are the law
	1st	We mean these instantiations	Instantiations are the law
	–	Confusion or mistake produced this text	Fix text (backup plan?)
Confusion	3rd	Confusion existed for this concept	Fix concept (backup plan?)
	2nd	Confusion existed for these criteria	Fix criteria (backup plan?)
	1st	Confusion existed for these instantiations	Fix instantiation (backup plan?)
	3rd	We assume the text means this concept	Concept is the law
Assumption	2nd	We assume the concept has these criteria	Criteria are the law
	1st	We assume these instantiations	Instantiations are the law
	3rd	We insist the text says this concept	Concept is the law
Projection	2nd	We insist the concept has these criteria	Criteria are the law
	1st	We insist these instantiations are covered	Instantiations are the law
	3rd	We never considered this concept	
Demurral	2nd	We never considered criteria	Reconstruct or consult a backup plan?
	1st	We never considered an instantiation	

And so, the question now becomes: how does an appeal to bystanders affect any of this? The answer depends upon what role they are supposed to play. Proponents of the new originalism must tell us who they believe is putting forth the statements in Table 8.2. Or as Larry Solum once said, "Who uttered the Constitution?"[27]

One possibility is the statements come *directly* from the bystanders themselves—so that they, in effect, are now "the speaker" of constitutional text. Another possibility is that Framers posit the statements, for which bystanders play the role of referee or judge (somehow). The former treats the bystander as the declarant; the latter treats it as a referee for someone else's act of speech.

Let's assume that bystanders are said to provide the answers, directly (*declarant version*). The next step is to identify who the bystanders are. If they are the delegates at the ratifying convention (Whittington's view), this idea merely puts forth a second-party understanding of constitutional text. This is *not* a new kind of originalism. It's text-centered, formalistic OI that uses a ratification-centric theory of Framers [9:§1(a)]. This belief system merely tells us which of the participants who passed the Constitution should be treated as being "the speaker." It therefore clearly endorses speaker's meaning. There is nothing philosophically new here.

However, if the bystander is taken to be "the observant public," this view *does* put forth a new kind of originalism. It puts forth a third-party understanding of constitutional text that does *not* endorse speaker's meaning. This is because the public cannot be said to be "the Framers" of the document without seriously changing the sense of that idea. As such, this view believes, quite simply, that the meaning of the Constitution is revealed though a past societal understanding of some kind that became hegemonic for its age. Knowingly or not, the view flirts with a celebratory understanding of the Constitution [Table 9.3], because it comes to understand the document from the perspective of the generation that secured it or the era that lent its blessing. I discuss this new version of originalism in the next two chapters.[28]

Now, let's see what happens when bystanders are *not* conceived to be declarants.

(a) Judging Language?

Let's assume that "Framers" (however defined) are said to offer the statements in Table 8.2, and that bystanders must play the role of *referee*. How does this idea even work?[29] Because new originalism is purportedly concerned with the real meaning of text, the point seems to be for bystanders to *validate* the statements *linguistically*. So, for example, the bystanders might say, "Yes, we can verify that the idea you have expressed is, in fact, something that we can understand in our time."

In this sense, bystanders are posited merely as a *rubber stamp*. They affirm that the speaker's (specific) meaning is, in fact, linguistically possible for the provision in question—so that one could read the text that way and make sense of it (if one wanted). And so, if the Framers of the Equal Protection Clause say, "We didn't intend it to apply to women," the only job for the bystander is to see whether the language game could support a genderless equality program under the phrase "equal protection of the law." For if such a cultural arrangement could be successfully spoken of with this phraseology during the time in question, one could then acquire a basis to say two things: (a) that this is what "they really meant"; and (b) it was, in fact, taken this way.

This approach, in essence, allows Framers to inculcate their specific sense of the text into the law, by use of the rubber stamp. So as long as Framers *thought* women excluded from equal protection, and so long as the ratifying agent or informed public could understand the text being read that way—in that it was intelligible to them—then the "true meaning" of the Clause must, in fact, exclude women. And the same with the Due Process Clauses (mentioned earlier). If they were intended not to apply to abortion—and if they were, in fact, taken that way—then a basis exists for saying "this is what that language actually means."

However, as I argue throughout this book, modern legal culture in America does not allow legislation to work this way [3:§3; 13:§2]. The only way that an act of legislation can *automatically* eliminate rival concepts, criteria or instantiations [2:§1-2] is for the text to explicitly say so, in definition sections or in sufficiently rigid nomenclature [3:§2]. Absent this, courts must choose what sense is best to give the text. In short, if any generation wants the phrase "equal protection" to exclude women, they need to legislate better. I don't claim this a priori; I claim it is the way that modern positivistic legal culture works in America [13:§2].

So, let's return to the initial question. How is this approach different from text-centered/formalistic OI—and does it, in fact, adhere to speaker's meaning? My conclusion is very simple. Any belief system that uses bystanders as a rubber stamp for "the speaker" surely adheres to both speaker's meaning and OI. This is because the point of the belief system is merely to find a perfunctory way to validate the communicative potential of the speaker's intention in the culture in which the utterance lived. One wants to say it this way: this view defends speaker's meaning, so long as it is intelligible in its time. Non-intelligible meaning, one assumes, is cast aside on the grounds that it should have been articulated better.

Therefore, the only credible theory of bystanders in the new originalism is one that uses the idea: (a) as a rubber stamp; or (b) as its very own declarant. And it also seems that all but one of the possible combinations of beliefs[30] amount to nothing more than a warmed-over version of text-centered, formalistic OI that adheres to speaker's meaning.

And this is why some scholars have rejected the talk of "a new originalism." Barber and Fleming, in particular, say that the only thing that has changed is the way originalists *speak* about the issue. They write, "The distinction between intention and meaning is a refinement that cuts no ice with us. Everyday speakers of a language confound 'meaning' with 'intent' because speakers normally pick a word that conveys what the word is generally taken to mean. 'What did you intend?' is thus often equivalent to 'What do you mean?'" [B&F, 79, note 1]

Of course, this is not true for at least one version of the new thinking. And that version will be taken up in the next two chapters.

Notes

1. [OV, 1249]: "Intentionalism eventually fell out of favor for reasons political and intellectual."

2. Larry Solum, for example, tells us that the scholarly consensus became such that Framers' intent "could not serve as the basis for a viable theory of constitutional interpretation and construction" [LS-1, 19].

3. For example, Whittington is against the idea of an economic interpretation of the Constitution, such as the one provided by Charles Beard, who, in 1913, claimed that Framers were primarily motivated by their private financial interests when setting forth the document. Whittington's point is that, even if such a thing were true, ulterior motives are irrelevant for saying what the provisions of the Constitution actually "say" [KW-1, 178]. The key enthymeme here is that the ability to pass law is purely a political power that itself is separate from what the enacted law actually means.

4. [KW-1, 59-60, 76, 84, 93-99, 175-79, 182-87, and 210-11].

5. A succinct account of Goldford's own views on the issue can be found in this passage:

> What is at stake here is, again, evident in the juxtaposition of these two familiar propositions:
> P_1: What binds the future is the text of the Constitution.
> P_2: What binds the future is the original understanding—in Whittington's formulation, the author's understanding—of the text of the Constitution.
> The essential originalist argument is P_1 and P_2 are identical, such that the rejection of P_2 entails the rejection of P_1. My own contention is that these two propositions are distinct rather than equivalent, so that we can affirm P_1 even as we reject P_2 [DG, 230].

6. Mad Libs is a humorous game for children wherein words are selected at random to create funny meanings. A similar idea can be found at this amusing website: http://writing-program.uchicago.edu/toys/randomsentence/write-sentence.htm (accessed June 12, 2012).

7. It's actually more than culture. It is cognition as well: the way the brain is hard-wired to receive and process language. Together, this is what Wittgenstein means when referring to the "form of life." You cannot have a private language unless you had a different form of life—in which case the language would *still* not be private, it would simply be different.

8. Whittington does this, in fact, when attacking a common caricature about Framers' intent. Knowing an author's intention, he says, does not require one to "penetrate some kind of alien mind" [KW-1, 59]. Unfortunately, however, he appeals to the private language argument when Wittgenstein's remarks on philosophy of psychology seem better:

> Even if I were now to hear everything that he is saying to himself, I would know as little

what his words were referring to as if I read *one* sentence in the middle of a story. Even if I knew everything now going on within him, I still wouldn't know, for example, to whom the names and images in his thoughts related [LW-9, 29].

. . . It's only in particular cases that the inner is hidden from me, and in those cases it is not hidden because it is inner [LW-9, 33]. . . . Indeed, often, I can describe his inner, as I perceive it, but not his outer [LW-9, 62].

. . . The "inner" is a delusion. That is: the whole complex of ideas alluded to by this word is like a pained curtain drawn in front of the scene of the actual word use [LW-9, 84].

. . . One could even say: The uncertainty about the inner is an uncertainty about something outer [LW-9, 88].

9. Even new words work like this. If I place a new word in circulation, all that the game entails is finding out what public criteria I have assembled for the usage (baptism). It also involves comparing other ways of speaking that are currently in circulation for similar (or same) phenomena.

10. Aside from the other quotes that I have already used to demonstrate this error, one could add these:

But if a sentence can strike me as like a painting in words, and the very individual word in the sentence as like a picture, then it is no such marvel that a word uttered in isolation and without purpose can seem to carry a particular meaning in itself [LW-1, 215].

. . . People say to us: "You understand this expression don't you? Well, I too am using it with the meaning you are familiar with." . . . This is to treat meaning as a halo that the word carries round with it and retains in any sort of application [LW-5, 44].

It isn't just Whittington who makes this error, however. It is also committed by Johnathan O'Neill. In the quote below, note that O'Neill is correct for the first sentence. It is the second that gets him into trouble:

[T]he insight of the later Ludwig Wittgenstein that speech was essentially communicative, arguing that an utterance or a text is a "speech act" undertaken to communicate the intention of the utter or author. Absent the conception of intent there is no communication. For communication to be successful it is impossible to conceive of interpretation as anything other than the reader's or auditor's attempt to comprehend the intention of the author or speaker. Johnathan O'Neill, *Originalism in American Law and Politics* (Johns Hopkins, 2005), 195.

Contrary to O'Neil's assertion, an author or speaker does not control whether something is intelligible (communicates), the language culture does. And as I have shown in Table 9.3 [9:§2(d)], it is indeed quite possible to conceive of interpretation along lines different from "speaker's meaning." Wittgenstein in no way would confine jurisprudence to this.

11. Stanley Fish writes, "[I]f you want to know what the words someone utters mean, you have to know what code or language he is using. . . . In short, intentions are prior to meaning . . . . The system of meanings belongs to [the speaker], not to something called a language." Stanley Fish, "The Intentionalist Thesis Once More," in *The Challenge of Originalism, Theories of Constitutional Interpretation*, ed. Grant Huscroft and Bradley W. Miller (Cambridge, 2011), 102.

12. This is a rather unbelievable stance. When I read it, I could not believe my eyes:

The Constitution, a statute, and a grocery list are in reality no different from an unintelligible string of letters—e.g., xbrzal—or some set of mysterious marks—e.g., Δ ¥ ≡ +— which we need the authors' key to decipher. No text can by itself declare the language, idiolect, or code in which it is written or even that it *is* a text. . . . But severed from their authors' intended meaning, the words will not themselves constrain. How will we know what language they are in? Is the Constitution in English . . . Perhaps it is Martian. Larry Alexander, "Simple-Minded Originalism," in *The Challenge of Originalism, Theories of Constitutional Interpretation*, ed. Grant Huscroft and Bradley W. Miller (Cambridge, 2011), 91-92, n.11.

13. Wittgenstein also offers these remarks, which suggest that we think in language, at least in some respect and in some situations:

When I think in language, there aren't "meanings" going through my mind in addition to the verbal expressions: the language is itself the vehicle of thought. . . . Is thinking a kind of speaking? One would like to say it is what distinguishes speech with thought from talking without thinking.—And so it seems to be an accompaniment of speech. A process, which may accompany something else, or can go on by itself [LW-14, 122, §329-30].

14. And even in ordinary language games (not involving legal behavior), if a person is told to "buy a dog" where the clear suggestion is to "buy a poodle," only *courtesy* requires that a poodle be purchased, not language—because the whole point of this exchange is merely to facilitate courtesy between one another, the violation of which amounts only to bad manners [4:§5; 6:§1, note 4].

15. Scalia offers the following remark, "When there are two statutes, the more recent one prevails. It implicitly repeals the older one. But when the Constitution is at issue, the Constitution prevails because it is a super-statute" [AS-3].

16. Whittington notes that, "[T]he constitutional text is meaningless unless and until it is ratified. It is the adoption of the text by the public that renders the text authoritative, not its drafting by particular individuals." The new originalism, he says, is "concerned with what the text meant to those who adopted it." [KW-2, 610].

17. Randy Barnett talks of what "the text might have meant to a reasonable listener" [RB-3, 93]. And Larry Solum writes:

However, all of the problems that attended the equation of constitutional meaning with Framers' intent seem to attach to ratifiers' intent. Moreover, evidence may be even more difficult to obtain and the problems of group intention—of multiple conventions with multiple members—even more confounding with respect to ratifiers' intent. To the extent that the ratifiers' understanding is rooted in the public meaning, the emphasis on ratifiers is merely a way station on the journey from original intentions to original public meaning. . . . The core idea of the revised theory is that the original meaning of the Constitution is the original *public* meaning of the constitutional text [LS-1, 19-20, 23].

18. Of course, if ratification of an Amendment occurs by popular vote, this distinction would seem to collapse. In this case, both views would be appealing to something called "the public meaning of the provisions" [4:§1].

19. This terminology is explained in Chapter 2.

20. See, e.g., Anonymous, *Original Meaning Jurisprudence: A Sourcebook* (U.S. Department of Justice, Office of Legal Policy, 1988). See also, Wikipedia: http://en.wikipedia.org/wiki/Original_meaning (accessed June 12, 2012).

21. See also [KW-2, 610-11; RB-1, 105; and RB-2].

22. [LS-1, 22-23]. Solum writes, "As early as 1986, Scalia gave a speech exhorting originalists to 'change the label from the Doctrine of Original Intent to the Doctrine of Original Meaning,'" citing Scalia's "Address Before the Attorney General's Conference on Economic Liberties" in Washington D.C. (June 14 1986) in *Original Meaning Jurisprudence: A Sourcebook* (U.S. Dep't. of Justice, 1987) at 106.

23. *See, e.g.,* Caleb Nelson, "Originalism and Interpretive Conventions," *U. Chi L. Rev.* 70 (2003): 554-55; Jamal Greene, "On the Origins of Originalism," *Tex. L. Rev.* 88 (2009): 9; [OV, 1249]: ". . . the focus of originalism gradually shifted in the early 1990s from original intent to original meaning . . ."; and [KW-2, 607].

24. The clause reads: "No State shall . . . deny to any person within its jurisdiction the equal protection of the laws." U.S. Const. amend XIV §1.

25. One clause reads: "No person shall be . . . be deprived of life, liberty, or property, without due process of law." U.S. Const. amend V. The other is identical for our purposes U.S. Const. amend XIV §1.

26. The clause reads: "The enumeration in the Constitution, of certain rights, shall not be construed to deny or disparage others retained by the people." U.S. Const. amend. IX.

27. Larry writes:

> Was the text uttered by the framers, the ratifiers, or the people of the United States? The most probative facts are not in dispute, and in some sense this question has no clear answer. But if we view the Constitution as a speech act, then the relevant question is what individual, collectivity, or set of corporate bodies had authority to utter a constitution . . . . A formal answer to that question might be—"the ratifying conventions." An answer rooted in a normative conception of legitimacy might be, "the people themselves." But there is an alternative story[:] . . . the Constitution could be viewed as the utterance of the Philadelphia convention, and that the relevant speech act was not "constitution" but "proposal" [LS-2, 40].

28. I also address celebratory theories of constitutional law in [App: 12-32].

29. The first thing to note is that the referee isn't allowed to judge the credibility or sincerity of the statements—the point isn't to ask whether Framers are lying to us in the table. Recall that Dumbledore's Pensieve took care of that issue [8:§3(a)].

30. Some may object that another possibility exists. Is it possible to use bystanders in a way that is *not* a rubber stamp? Could there ever be a difficult standard imposed upon Framers? Imagine this view: "genderless equality" is meaningless or senseless, because the word "equality" means something fixed. Or, "substantive due process" isn't allowed because the words clash inappropriately. This view seems to indulge the idea that "meaning isn't use," something I covered in Chapters 5 and 6. I direct the reader there.

Chapter 11

The Constitution as Old Society

This chapter is not concerned with what Framers meant for constitutional text. Rather, it is concerned with what "neutral bystanders" (onlookers) living during the act of framing would have said about the document's provisions. I call this the *societal perspective*. This chapter is exploratory at first and critical toward the end.

§ 1. Whose Preferences Count?

The idea that constitutional text "truly means" only what reasonable people living during the framing understood, is, perhaps, one of the central faiths of the new originalism.[1] Predictably, the genesis of the idea comes from Justice Scalia, who believes that judges should focus "upon what the text would reasonably be understood to mean" [AS-1, 144]—i.e., the "meaning that its words were understood to bear at the time they were promulgated."[2]

The first question that must be asked is: who are these onlookers, anyway? Are the preferences that women and slaves held about the Constitution included in the subject—or only the views of white males? Are the preferences only those of social elites who dominated the occupations of law, politics, plantation-owner and trading company—or do we consider the views of the commoners, the laborers, the indentured and so forth? Are the views that we "pluck" decidedly English in their heritage or are they from people with different traditions or customs? Are the preferences specifically those of Enlightenment philosophers or do they come from the clergy? The plantation crowd or the money lenders?

These questions raise an interesting conundrum. Because American political culture was not especially democratic or egalitarian by the standards of our age, one must ask what the goal is of saying "the society believed in such-and-such." Is it to capture the segment of the society that was dominant for *its* time or to reconstruct views that would prevail under forces dominant in *our* time?

(a) Aggregating Philosophy

Trying to aggregate constitutional preference in 1789 American history, the year the Constitution was adopted, is tricky business. This is not only because governments with three equal branches and written constitutions were a new phenomenon, but also because there was very strong sentiment against forming the government in the first place.[3] As such, beliefs about the Constitution—both whether to have enacted one and what it meant—were in flux and had a changing dynamic, depending upon the political affiliations that dominated the era.

In Table 11.1, I propose four different assumptions that one can make when aggregating societal preference. One option is to simply pick those who "won out" and dominated in their time (*alpha-constituency*). If we applied this logic to 1789 American society, it seems that the result has no choice but to be Federalist-minded. This is because the Constitution's success was largely the product of Federalist-spirited social elites who not only were instrumental in framing the document, but who tended to dominate the first eight to twelve years in American government.

Table 11.1: The Four Constituencies of Societal Preference	
Type	**Description**
Alpha Constituency	Preferences that persevered in a political struggle
Beta Constituency	Preferences that were defeated in a political struggle
Negotiated Constituency	Compromised preferences of Alpha and Beta that are constructed after the fact.
Reconstructed Constituency	Preferences that can be recreated if the society had used contemporary or egalitarian means to capture them

Accordingly, this alpha constituency would believe that the Constitution, when passed, had *already included* a world view that endorsed strong central authority, taxation, judicial review, public works (e.g., roads), finance capitalism, banking, manufacturing, urbanization, stock markets, oligarchic political institutions, non-partisanship, the practice of showing deference for natural elites (meritocracy), skepticism towards slavery (Quaker Petition), and being friends again with Great Britain (Jay's Treaty).[4]

What this argument basically says is that Alexander Hamilton, George Washington, John Marshall, John Adams, John Jay and other Federalist-spirited elites hold the important (and correct) views about what the Constitution "really means." This leaves the plantation crowd out in the cold—Thomas Jefferson, George Mason, James Madison,[5] Patrick Henry, James Monroe, etc. One who accepts this view might see Abraham Lincoln as finishing the work of the Federalists and vindicating "the true constitution" against the illegitimate heritage that had initially opposed it and had incorrectly hijacked its principles after it was passed.

By contrast, if you believe that "the real constitution" is reflected in the Jeffersonian spirit, you are advocating for the *beta constituency* in 1789 (the alpha of 1800). Seeing the Constitution through these eyes would see it as having affinity for confederacy, plantation slavery, state nullification, favoring France over Britain, and increased democracy for white men (only). It would also have significant hostility toward central authority, the United States military, judicial review, finance capitalism, banking, federal spending, taxation, manufacturing, stock markets, urbanization and the practice of social deference for "natural elites"—except, of course, on the plantation, where racial deference was overtly celebrated.

Seeing the Constitution from this vantage point would resent the New Englanders who harbored so much Loyalist sentiment during the revolution and who wanted to secede in 1812. And who had done so much to undermine the outcome of the American Revolution by corrupting the halls of Congress with northern economic interests that were "in bed" with English and Scottish "money lenders"—the very same people who had threatened the power of the plantation state, and who lived by swindling the "common farmer" with economic gambling, rather than working honestly in the bosom of the earth [JF, RC, JE-1].

If one doesn't like either of these options, one could pretend that no winners or losers existed in 1789 and simply superimpose a compromise between the pro and con forces (*negotiated constituency*). Or, if one could reconstruct what this society might have believed had women and slaves not been in castes, this would be a *reconstructed constituency*.[6]

(b) Qualitative Factors

Instead of aggregating past preference, one can also break it down. The way to do this is to deny that preferences are equal. If truths about the Constitution are said not to come from just *any* past beliefs, but only from *reasonable* ones, this admits that some are "inferior."[7] Differentiating beliefs by their supposed merit is an *epistemic* task. As Illustration 11.1 indicates, beliefs can be differentiated along more than just two dimensions: some are "superior" even to the reasonable ones.

Illustration 11.1: Hierarchy in Belief

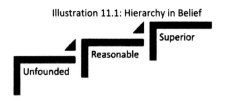

The introduction of epistemology adds a new dimension. As Table 11.2

shows, juristic beliefs can be understood along three lines: (a) the level of analysis for the provision [2:§1-2]; (b) the standard for how good it is; and (c) and how to aggregate it. Theoretically, this makes the number of juristic views one can hold about past preference much more varied than is currently discussed.[8]

Table 11.2: Three Dimensions to Past Constitutional Beliefs		
Standard of Belief	**Level of Analysis**	**Aggregating Philosophy**
Reasonable Preference	Beliefs about concepts	Alpha Constituency
Specialist Preference	Beliefs about criteria	Beta Constituency
Single-Great Person	Beliefs about instantiations	Negotiated Constituency
		Reconstructed Constituency

There are three standards of belief listed in the table. "Reasonable preference" simply means the views that are prudent.[9] "Specialist preference" wants to be more than prudent. It purports to lead the field and be possessed of the absolute best in the knowledge, information, training and experience for its time.[10] Finally, the "single great person" is one who contributes so much that the person becomes lionized, and his or her views are still read today as a giant in the field.[11] Perhaps one would attribute this status to William Blackstone.[12]

§ 2. Criticisms

Having just explored how beliefs about the societal perspective might be structured in jurisprudence, I now offer a short critique. The meaning of the Constitution simply cannot be reduced to the beliefs held by past society, no matter how you slice it. There are four reasons why.[13]

(a) Social Learning

The first criticism that I levy concerns *social learning*. This idea says that people often have to learn what is "correct" by making use of life experience and trial-and-error. Because three-branch governments and written constitutions were a new phenomenon, and because the Constitution itself was an insecure creation—it was almost voted down—the details of how it would be administered were unclear. Even those who helped engineer the new American experiment did not know how the creature would work in detail. Because of this, American society could not form intelligent constitutional opinions until it first *learned*, socially, how the new institutions appeared to *function*.

To understand this idea, examine Table 11.3. It lists several views about the Constitution that American culture had to *learn* to reject (or accept).[14] The items are taken primarily from the Washington Administration, but also include a few other notables. In each case, the "proper meaning" was counter-intuitive to what proponents first thought. The preferred arrangements had to be socially learned.

Table 11.3: The Constitution and Social Learning

- **Separation of Powers.** Washington would not allow his vice president, John Adams, to participate in cabinet meetings because he thought it violated separation of powers, since the Vice President presided over the Senate.[15]
- **Parliamentary System?** James Madison thought the Congress would be the most important branch of government and that it would even manage the executive branch, not unlike the way prime ministers were "managed" in Parliamentary Systems. (Madison's Virginia Plan had proposed a parliamentary system at the convention). Alexander Hamilton thought otherwise.[16]
- **Advice and Consent.** When making an Indian treaty, Washington tried to use the Senate as a literal consulting body because of the Advice and Consent Clause. He brought several proposals to discuss. He ended up waiting for long hours while each member debated on the floor. The end result was nothing—the matter was referred to a committee. After this, Washington gave up on the idea of consulting with the Senate. He and other presidents simply learned to consult with their own executive-branch personnel, making treaty-approval in Congress purely a political process.[17]
- **Foreign Policy.** Washington initially thought the Executive had the power to unilaterally proclaim neutrality towards other nations and to authorize punishment of the citizenry who violated the stance. Others thought such policies should be enacted by the Congress.[18]
- **Nullification?** Jefferson thought the States could nullify federal laws that were declared by those states to "violate the Constitution."[19]
- **Approval of Treaties.** Jefferson thought the House had the constitutional authority to approve treaties, because it was closer to the people, and that this was one of those self-evident truths dictated by "fundamental (natural) law."[20]
- **Judicial Review.** Numerous disputes existed about whether courts had the power of judicial review, which showed (again) the social confusion over how constitutional systems worked versus parliamentary systems.[21]

(b) Presentism

A second objection comes from what historians call "presentism." In 1789 American history—or in 1791, when the Bill of Rights was passed—views about the meaning of the fundamental law may not have been strictly limited to what any provision in the Constitution said. In the intellectual culture of the Enlightenment in the late 1700s, talk of "fundamental law" tended to be guided by a natural-law paradigm.[22]

Therefore, in some corners of thinking, the so-called "true meaning of the Constitution" could be understood as something in the service of a priori notions and self-evident truths—or some other natural-law invention, such as the indisputable wisdom of the common law or of sacred tradition. It's not that these things supplanted the Constitution. It's that the Constitution was only "true" to the extent that it accurately captured them. For some, this is precisely what a constitution was for—the reason why you would even have one. Hence, this is why Jefferson argues that the House is the rightful body to approve Treaties.[23] In such a culture, therefore, it may be problematic to assert that the meaning of "fundamental law" was legalistic and provision-bound, as if it had to first be codified by government before it could exist.[24]

Note also that the argument for "expectations originalism"[25]—which I simply call instantial judgments [2:§1(c); 8:§3(b)]—is far worse in this respect, when it is argued from the societal perspective. This is because the argument focuses upon the actual case *decisions* expected by the framing society. The argument asks that American society in 1789 not only have a preexisting understanding of how cases arising under the Constitution would be judged, but also by whom. Hence, it would seem that this approach implies a pre-packaged clairvoyance of what the institutions of American government are supposed to do with constitutional cases, and how. This means that the role of the judiciary is already assumed to be known, no matter what it believes about judicial review.[26] So, whether it is the Court, Congress or Senate deciding the cases, expectation originalism seems already to know: (a) who will do it; and (b) how.

And so, the point is that one could levy the charge that all of the societal perspectives are presentistic by requiring the meaning of the Constitution in 1789 to be either provision-centric or Court-savy. Because both of these understandings develop over time, and because social learning is an important ingredient, one could easily find preferences in 1789 to be a *poor* resource for the Constitution's meaning.

(c) Wrong Unit of Analysis

Perhaps the central problem with the societal perspective is simply that is has the wrong unit of analysis. Instead of being concerned with the best possible meaning to give to any provision, it is concerned with the welfare of an adjacent entity. The focus is upon the desires of a past *society* rather than the ideas in the Constitution for their own sake.[27]

First, the Constitution itself does not confer jurisdiction upon the framing society to be its official expositor. Nowhere is it mentioned that: (a) the society is an Article II or III judge; (b) there should be a referendum or initiative for Court decisions;[28] or (c) that judges are to adore 1789 societal preferences as the secret law.

And of course, the Constitution doesn't automatically enact *any* specific societal preference unless the language of the document explicitly says so. This isn't an a priori claim; it is the way modern legalistic culture in America behaves. The only thing that generations pass along to one another is the *language* they enact. And absent language that specifically codifies a discreet societal preference, the matter is left open for each era to impose the arrangement it believes best *for its age*. And this is precisely what happens. The domination of any societal preference within any age is always in flux as time goes by and is only rendered (apparently) clear in its own time by political triumph.[29]

The problem with having the wrong unit of analysis is more severe than one might think. It isn't a small mistake. As I show in [13:§2], and also in Chapter 7, it makes the entire *behavior* the wrong sort of behavior. If one takes the position that the enacted law cannot speak solely for itself in the legal system, it means that the Constitution becomes something subservient to a greater authority—that it retains a hidden expositor or custodian. It means that the document becomes symbolic to some other intelligence and must be read only as a *gesture* to that thing.

Finally, recall from Chapters 8 and 9 that "Framers' intent" was guilty of trying to personify the messy administrative process used to pass law [8:§4; 9:§1]. It was said to have amalgamated selected minds into a kind of "Frankenstein" that it imagined as a singular consciousness. Although juristic beliefs centered upon framing society do not do this explicitly, they do something similar. They reify society as being one living thing. They imagine "the society" as a singular being. The ultimate culprit in these sorts of claims is the desire to make too much out of typicality or central tendency.[30] It's like saying on the night of a presidential election, "The American people have spoken," when, in fact, the split is 52% to 48%. In such a scenario, "the people" are almost as much in favor as against.[31]

(d) Domination Isn't Special

The final problem with past societal preference concerns the relationship it has to cultural transformation and political triumph. Just because a view becomes popular or socially dominant does not mean that it is necessarily a *better* or more genuine constitutional idea. It merely means that the cultural orientation in place supports it, and that political triumph has occurred.

We wouldn't say, e.g., that the "true meaning" of the Second Amendment[32] *had* to be the view that existed throughout the vast majority of American history, merely because of its social dominance, versus the new one that is now emerging at the hands of conservative American justices in the *Heller* case.[33] If anything, the popularity of each view reflects only the political and cultural orientation toward the various things that the Second Amendment could be *taken* to say.[34] And so, if it works like this for us, today, it works the same for the views that were in vogue in 1789 (or at any time). Those views aren't made special merely because they were popular or became dominant.

Similarly, we wouldn't take the position that the "true meaning" of the Commerce Clause had to be what the post-Roosevelt world came to believe about it, merely because this program became so socially dominant. Rather, what we say is that the post-Roosevelt world ushered in a new political and cultural arrangement when America shifted from an agrarian to industrial/post-industrial society. Therefore, the constitutional attitudes that surfaced came about through cultural change and political triumph—and this is all that the social dominance ever indicated. And, again, if it works this way for the Roosevelt program, it works the same exact way for the things that dominated the framing society.

The fact of the matter is that comparing what any one generation believes about its constitution versus another is no different from comparing the views of two individuals. The issue isn't resolved by asking: "who was first in time?" Whether the first generation (or any) is taken to espouse "the best view" is going to be a function of something independent of them being first.

Notes

1. [KW-2; RB-2, 621]. See also Ozan Varol, who writes, "New originalism seeks to discern, not the subjective original intentions or expectations of the founders, but the objective meaning that a reasonable observer would have assigned to the Constitutional provision when it was enacted" [OV, 1249].

2. Scalia writes, "[O]riginalism treats a constitution like a statute, and gives it the meaning that its words were understood to bear at the time they were promulgated" [AS-4]. Of course, one should bear in mind Chapter 4, which stresses that the meaning of language is not elected or voted upon by societies. The ordinary words and phrases in the Constitution mean what they do in the language culture; you can't vote intelligibility out of existence. Therefore, all that the framing society has control over (in theory) is the text that is codified. One must read Justice Scalia, then, as arguing only that the preferences of the framing-society about its Constitution amount to "fundamental law," period. Not that the text *means* those preferences.

3. Indeed, Joe Ellis estimates that, during the middle of the revolutionary war, only about a one third of the country supported independence from Britain, while another third opposed it (the remaining being pretty much neutral) [JE-3, 33, 43]. In New York, enlistments for the British army outnumbered Washington's Continental Army [JE-4, 88, 96, 101]. It is also widely accepted that the Constitutional Convention had been an elite rather than mass-driven endeavor. And the views that drafted the Constitution were not representative of the rest of the nation, which is why the anti-Federalist sentiment opposing the Constitution was so strong. Also, the Constitution's passage was extremely close and benefitted from the fact that it was "take it or leave it" idea—most eligible voters probably would have wanted a more watered-down version [JE-2, 115; JE-3, 33, 43].

4. For a general account of the ideological and policy positions referred to in this paragraph, see [JF; RC, JE-1].

5. Madison, of course, wore one hat when drafting the plan of government, but another when holding office in the new system. If one were inclined to speak of two Madisons, the reference here is to the second one.

6. Note that we could also transform any of these preferences into modern ones the way that dynamic-intent was described in note 8 in Chapter 8.

7. Or as Steven Smith writes:

What matters is not what flesh-and-blood members of the public at the time a provision was enacted actually thought it meant, but rather what . . . an idealized audience would have understood it to mean. We look for "something a bit more hypothetical," Gary Lawson explains, "such as the understanding that the general public *would have had* if all relevant information and arguments had been brought to its attention." Steven D. Smith, "That Old Time Originalism," in *The Challenge of Originalism, Theories of Constitutional Interpretation,* eds. Grant Huscroft and Bradley W. Miller (Cambridge University Press, 2011), 225, citing Gary Lawson, "Delegation and Original Meaning," 88 Va. L. Rev. 327 at 341 n 51 (2002).

8. There could be an elaborate analytical map here. Imagine one who believed that specialist-preferences about a concept or criteria held by alpha constituencies in 1789 was "the true meaning of the Constitution," but only if text-centered and formalistic [8:§3].

9. They come from people who have sufficient information and capacity, and who engage in a rational chain of thought with requisite effort and sincerity. The things agreed to constitute "the reasonable opinion," and the things not constitute "reasonable disagreement." The views failing this threshold would not even make it into the conversation.

10. Note that elite publics still need aggregated. One could think, e.g., of a beta-elite preference (the elites that lost). Or a reconstructed-elite preference that includes, e.g., certain women who should have qualified as elites in their day, but were not allowed.

11. Despite the label "single-best," it could apply to any individual who merited it.

12. See. e.g., William Blackstone, *Commentaries on the Laws of England.*

13. I also expand upon these points in Chapter 12.

14. The list is illustrative only; it is hardly meant to be comprehensive.

15. David McCullough, *John Adams* (Simon and Schuster, 2001), 415: "Other than a few still social occasions, Adams had little contact with the president and no influence . . . ." Joseph Ellis writes about John Adams during the Washington administration:

> To make matters worse, his duties in the Senate removed him from the deliberations of the cabinet. Washington seldom consulted him on policy questions, apparently believing that the vice presidency was a legislative office based in the Senate; therefore, to include Adams in executive decisions violated the constitutional doctrine of separation of powers. When asked by friends about his isolation from the presidential councils, Adams half-heartedly endorsed the same constitutional explanation. "The executive authority is so wholly out of my sphere," he observed, "and it is so delicate a thing for me to meddle in that, I avoid it as much as possible" [JE-1, 167]

16. Ron Chernow writes:

> Hamilton's seeming omnipotence unnerved Madison because it further skewed what the latter deemed the proper balance between executive and legislative power. For many delegates at Philadelphia in 1787, Congress was supposed to be the leading branch of government, the guardian of popular liberty that would prevent the restoration of British tyranny. That was why the legislative duties were spelled out in article 1 of the Constitution. Consistent with this view, Madison thought the treasury secretary should serve as an adjunct to Congress, providing legislators with reports from which they would shape bills. Jefferson likewise balked at the way Hamilton both submitted reports and drafted bills based on them. Hamilton, in contrast, envisioned the executive branch as the main engine of government, the sole branch that could give force and direction to its policies, and time has abundantly vindicated his view [JE-1, 167].

17. Joe Ellis writes:

But when he brought his proposals for treaties with several southern Indian tribes to the Senate, the debate became a prolonged shouting match over questions of procedure. The longer the debate went on the more irritated Washington became, eventually declaring, "This defeats every purpose of my coming here." He abruptly stalked out of the sessions, as one witness reported, "with a discontented Air . . . of sullen dignity." From that time onward, the phrase "advise and consent" meant something less than direct executive solicitation of senatorial opinion, and the role the Senate as an equal partner in the crafting of treaties came to be regarded as a violation of the separation of powers principle [JE-4, 194-95].

18. *The Almanac of American History*, ed. Arthur M. Schlesinger (Barnes & Noble Books, 1993), 163: "Madison questioned the president's authority to issue the proclamation." Gordon S. Wood, *Revolutionary Characters: What Made the Founders Different* (Penguin Books, 2006), 37: "When the president issued his Proclamation of Neutrality in 1793, he did not even bother to ask for the consent of the Senate, and thus he further established the executive as the nearly sole authority in the conduct of foreign affairs." The Proclamation reads:

And I do hereby also make known that whosoever of the citizens of the United States shall render himself liable to punishment or forfeiture under the law of nations by committing, aiding, or abetting hostilities against any of the said powers, or by carrying to any of them those articles which are deemed contraband by the modern usage of nations, will not receive the protection of the United States against such punishment or forfeiture; and further, that I have given instructions to those officers to whom it belongs to cause prosecutions to be instituted against all persons who shall, within the cognizance of the courts of the United States, violate the law of nations with respect to the powers at war, or any of them. George Washington, "Proclamation 4—Neutrality of the United States in the War Involving Austria, Prussia, Sardinia, Great Britain, and the United Netherlands Against France," April 22, 1793, *The American Presidency Project*, ed. Gerhard Peters and John T. Woolley, http://www.presidency.ucsb.edu/ws/?pid=65475 (accessed June 12, 2012).

19. Ellis writes:

Working alone in Monticello, Jefferson composed what became known as the Kentucky Resolutions in August and September. His core argument was that the Sedition Act was unconstitutional because it violated the natural rights of the citizens of each state to control their own domestic affairs. Moreover, each state "has a natural right in cases not within the compact"—that is, in all cases not specified as under federal jurisdiction in the Constitution—"to nullify of their own authority all assumptions of power by others within their limits." Here was the classic states' rights position, topped off by the sweeping claim that federal laws could be nullified by the states, which then had a legitimate right to secede, what Jefferson called "scission," if the federal Congress or courts defied their decision [JE-1, 199-200].

20. Joseph Ellis writes regarding Jay's Treaty:

Jefferson could not believe that a treaty so unpopular could ever become law, since it was, as he said, "really nothing more than a treaty of alliance between England and the Anglomen of this country against the legislature and people of the United States."

Though the Constitution nowhere specifically mentioned it, Jefferson persuaded himself that the "true meaning of the constitution" gave the House of Representatives sovereign power over all legislation, including treaties [JE-4, 229].

. . . Jefferson managed to conclude that the House was intended to be an equal partner in approving all treaties, going so far as to claim that that body was the sovereign branch of the government empowered to veto any treaty it wished, thereby "annihilating the whole treaty-making power" of the executive branch" [JE-1, 138].

21. See the dissent by Justice Gibson in *Eakin v. Raub*, 12 S. & R. 330 (Pa.1825), arguing, in essence, for a parliamentary system where the statute is the highest form of law. Gibson would later change his mind, "both because an intervening state constitutional convention had silently 'sanctioned the pretensions of the courts' and because of his 'experience of the necessity of the case.' *Norris v. Clymer*, 2 Pa. 277 (1845)." Gerald Gunther, *Constitutional Law*, 11th ed. (The Foundation Press Inc., 1985), 17.

22. The overthrow of monarchy, of course, was commonly predicated upon natural law and Enlightenment thinking. The Declaration uses natural-law reasoning (inalienable rights, self-evident truths). The drafting of the Constitution was thought to be in the service of what was both empirically true (in nature) and rational. *See, e.g.*, Henry F. May, *The Enlightenment in America* (Oxford, 1976), 96-101, discussing the Enlightenment's influence upon the Constitution, and 163-164, discussing the Declaration of Independence. And it is worth noting that, during the First Congress, James Madison had proposed re-writing the Constitution and creating a natural-rights preamble, like the Declaration had. Richard Labunski, *James Madison and the Struggle for the Bill of Rights* (Oxford, 2006), 198-199. Also, Madison thought that government could not accurately codify all of the true natural rights because the people might vote them down or would not respect them. Madison writes:

> [T]here is great reason to fear that a positive declaration of some of the most essential rights could not be obtained in the requisite latitude. I am sure that the rights of conscience in particular, if submitted to public definition would be narrowed much more than they are likely ever to be by an assumed power.
>   . . . It has been objected also against a Bill of Rights, that, by enumerating particular exceptions to the grant of power, it would disparage those rights which were not placed in that enumeration; and it might follow by implication, that those rights which were not singled out, were intended to be assigned into the hands of the General Government, and were consequently insecure. This is one of the most plausible arguments I have ever heard against the admission of a bill of rights into this system; but, I conceive, that it may be guarded against. I have attempted it, as gentlemen may see by turning to the last clause of the fourth resolution. John Hart Ely, *Democracy and Distrust* (Harvard, 1980), 35-36.
>   . . . Repeated violations of these parchment barriers have been committed by overbearing majorities in every State. In Virginia I have seen the bill or rights violated in every instance where it has been opposed to a popular current. (Labunski, above, at 160).

See also, Gordon Wood, *The Radicalism of the American Revolution* (Vintage Books, 1991), 189-212, discussing the Enlightenment; Gordon Wood, *Revolutionary Characters, What Made the Founders Different* (Penguin, 2006), 11-28, discussing the Founders and the Enlightenment.

23. See note 20, above.

24. The Ninth Amendment presents an interesting paradox. It explicitly sets forth a

provision telling readers not to let the text be the end of the story. This seems to be a case of positivism (codification) franchising its competition—saying, in essence, "We have a written Constitution, but even *it* says not exactly for everything" U.S. Const. amend. IX.

25. This is the view that the Constitution means only what framing society would have expected it to mean, often called "expectation originalism." See [8:§3(b), note 15].

26. The point is this: the view presumes that the framing culture would expect the decisions to be issued by *some entity*. Even if that entity was an institution other than the Supreme Court (e.g., the Senate), the view *still* presumes a settled expectancy for *both* what the Court is to do and how the pronouncer of a constitutional decision is to behave.

27. Note that this is no different from Framers' intent, which focused its energies upon the welfare of specific actors ("Framers") rather than allowing constitutional text to speak solely for itself. As such, the criticisms one can levy are very much the same.

28. In fact, what the document appears to "say" is that the Supreme Court is its own branch of government, with life-tenured judges, possessing the judicial power of the United States. U.S. Const. Art. III cl.1.

29. See, e.g., Mark A. Graber, *Transforming Free Speech, The Ambiguous Legacy of Civil Libertarianism* (University of California Press, 1991), showing how different conceptions of the First Amendment existed throughout American political development.

30. One should note that alpha, beta, negotiated and reconstructed constituencies covered in [11:§2(a)] work very much like the concepts of mean, median and mode in statistics. Both concern how to construct central tendency.

31. Also, typical doesn't necessarily mean *better*. Given what we know about social learning and bell curves, one could indulge exactly the opposite idea: typical preference suffers from the drag of the common denominator.

32. The Amendment reads, "A well regulated Militia, being necessary to the security of a free State, the right of the people to keep and bear Arms, shall not be infringed." U.S. Const. Amend. II.

33. *District of Columbia v. Heller*, 554 U.S. 570 (2008).

34. And there's no doubting that America has a "unique" gun culture that has been given its expression in the new ruling, whether one likes it or not. The point: where else could such a ruling have occurred in the West other than America? As dismal as it may be, there is a cultural orientation in place that supports the *possibility* of such a decision.

Chapter 12

Cultural Construction

§ 1. Abortion, Sodomy and Time Travel

Let's imagine two cases of first impression in the American legal system. They argue, respectively, that the Constitution protects "the right to choose" and the right to engage in sodomy. For simplicity, let's call the abortion case *Roe* and the sodomy case *Lawrence*. And also, to keep things a little less hairy, let's assume that the issue in *Roe* concerns the right to abortion by surgical or clinical procedure, meaning that neither the abortion pill nor any ingestible substance is the factual issue in the case. And also, let's assume that the fetus has not yet reached the point of "quickening," which is the point at which women can feel the fetus move in the womb, around 18-20 weeks.[1]

Let's also imagine that a hypothetical person exists who comes to exemplify the dominant societal preference for his or her historical age with respect to "surgical abortion,"[2] sodomy and constitutional rights. And let's further assume that there are two such individuals covering (together) both historical periods that interest us: the year of the adoption of the Ninth and Fifth Amendments (1791), and the year of the Fourteenth (1868). Finally, let's assume that these two people are transported through a time portal and, right now, stand before us.

The question that must be asked is extraordinarily simple. What would they say that would show us how to resolve the cases? What could they offer that reveals "the true meaning" of the constitutional provisions in question?

(a) Mystery Rights

To begin, let's consider those provisions. The Ninth, Fourteenth and Fifth Amendments read as follows:

○ The enumeration in the Constitution, of certain rights, shall not be construed to deny or disparage others retained by the people. Amend. IX.

◦ No State shall . . . deprive any person of life, liberty, or property, without due process of law. Amend. XIV, §1; Amend. V.

◦ No State shall make or enforce any law which shall abridge the privileges or immunities of citizens of the United States. Amend. XIV, §1.

◦ No person shall be . . . deprived of life, liberty, or property, without due process of law. Amend. V.

The view that the Constitution protects liberties not specifically listed in the document is called the *mystery-rights thesis*. Several provisions speak to it. The Ninth pointedly mentions that some constitutional rights are simply not specified. The Privileges and Immunities Clause could also be read in the service of this idea. It could be taken as protecting, in a stylish prose, all of the American rights and prerogatives, including the unmentioned ones.[3]

However, the more frequently-cited clause promoting mystery rights is the Due Process Clause. This sparks more linguistic controversy. Read narrowly, the clause could be said to mean only that liberty can be taken if fair election processes exist and if representatives duly enact the laws. But read in a different sense, the term "process" can mean not just the workings of a *legislative* body, but executive and judicial as well. Thus, the idea could mean that liberty is protected by the proper handicraft of the *entire* American experiment, which includes the Court's role in guarding fundamental liberty.

Also, consider the sense of the word "law" that one could give to the Due Process Clause. If the word is given a pre-Austinian vernacular [JA]—or, at least, one of the grammars that Austin was rebelling against—it would mean something like "an immutable truth," as with the expressions, "the laws of physics" or "the law of God." These expressions give the word "law" the sense of immutability, something universally correct. Therefore, the Due Process Clause could mean that liberty cannot be taken without the due workings of "the great truths"—or in short, without undeniable *justice*.

And so, there are many ways that one could come to believe that the Constitution protects mystery rights. And the only question left for those who hold such a belief is whether surgical abortion and/or sodomy should be regarded as one of them.

What would the time travelers say about these assertions?[4]

(b) Past Populism

After reviewing *Roe* and *Lawrence*, let's imagine that the time travelers begin by telling us something very basic. They say that the most considerate preference for their respective historical eras is that neither surgical abortion nor sodomy would ever be taken as constitutional rights. This is because, they say, surgical abortion and sodomy were thought to be uncommon, irregular and unpopular by the main of society. Most people either didn't do it or thought negatively (snooty) when they heard about it.

Assuming for the moment that this is true, does it resolve the cases for us? The answer is quite obviously "no" for numerous reasons. But what may not be clear is that the answer is "no" even for the era of the *time travelers*. This is because, if the cases are denied on these grounds, it will have said something problematic about fundamental law. It will have said that the Constitution amounts only to one of two things: (a) a kind of dominant populism in outlook; or (b) a state of normalcy in certain behavior (dominant norms). Yet, one could never accept the naked idea that the Constitution was *forced* to always mean whatever is overtly popular[5] or normal.

That is, one could surely think of examples, today, where the Constitution reasonably came to endorse a right that was surprising for its day or otherwise unpopular (e.g., flag burning). And surely there are examples of valid criticisms of the Court, in retrospect, after it caved to populism or the status quo in the face of great injustices (e.g., the Japanese Internment,[6] *Plessy v. Ferguson*, etc.). And so, if populism and normalcy cannot be reasons in themselves for selecting outcomes for us, today—surely it is not proper to superimpose an antiquated rendition of it from the past. To the contrary, the good logic here would seem in reverse: if populism or normalcy did dispose of the matter, one could simply say to the travelers, "Well, most people in our age support the idea." That would seem to serve as the perfect refutation for the point being made.

And of course, there is always this familiar objection. If the generations of the respective time travelers wanted the things that were popular and normal in their lives to be "the law of the land" indefinitely into the future, they had a duty to specifically set forth those ideas into the Constitution, with clear and precise language. They simply cannot expect new rights (they oppose) to be precluded from consideration when the constitutional text authored across time opened the door to the mystery-rights thesis. Accordingly, the same requirements of clarity that the enacted law is said to require for the legislative ambitions of lawmakers must also attend to the ambitions of the time travelers. If Framers cannot secretly make the law with their private wishes, surely the travelers cannot.

(c) Past Culture

Let's say that the time travelers offer this line of inquiry. They say to us, "Sodomy cannot be legalized because the prevailing view among the learned authorities is that homosexuality is both abnormal and unnatural. Everywhere it is outlawed,[7] and with very extreme punishment."[8] Note that this view doesn't merely say that sodomy is unpopular, it makes an epistemic claim in cultural time: it says, in essence, that "All we know about the subject during the time in which we live would disapprove." It says, in short, that the *knowledge* on the subject does not permit it. And let's say that the time travelers offer something similar about abortion. They say, "Surgical abortion cannot be allowed because it results in death or injury to the mother in a high percentage of cases, and because the medical community is resolutely against it as a procedure."[9] And they add, "Even when not injured by it, women would be prone to scandalous conduct."

Notice what this idea is doing. It reveals something interesting about the travelers: it shows they can only understand the idea of surgical abortion and sodomy as it exists in *their* time. This means that their opinions are prestructured by their cultural life and what they regard as "prevailing authority."

This is particularly revealing for the issue in *Roe*, which becomes culturally processed by the travelers as a *medical-patriarchal* issue. This is because of three things. First, medical technology was such that surgical abortion posed a significant degree of risk.[10] Second, women were in a patriarchal caste, which meant that their welfare was often rendered petty, subservient, confined and protective. And most importantly, the best thinking of the day held that the quickening was an important indicator of the moral status of life. Once the fetus became "animate," it was said to have acquired its soul and to have become a higher priority.[11] Prior to that, its status was lesser.

And so, it is the *culture* of the time travelers that processes their opinions. And this means they are at a severe disadvantage when trying to form the best opinions possible about the matter at hand, *today*. The way that life is arranged for the travelers—technologically, socially, intellectually, politically—simply doesn't allow for the social behavior of surgical abortion and sodomy to become constitutional rights.[12]

In fact, even their *sense* of these ideas—the way they speak and think of them—is different. They don't live in a culture with the "morning after pill" or with the theatrical behaviors and outlooks of those depicted in the movie, *Juno*. To them, speaking of the very idea of surgical abortion conjures up different pictures in the mind and different arrangements of thoughts. And the same is true for sodomy. They don't see the movies that we see. There are not gays in popular sitcoms. The polls don't show a 50/50 split on gay marriage in their time. And they surely don't have a porn industry and the sexualized culture that broke out in America in the last half of the 20th century—or even the same higher-educational curriculum.

Because of this, one might even be tempted to say that the law truly *does* outlaw their *sense* of these ideas, which is not at all the same as our sense (how we've arranged our thoughts and social life). And hence, what is said here is only this: for them, the idea that surgical abortion and sodomy are constitutional rights is *culturally foreign*. For us, it's not—it's just a pro/con debate.[13]

But wait . . . I hear an objection from one of the lawyers in *Roe*. Is it unfair that I have allowed the travelers to judge surgical abortion as it existed in the *past* rather than the procedure today? After all, no one is trying to say that the procedure used to surgically abort in the late 1700s or mid-1800s should be the one constitutionally blessed. So, why not test the real issue in the case?

Here's the problem. You can't—not even theoretically. For them to judge the current procedure *knowingly* requires that they first be *culturally acclimated*. They would have to know all that we do about the issue. They would have to understand what happened to the patriarchal state and how the role of women today is completely different. They would have to know how the quickening became an outdated metaphysical indicator. And how scientific reductionism (DNA material) and photographic imagery began to compete for conceptions of what has the right to live, against philosophic ideas about the state of consciousness and the sense of "I."[14] They would have to know what cultural and intellectual developments took place over the last 150-200 years. And importantly, once all of this took place—once the transformation occurred—the opinions of the time travelers would *still* remain *irrelevant*. Why? Because their views would have become sentiments already readily available in our time (we don't need them to teleport in).[15]

And so the point comes down to this. The time travelers simply cannot reveal "what the Constitution means." They can only offer considerate ideas of how the issue in question would fit *their* lives. As such, their opinions would only be paramount if we had been asked to travel in time and become the judges for *their* Court. Indeed, in such a situation, their views would be of monumental importance to us. We would be blithering idiots were we to judge in their culture, without their direction.

So, it seems that the new originalism has the entire thesis *backward*. If past societal preference reveals anything constitutionally admissible, it is what might be good for *yesterday*. The simple fact of the matter is that the travelers can show us *nothing* that is authoritative on the issue. What they would tell us could never be used as policy expertise today. We could never count it as a revelation in any academic field. They wouldn't be giving us something that history and philosophy didn't already know.[16] All they would be providing is their *opinion* based upon 18th and 19th century religious, scientific and technological understandings; and upon attitudes about sexuality, marriage and children in an era where family, gender roles and promiscuity are radically different.

And if historic opinion really did constitute "the ultimate law" in the American legal system, one wouldn't need a Supreme Court. One would simply submit the issue to an unquestionable authority like historian Gordon Wood. And if we did appoint Gordon Wood as the sole and just expositor of "the true constitution," note how it would seem similar to those societies that might appoint a sage or an elder to keep certain social arrangements (faiths) in order. It would hardly seem like acceptable professional behavior in a legalistic culture.

(d) Perspectival Views

Let's assume that the lawyers in *Roe* and *Lawrence* make an objection to what has just transpired in the preceding section. They argue that the kinds of opinions provided by the time travelers (so far) are not the ones that are truly relevant. This is because they are only *policy preferences*. They only tell us whether surgical abortion or sodomy would be regarded as acceptable social policy. Therefore, the lawyers say, we are consulting the wrong thing. We need to consider what the travelers say about the best *legal* opinion that existed in their day for the meaning of constitutional law.

To understand this idea, consider five such views found in Table 12.1, which I call *orthodox views*. They each address the subject of "mystery rights." They range from the idea that no mystery rights are created by the Constitution, to the idea that such rights exist only if they concern matters fundamental to ordered liberty. Other views have them exist if it is politically palpable, or if it is consistent with tradition or common law at the time of the framing.

Table 12.1: Five Potential Orthodox Views Affecting Abortion Rights

View	Position
Deactivation Thesis	No mystery rights exist in the Constitution.
Common Law Thesis	Mystery rights do not exist unless the common law at the time of the framing had endorsed them.
Political Pragmatism	Mystery rights exist only where enough people support those rights and where too many states do not enforce laws to the contrary.
Sacred Tradition Thesis	Mystery rights exist only where vindicated by the sacred traditions of the society.
Fundamental Rights Thesis	Mystery rights exist only if they are fundamental to ordered liberty.

To see why past orthodox views are not "special," imagine the following scenario. A professor assigns a paper in which students must determine which orthodox view in Table 12.1 is the most justified. This doesn't mean the view that was most popular in the past. Rather, the question is on the merits: if all the views are equally announced for the first time, today—as if the issue were fresh—which of them could be defended as the best principle of law, and why?

Here is what the issue boils down to: how would the professor even judge the paper? The only way the paper could be fairly judged, it seems, is based upon how well the student could *defend* his or her thesis, not what that thesis is. The professor looks for the view that can account for all the inconsistencies, problems, warts and "issues." In short, the professor looks for the view that has a rich perspective in that it successfully confronts all of the problems to the *best* of our current thinking *abilities* (developments).

For example, consider the Common Law Thesis. It argues that the common law inherited from England tells us what the mystery rights are. A similar position is taken by the Sacred Tradition Thesis. It argues that longstanding and "sacred" practices handed down to the American people through history tell us what the unmentioned rights are. But there are *numerous* obstacles that these views must confront.

First, what is the true nature of the common law? Is it an autonomous and indisputable achievement of "right reason," as the famous English jurist Lord Coke said it was?[17] Or, is it merely the "intuitions of public policy"—and even prejudices—as famous American jurist Oliver Wendell Holmes described it in 1881?[18] And, when one does the method, are they simply *legislating* as Justice Scalia appears to describe it (surprisingly)?[19] He writes:

> [First-year law school] consists of playing common-law judge, which in turn consists of playing king—devising, out of the brilliance of one's own mind, those laws that ought to govern mankind. . . . It is an art or a game rather than a science . . . [growing] like a Scrabble board. . . . [T]he skill to perform the broken-field running through earlier cases . . . leaves him free to impose that rule: distinguishing one prior case of the left, straight-arming another one on the right, high-stepping away from another precedent about the tackle him from the rear, until (bravo!) he reaches the goal—good law [AS-1, 7-9].

And so, the point is this. If judge-made common law cannot be defended as being inherently righteous (just), then any mystery-rights thesis that chained itself to old renditions of this idea would have to account for *why* it did so. Or, it would have to account for why judges couldn't continue creating mystery rights under the auspices of interpreting a clause in the Constitution that can be fairly said to allow them to do just that. Isn't it difficult to both *endorse* the common law of the past as a *true* declaration of "fundamental liberty" prior to the passage of the Constitution, and then to shun the process of judge-pronounced rights altogether under a document that seems to license it? Note that this would be a perfectly rational thing to do if one took the position that the passage of the Constitution *closed the door* to new rights. Yet, isn't this precisely what the Ninth Amendment addresses?

Another problem that must be confronted is the *fallacy of received authority*. During the scholastic period in the High Middle Ages, certain ancient authorities were not questioned. They were simply handed down as "received." Education, in fact, consisted only of learning the stipulations of knowledge bequeathed by Church authorities and reconciling the same with the body of knowledge generated by "giants" like Aristotle, Plato, Aquinas and the esteemed treatises. In fact, in this culture, this is what the very act of intelligence consists of (reconciling stipulations with "giants"). It's often referred to as *classical scholastics*. But once the Enlightenment comes around, this model is overthrown, and intelligence becomes something that never has a fence or boundary: all answers must be subject to the best thinking science and philosophy can offer—there are no "freebies."

And so, when one suggests that the meaning of constitutional text must now, today, bow to the common law or sacred traditions from the past, the question that must be asked is: why? Is it because they are "received authorities" that must be administered in the same way that unquestioned postulates were handed down in the "dark ages?" Are we being asked to behave intellectually as though it were medieval times again? Or, are the authorities being offered under warranty that they still constitute the best thinking we have, *today*, for the subject at hand?

To see this more clearly, consider the received wisdom in *Roe* and *Lawrence*. In *Roe*, the received authority would be centered upon "the quickening." This was said to be an indication of when the soul entered the body. Once the creature moved, it was then life of a different sort.[20] And in *Lawrence*, the received authority would simply declare that homosexuality is "unnatural." Now the key question must be posed: are we being asked to accept these postulates uncritically, in the way a medieval mind would? Or, are these answers being espoused under warranty that they, themselves, *right now*, constitute the best thinking that our intellectual culture has about these subjects?

Because, it seems to me that Lord Coke and Blackstone were offering the best judgment that their *culture* could offer for the law: the best that their schools, information, politics, education, etc., could muster. So, if we offer the very same postulates that they did, we are in danger of being either mindless fools who are parroting the intellectual behaviors of the dark ages or misinformed fools who are saying that such answers are the best that we possess. It seems to make no difference in this case whether the mind is blank or wrong.

The simple fact is this. If any thesis that promotes received authorities does not have acceptable answers to *all* of these challenges, it makes for *poor philosophy*. It makes for an unrefined or "bent" perspective. And the same is true for every orthodox view in Table 12.1. The Deactivation Thesis, for example, must show *why* the Constitution doesn't appear to mean what it says. And in doing so, it must show that the thesis is free from a troublesome account of what fundamental law is in the American legal system (Framers' intent, an antiquated cultural arrangement) [13:§1-§2].

Once all of the problems inherent with each orthodox view is acceptably known and accounted for by the student, only then can the professor say that he or she has a defensible perspective. And that's exactly the point: all of the orthodox views are *perspectival* in some way. And as such, it matters *nothing* if one of them is historically older—at least, nothing beneficial. All that matters is which of the perspectives can be thought to provide the most considerate, informed, workable and refined framework—something that can change as time moves forward and can even be reasonably disagreeable (depending upon the theses being considered).

Therefore, what the Constitution means is ultimately a question involving allegiance to a defensible intellectual framework (paradigms),[21] similar to the way that meaning works for the Bible. And just as one might say that a fire-and-brimstone, millions-going-to-hell theology doesn't seem to espouse a very refined God concept, one can look at "fundamentalist constitutionalism" with equally suspicious eyes.

But the key point I am making is that constitutional meaning requires that one take stances of some kind that are philosophic in nature. All orthodox claims must, by definition, be *opinionated* in some way. And the reason why old juristic opinions favoring any concept, criteria or instantiation[22] should not automatically be accepted as constitutional gospel is simply because they must first be compared with competing views that have the benefit of developments in information, knowledge, culture, science and philosophy. Orthodox views are not like wine: they do not grow more valid with their age. Once any framework becomes antiquated or local to its world, it becomes of no use to us.

This means that, if one wanted the most inherently superior perspective about constitutionality, one would never rule out developments in thinking that take place *after* the point of adoption (framing). Indeed, adoption is probably best understood as the point that *starts* the heavy thinking. If this is true, it means that originalism never seeks to provide the *best* constitutional meaning. Rather, it only seeks to find the meaning that dominated an antiquated point in history—an old hegemonic framework.

Finally, it must be remembered that any generation's orthodox views are never specifically enacted into the Constitution. To the contrary, the document is set up so that such views must be *supplied* by anyone wishing to offer a considerate account of what it means. This is the same idea that I already presented elsewhere in this book: that any ordinary-language constitution, by definition, requires its interpreter to eliminate rival concepts and criteria before it can be productively used [2:§1-2; 3:§1-2]. One can't make the text operational without doing this. Because this labor must be *supplied*, it cannot already be enacted.

§ 2. Cultural Development

To finish off this chapter, I must quickly discuss a point that I have frequently alluded to: the meaning of the Constitution depends upon cultural development. What American culture has historically said about its Constitution, and what the judges are to do with it, has always been a matter of significant debate. I now briefly sketch the important developments of that conversation.

Take, for example, the very question of where the great truths of the American Constitution, if any, come from. The answer we are told in early American history is not the same as in later. American colonial culture was agrarian and educated in the classics. It was participating in Enlightenment political philosophy.[23] As such, its elites held views about "ultimate law" that arose from a natural-law discourse. The fundamental law, it was said, came from "self-evident truths" that revealed themselves in undeniable nature captured by Enlightenment science and learned philosophy. It is for this reason that social elites drafted the Constitution in secret, separating the branches of government per the new "scientific thinking" revealed by Montesquieu.

By contrast, once the industrial and post-industrial culture forms, intellectual culture turns much more positivistic. In this world, people begin to argue that the great truths don't pre-exist the machinery of government. Instead, fundamental law arrives in the legal system *only* from its naked passage during a political process. Therefore, if government doesn't specifically bless the law, it doesn't exist (in the system).

Also, how judges were said to carry out their craft was (and is) something always in flux. In the 1600s, judges made decisions by pointing to the great maxims or platitudes.[24] By the time American judges began writing opinions in the early republic, they purport to reach conclusions through the craft of rhetoric that is advertised as its own stately logic. The decisions contain very little citation to precedent or enacted law, and seem very much like "bad philosophy." But by the time of the 20th century, the judicial opinion becomes decidedly positivistic and dense, with judges daring not to make any assertions of their own unless they can point to some other citation or authority giving it license.[25]

Relatedly, how the judges were supposed to *think* is something that developed over time. If we look to the mid-to-late 1800s in America, an intellectual era sometimes called "the moral sciences period," one sees the idea that law is its own self-contained "science."[26] Sometimes, the inheritance of this orthodoxy was Blackstonian: great traditions were said to be the lynchpin of the thinking. At other times, the inheritance comes from famous Dean of the Harvard Law School, Christopher Columbus Langdell, who played an important part in the proliferation of analytical formalism ("law as geometry").

But by the time the century turns, the world begins to change several times over again. It begins with the Holmesian and realist idea that comes to dominate legal elites: that judges merely make the law into something that they want it to be. Faced with this apparent "problem," the empiricist intellectual culture provides a short-lived experimental remedy, called sociological jurisprudence [1:§1(c)]. This idea held that the best legal opinions should be based upon the most empirically-sound behavioral science of its day. This thinking is what rationalizes, in theory, the historic decision in *Brown v. Board of Education*.[27]

But as the century moves on, one begins to see intellectual culture produce a schism. It produces thinkers like Dworkin, who stresses the model of "best thinking" [3:§4(a)]. The idea is that a good judge is a considerate, deep, philosophic sort of thinker who sees that constitutional choices reduce themselves to compelling moral principles that are defended in considerate arguments. And that this, when undertaken properly, is not an activity that is subjective or "political" (in a negative sense). Contrary to this view are the pragmatists, popularly voiced in American legal culture by Judge Richard Posner, who preach the idea that constitutional questions do not require philosophic pontification. Instead, for Posnerians, the judge need only make pragmatic decisions that pay attention to social utility.[28] Finally, the century also saw the influence of postmodern frameworks, such as critical legal studies, which promote skepticism in jurisprudence.[29]

And so, the point comes down to this. It would be quite problematic to say that the Supreme Court could never violate the orthodox views dominant in the legal academy at any discrete point in time. The simple reason is that the story of intellectual culture cannot ever be frozen at any stagnant point. What the Constitution is said to mean is socially, politically and culturally contested, and is dependent upon intellectual, scientific, philosophic and informational developments that arise as culture changes. All that one could ever do is properly absorb those developments and provide the best defensible account that one could muster.

Notes

1. See *American Medical Association Encyclopedia of Medicine,* ed. Charles B. Clayman, MD (Random House, 1989), 842.

2. When I refer to "surgical abortion," I mean the use of clinical or medical implements to extract the fetus from the uterus during any point in history where such behavior occurred. Today, I believe it is called "vacuum aspiration" or "dilation and curettage." See section 2.3.1, vacuum aspiration, in *Safe Abortion: Technical and Policy Guide for Health Systems* (World Health Organization, 2003), 32.

3. This is not the way, of course, that the Court read the clause. It was famously "gutted" in *The Slaughter-House Cases*, 83 U.S. 36 (1873).

4. At the outset, one should note some ground rules. The time travelers cannot offer inside information about the events of the law-making process. They can't, e.g., reveal what lawmakers secretly did, thought, assumed or expected when they passed the constitutional provisions. This is because I've already addressed the issue of Framers' intent in Chapters 8 and 9. Therefore, this issue cannot be a masquerade of that one.

5. That's not to say that popular belief is automatically meaningless or irrelevant. Whether any belief is helpful consists upon what it rests, not how many people believe it. You never resolve the *merits* of any issues with a headcount, though you may resolve the politics. If what people believe about anything in any era can be defended, then it is the *reasons* that may prevail, not the people. As such, populism might be *evidence* of good belief, but it easily might not be. Ultimately, the question depends upon what the assertion is.

6. *Korematsu v. United States*, 323 U.S. 214 (1944); *Hirabayashi v. United States,* 320 U.S. 81 (1943); *Yasui v. United States,* 320 U.S. 115 (1943).

7. According to Mahoney, "Modern American and European law is based on ancient Roman law, which prescribed the death penalty for anal intercourse in A.D. 390 (Bullough, 1979). In England, homosexuality was punishable by death until 1861 and by life in prison until 1967." E.R. Mahoney, *Human Sexuality* (McGraw-Hill, 1983), 303.

8. Sodomy appears to have been punished by death in the colonies until the time of the American Revolution, when there was a movement for "less severe punishment," like castration (proposed by Thomas Jefferson) and lengthy prison terms. See Gary David Comstock *Violence Against Lesbians and Gay Men* (Columbia University Press, 1991), 15.

9. This actually is a thorny issue. In 1857, the AMA formed a committee against abortion that culminated in its official stance in 1871. (See *Roe*, cited below). However, the issue isn't quite so clear for 1791 because of medical norms. James Mohr notes that, because early pregnancy could not be medically verified, pre-quickening abortion could be treated as a "menstral block," for which a variety of homeopathic-sort of remedies existed, such as: bloodletting, bathing, purgative herbs, and "doses of calomel and aloes" (cited below).

Putting aside the efficacy of such treatments, this isn't what the hypothetical is concerned with. It seems more concerned with the behavior described by King, who notes that women in the 1800s "often resorted to using sharp instruments, wax candles, penholders with attached wires, glass rods, hair curling tongues, sticks, spoons, knives, and catheters" to perform surgical abortion (cited below). Even Mohr notes that some doctors could perform an abortion with "surgical techniques." But it is also said regarding this that "patients ran the risk of complications, such as perforated uteruses and septicemia" (cite below). Finally, it is said that the whole process was risky because of the failure to have antiseptics, which was not invented (and in wide use) until much later. (*Roe*, cited below).

Citations are as follows: *Roe v. Wade* 410 U.S. (1973) at 141, 148-149; James C. Mohr, *Abortion in America: The Origins and Evolution of National Policy* (Oxford, 1978), 3-19 (quote about "surgical techniques" on page 15; everything else throughout the chapter); C.R. King, "Abortion in Nineteenth Century America: a Conflict Between Women and Their Physicians," *Women's Health Issues* 2, no. 1 (Spring 1992): 32–39 (the official publication of the Jacobs Institute of Women's Health at George Washington University); and *The Selected Papers of Margaret Sanger*, ed. Esther Katz (University of Illinois Press, 2003), 73n3.

10. Justice Blackmun states in *Roe*:

[T]he procedure was a hazardous one for the woman. This was particularly true prior to the development of antisepsis. Antiseptic techniques, of course, were based on discoveries by Lister, Pasteur, and others first announced in 1867, but were not generally accepted and employed until about the turn of the century. Abortion mortality was high. Even after 1900, and perhaps until as late as the development of antibiotics in the 1940's, standard modern techniques such as dilation and curettage were not nearly so safe as they are today. *Roe v. Wade* 410 U.S. (1973) at 148-149.

See also, *Culture Wars, an Encyclopedia of Issues, Viewpoints and Voices*, ed. Roger Chapman (M.E. Sharpe, Inc., 2010), 1, stating: "These 'back alley abortions' resulted in many deaths and injuries." And *Encyclopedia of the Supreme Court*, ed. David Schultz (Facts on File, Inc., 2005), 2, stating: "The American Medical Association (AMA), founded in 1847, created a Committee on Ethics that launched a campaign in 1857 to make abortion illegal at all stages. The campaign failed to stop abortions; it simply sent them underground. Scores of women died or became sterile from self-induced abortions or botched abortions—'back alley' abortions."

11. See *Roe v. Wade* 410 U.S. (1973) at 133. Justice Blackmun also offers this background information in Footnote 22:

Early philosophers believed that the embryo or fetus did not become formed and begin to live until at least 40 days after conception for a male and 80 to 90 days for a female. See, for example, Aristotle, Hist.Anim. 7.3.583b; Gen.Anim. 2.3.736, 2.5.741; Hippocrates, Lib. de Nat.Puer., No. 10. Aristotle's thinking derived from his three-stage theory of life: vegetable, animal, rational. The vegetable stage was reached at conception, the animal at "animation," and the rational soon after live birth. This theory, together with the 40/80 day view, came to be accepted by early Christian thinkers.

The theological debate was reflected in the writings of St. Augustine, who made a distinction between embryo inanimatus, not yet endowed with a soul, and embryo animatus. He may have drawn upon Exodus 21:22. At one point, however, he expressed the view that human powers cannot determine the point during fetal development at which the critical change occurs. See Augustine, De Origine Animae 4.4 (Pub.Law 44.527). See also W. Reany, The Creation of the Human Soul, c. 2 and 83-86 (1932); Huser, The Crime of Abortion in Canon Law 15 (Catholic Univ. of America, Canon Law Studies No. 162, Washington, D.C.1942).

Galen, in three treatises related to embryology, accepted the thinking of Aristotle and his followers. Quay 426-427. Later, Augustine on abortion was incorporated by Gratian into the Decretum, published about 1140. Decretum Magistri Gratiani 2.32.2.7 to 2.32.2.10, in 1 Corpus Juris Canonici 1122, 1123 (A. Friedburg, 2d ed. 1879). This Decretal and the Decretals that followed were recognized as the definitive body of canon law until the new Code of 1917.

12. I'm trying to think of a modern analogy for this. It would require imagining a medical procedure with a degree of risk being inflicted upon someone in a paternal caste. How about this? Imagine that breast implant surgery in the 1950's was every bit as risky as surgical abortion in late 1789 or 1868. The risk, let's say, is from harmful substances that can leak from the implant and cause all sorts of unwanted maladies. And let's imagine a law being passed that forbade doctors from performing the procedure upon unemancipated teens. It would seem quite strange, in that cultural circumstance, for a person to say that the Constitution protected the right to teenage breast implants. In this situation, the culture of the 1950s simply couldn't process the idea seriously. Now, compare this picture to how liberal segments of California might react to the idea, today.

13. I don't mean to imply that each side of the "debate" has equally valid opinions, either. I just mean that, for our generation, these matters were culturally contested. As time moves on, the loser in this contest will take on the appearance of being quite unreasonable indeed.

14. See Derek Parfit, *Reasons and Persons* (Oxford Clarendon Press, 1984).

15. In fact, truth be told, we never needed them to come here. We already have plenty of people in our current times who say the same things that they do—because, unfortunately, having a 19th century mind on these issues is something that some in our time still possess. So those sentiments are already here and can be considered for what they are worth. We don't need anyone to teleport in.

16. And if they did reveal something that history did not know, that would be most relevant to history, not to the best meaning we should give to any plain-language sentence in the Constitution.

17. *Thomas Bonham v College of Physicians*, 8 Co. Rep. 107a, 114a C.P. (1610) (Bonham's Case). Lord Coke writes, "[I]t appears in our books, that in many cases, the common law will controul Acts of Parliament, and sometimes adjudge them to be utterly void: for when an Act of Parliament is against common right and reason, or repugnant, or impossible to be performed, the common law will controul it, and adjudge such Act to be void." See also, *The First Part of the Institutes of the Laws of England,* Section 97b,

which reads:

> [F]or reason is the life of the law, nay the common law itself is nothing else but reason, gotten by long study, observation, and experience, and not of every man's natural reason." And see Section 183b, which reads, "The reason of the law is the life of the law; for though a man can tell the law, yet if he know not the reason thereof, he shall soon forget his superficial knowledge. But when he findeth the right reason of the law, and so bringeth it to his natural reason, that he comprehendeth it as his own, this will not only serve him for the understanding of that particular case, but of many others.

18. Here is the full quote, which, of course, is legendary:

> The life of the law has not been logic: it has been experience. The felt necessities of the time, the prevalent moral and political theories, intuitions of public policy, avowed or unconscious, even the prejudices which judges share with their fellow-men, have had a good deal more to do than the syllogism in determining the rules by which men should be governed. The law embodies the story of a nation's development through many centuries, and it cannot be dealt with as if it contained only the axioms and corollaries of a book of mathematics. Oliver Wendell Holmes, *The Common Law* (Belknap, 2009), 3.

19. Surprisingly, because, earlier on, he said something (from the bench) that sounded a little different:

> The very framing of the issue that we purport to decide today—whether our decision . . . shall "apply" retroactively—presupposes a view of our decisions as creating the law, as opposed to declaring what the law already is. Such a view is contrary to that understanding of "the judicial power," . . . which is not only the common and traditional one, but which is the only one that can justify courts in denying force and effect to the unconstitutional enactments of duly elected legislatures. . . . To hold a governmental act to be unconstitutional is not to announce that we forbid it, but that the Constitution forbids it . . . (Emphasis in original). See *American Trucking Associations v. Smith*, 496 U.S. 167, 201 (1990).

One year later, however, Scalia appears to have tempered his views. He writes:

> I am not so naive (nor do I think our forebears were) as to be unaware that judges in a real sense "make" law. But they make it *as judges make it*, which is to say *as though* they were "finding" it—discerning what the law *is*, rather than decreeing what it is today *changed* to, or what it will *tomorrow* be. Of course, this mode of action poses difficulties of a . . . practical sort . . . when courts decide to overrule prior precedent. *James B. Beam Distilling Co., v. Georgia*, 501 U.S. 529, 549 (1991).

20. See *Roe. v. Wade* 410 U.S. (1973) at 133, n. 22.

21. Ian Bartrum has an article that appeals to Kuhn's idea of paradigm shift to explain changes and developments in constitutional law [IB-3].

22. "Concept, criteria and instantiation" are explained in Chapter 2.

23. See the lengthy note on the Enlightenment [11:§2(b), note 22].

24. See, e.g., Herbert Broom, *A Selection of Legal Maxims*, 7th American ed. (from the 5th London ed.) (Philadelphia, 1874), also called "Broom's Legal Maxims." See also, Francis Bacon, *Collection of Some Principal Rules and Maxims of the Common Law* (1630).

25. See, e.g., *Neal v. United States,* 516 U.S. 284 (1996). Also, I think this whole phenomenon is why American justices are scared of the Ninth Amendment. They don't know how to process a legal command that says, in effect: "Perfect the thing yourself." So, when they do select rights, they pretend all along that the Due Process Clause had required it. They simply can't say: "We are penciling in this little perfection."

One wonders how this cultural orientation also affects legal scholarship. For law professors also cannot seem to say anything in an article without showing others that a citation can be found for it. And if a proposition of their very own were ever to be offered merely for its own sake, it would be as though something naked had appeared in their intellectual house. And they simply wouldn't know what to do with it.

26. Perry Miller, *The Life of the Mind in America: From the Revolution to the Civil War* (Harvest Books: 1965), 159-163. See also, M.H. Hoeflich, "Law and Geometry: Legal Science from Leibniz to Langdell," *American Journal of Legal History* 30: 95, 112-121 (1986).

27. See footnote 11 in *Brown*, citing the doll studies by Kenneth Clark and other social scientists. They serve as the basis for Warren's statement, "Whatever may have been the extent of psychological knowledge at the time of Plessy v. Ferguson, this [new] finding is amply supported by modern authority." *Brown v. Board of Education,* 347 U.S. 483 (1954), at 494, n. 11.

28. Richard Posner, *Overcoming Law* (Harvard, 1995).

29. See Gary Minda, *Postmodern Legal Movements, Law and Jurisprudence at Century's End* (New York University Press, 1995). Also, for the meaning of the term "skepticism" in philosophy, see Chapter 1, note 17.

Chapter 13

What Originalism Really Is

§ 1. A Formal Definition

What, if anything is common to all forms of originalism? If one tries to answer this question by listening to American legal scholars today, one is left with quite a chore. The term has become convoluted. Keith Whittington, for example, once took the position that "originalism" simply meant the legal arguments that conservatives espouse. So, for him, when conservatives opposed the Warren Court in the 1960s and 70s, originalism stood for judicial restraint, certain kinds of populism ("common sense") and opposing "legislating from the bench."[1]

Yet, Ozan Varol tells us something different. To him, originalism is the use of history to render a decision, even in situations where the law requires this. For example, imagine that the American Constitution had said: "No state shall pass any law respecting an establishment of religion, *according to the views of Thomas Jefferson.*" If justices then render legal opinions premised upon Jefferson's views, this, Varol says, is "originalism" [OV, 1245-46].

And then there is Jack Balkin, who calls "original meaning originalism . . . a version of living constitutionalism" [JB-2, 449]. Add to this Mitch Berman, who tells us that originalism only refers to how strongly a person advocates for "original meaning"—declaring, "I know of no self-described non-originalist who maintains that original meaning is irrelevant to constitutional interpretation" [MB, 251, n.7].

Larry Solum is a scholar who appears to endorse the current diversity of opinion. He believes in a big tent, describing originalism as a broad family of ideas [LS-1, 32-33]. This view affects his lexicon: he speaks of such things as "original public meaning originalism," "semantic originalism" [LS-2], and "original methods originalism."[2] Likewise, Sotirios Barber and James Fleming make liberal use of the term: they speak of broad, narrow, abstract, concrete and even "mindset originalism."[3]

Because of the frayed discourse, some law professors, such as Thomas Colby and Peter Smith, believe the conversation has become incoherent.[4] I wholeheartedly agree. To help this situation, I'm going to introduce a technical or professional sense of the term. My hope is that this particular language game will benefit from more structure.[5]

(a) Does Law Speak For Itself?

To begin, here is an excellent rule of thumb: an originalist cannot believe that an ordinary-language constitution speaks for itself, free from the guardianship of another entity from the past. Originalism always believes that some entity (Framers, framing-society) can reveal the true concepts, criteria or instantiations [2:§1-2] for any text in need. One wants to say it this way: originalism regards the Constitution as a kind of child. Always, there is a caretaker for it somewhere—a hidden historical resource that comes to the rescue of plain words.

But this definition is not perfect; it needs better clarity. It's not just the summoning of the past to assist ordinary language that makes someone an "originalist." Specifically, it is the summoning of the *origin* of the enacted law in question, and the vesting of that origin with a certain domain (power) over the provisions.[6] Therefore, originalism has two critical features: (a) it does not let constitutional text speak solely for itself; and (b) it invents a guarantor of meaning that always resides at the birth of the text (passage).

(b) Positivism and Natural Law

Notice that originalism shares a curious relationship to both positivism and natural law. Positivism believes that one must always follow the enacted law. But natural law believes in circumstances when the sovereign command can be disobeyed—with, paradoxically, the law still being "followed." The answer to this riddle lies in the fact that natural law posits an additional substance for legal systems: something beyond that which is formally codified, yet still operates (somehow). An example would be those who believe that the great precepts, right reasons and sacred traditions of the polity operate as "the fundamental law," voiding any enactment that clashes with them—which is what Bonham's Case purported to do.[7]

The American contribution to these ideas was, of course, novel. Americans set forth the fundamental law in a written instrument. As such, fundamental law itself became duly *enacted*. It became codified in the legal system. And so, American justices could say that they were not, in theory, judging "in the clouds," but were merely making judgments about whether one legal provision (a statute) conflicted with another (in the Constitution), the latter being of the highest rank.

But the problem—or the genius—is that the American Constitution was set forth as a plain-language document. And hence, a decision had to be made: was it allowed to speak solely for itself? If it was, it could be said to command a host of things that the judges *themselves* would have to arrange. But if the plain-language document could be placed into the custody of something else—some guarantor of its meaning—then it could be treated as though it were more articulate, like most legislatively enacted law is, especially since the advent of active government in the 20th century.

And hence, originalism was born. What makes the belief system distinct from natural law is that it focuses exclusively upon the events that occur during the passage of the law.[8] In fact, the behavior of codifying is considered the most precious event in the system. This is why originalism delves into the past *only* to the point of the origin of the legislation.[9] This is unlike various forms of natural law, which delve amorphously (and distantly) into the past—tracing sacred customs to times and eras far before an act of legislation.[10] Originalism, by contrast, needs only to travel to the events that gave birth to constitutional text.[11]

But although originalism is centered upon the codification of law, that doesn't mean it is harmonious with positivism. There is one critical difference: originalism does not let the law speak solely for itself. Instead, it places the text in the custody of a guarantor from the origin of passage—an historical entity that must, at times, play the role of speaking for it.

Yet, in modern positivistic legal cultures like America's, legislation is treated as speaking for itself. The enacted law only ever says: "follow these words." As such, if the text in question does not specifically exclude rival concepts, criteria or instantiations—which ordinary-language constitutions will not—the *judges* are forced to *supply* these things, knowing full well that they are doing just that. If judges admit that they are arranging the meaning of a constitutional provision—it is *their* intellectual exposition (they are completing the law)—they are not being "originalist."[12]

This is why non-originalists shun the expression "the true meaning" when referring to any specific arrangement of flexible text. Instead, they talk only of the *potential* things the text could afford in the language game—each of which is "truthful." Perhaps, at best, they can speak of the first social construction of the law—its first arrangement—but not its "original meaning." Always, among non-originalists, there is a separation between language that asks for you to arrange it, versus any one of the arrangements chosen in history. Indeed, for non-originalists, all that a plain-language document ever amounts to are its possibilities [Chapter 5].

(c) History and Living Constitutionalism

Suppose that someone offers the following objection to how I have just described originalism. They say, "I know plenty of 'originalists' who espouse historical things, but who don't believe they are already embedded in the text itself—they just think those things would make for the best rulings."[13] This objection says, in essence, that a person can offer old arrangements of constitutional text using the same license that a living constitutionalist[14] uses when offering a theory of *justice*. This is, of course, true, but it misses an important point.

First, one who argued for old solutions and policies using a theory of "living constitution" would have to share all of its burdens. That is, the person would have to show that those policies are worthy of being adopted in their own right, today, given all that we know about knowledge, culture, science, philosophy, etc. In other words, the past must be treated as being only a *candidate*, among others, for consideration.

But note what this does as an assertability condition. It seems to preclude the talk of adopting the old solution for reasons of it being "the original meaning" or for vindicating "the true constitution."[15] So, to advocate for the past without being originalist, one must shed this kind of talk. A person who argues for old solutions while using living-constitutional principles is a living constitutionalist, plain and simple.[16]

To understand this idea better, consider an admission made by Justice Scalia, who once called himself a "faint-hearted originalist" [AS-2]. Joan Biskupic's biography notes the following about the remark:

> "Oh, that was so long ago," the justice responds . . . . Scalia explains that he had used "faint-hearted" because he did not see how he, or any other judge, could vote to uphold, say, ear notching of criminals, as was allowed in the eighteenth century. If he were a true originalist, Scalia says, he would have to find ear notching today perfectly constitutional despite the Eighth Amendment ban on cruel and unusual punishment. Then he quips to the Federalist Society home crowd that maybe he could be a complete originalist these days: "I've gotten older and crankier." The audience laughs heartily.[17]

This is the key to understanding the issue. If Scalia believes that the *real* meaning of Eighth Amendment includes ear notching,[18] but chooses not to rule that way for pragmatic reasons, he is still an "originalist."[19] This is because of his belief that history provides the *truth* of the legal provision. So he is correct when he calls himself "faint-hearted." Likewise, because Scalia also sincerely believes that the Equal Protection Clause doesn't apply to women,[20] his belief that history provides this "truth" is what makes his claim originalist—not whether he would act upon it.[21]

However, there is another possibility. Had Scalia believed that the real meaning of the Eighth Amendment did *not* include ear notching—even though it was historically so—any crankiness that caused him to put forth the idea as a ruling (today) could only be classified in one of two ways.

First, let's assume he believes in ear notching as a cultural practice: he thinks it's a good fit for current society. Therefore, if he believes it is not intrinsically cruel or unusual by today's standards—and he can defend it as a good idea—he would be a living constitutionalist, as much as the next guy who says we should abolish death sentences. But, as such, this (mythical) Scalia must *prove his case.* He must show that ear-notching, today, is both: (a) non-cruel and non-unusual; and (b) fits well into our current program.[22] And he would also have to admit that his offering is only one example of many others—like outlawing death—that could also be truthful arrangements of the text. That's what the past looks like when it dons a living-constitutional dress.

But there is still another possibility—a middle ground. Let's suppose Scalia puts forth his program for ear-notching *apologetically,* laying a guilt trip on us to respect the past, even though he believes it is not "the true meaning" of the text. I call this *apologetic historicism.* It argues that the past should be given a handicap or special treatment in our constitutional calculations, even though it is not "the law itself."[23]

One wonders to what extent Larry Solum's contribution/constraint theses represent a good example of this. These argue, in effect, that the past "should make a substantial contribution to . . . constitutional doctrine," and that only "weighty reasons" could see it disregarded [LS-1, 35; LS-2, 6-10]. This only seems to say that we should feel morally guilted if the past does not compel us in some way. So, if one advanced these ideas while simultaneously believing that constitutional text hasn't codified the past, it would be an example of apologetic historicism, not originalism (technically speaking).[24]

Table 13.1. Historical Jurisprudence

Name	Reduction	Law School Name
Institutional-Leader Originalism	Plain-language constitution means what Framers wanted [Chapter 8].	Original-Intent Originalism
Cultural Originalism	Plain-language constitution is an historical cultural arrangement/hegemony [Chapters 11, 12].	Original-Meaning Originalism
Content-Prescriptive Hermeneutics	Plain words in the Constitution must adopt artificial sharp boundaries imposed from the past, such as stereotypes, archetypes or dominant behavior [4:§1(a)-(c)].	Original Public Meaning Originalism
Classical Legal Thought[25]	Judges should decide cases using the style-craft (and outlook?) of judges from the 1790s and 1800s.	Original Methods Originalism
Apologetic Historicism	Plain-language constitution speaks for itself. But in our own free choices for it, we should pay respect to the past choices.	Originalism

So the key to everything depends upon the attitude one has about the text—namely, whether history reveals its "truth." Absent this, all we need to know is why the person likes the past. If it's because it still provides the best answer (the best program), you don't need to be "originalist" to advocate for that. You just present the case on its own merits. But the moment one starts arguing that the past is owed some *favoritism* in the tabulation of points, the person begins to venture into the other camp. And the moment he or she declares that the past is already secretly enacted—it is the "real meaning" that would otherwise be "cheated"—then the person becomes an originalist, no matter whether he or she is faint-hearted.[26]

And such a person, of course, would sincerely believe that "the true law"— the true Constitution—had, in fact, enacted ear notching as permissible punishment and had excluded women in the Equal Protection Clause. By contrast, one who sees that clause as speaking solely for itself would see that these lost cultures enacted no such thing. They never properly legislated upon those subjects.

Table 13.1 presents a summary of my views. This concludes my explanation of what separates originalism from other systems of belief.

§ 2. Legal Behavior?

I now want to explore a rather unfortunate confusion. It stems from the idea that one can properly treat the Constitution as being a modern legal document while simultaneously disallowing its plain language to speak solely for itself. Modern legal culture in America, I contend, cannot allow this because of what the act of legislation is as a *behavior* in the system.

To see this, ask yourself what an act of legislation would have to say, right now, if it wanted to make ear notching and other punishments from the late 1700s forever permissible. That is, ask yourself what the positivistic legal culture[27] would have to enact for this to be the unquestionable law of the land. Consider this example of what the Eighth Amendment *might* have said:

> Criminal punishments are prohibited only if they are clearly considered extreme or harsh as understood by the standards of the American states in 1787, with any official punishment practice occurring therein not becoming later excluded for reasons of its abandonment into the future, no matter how cruel or unusual the said punishment comes to be seen, and notwithstanding any provision of law to the contrary, including but not limited to the liberty and rights clauses contained in this Constitution or any Treaty entered into.

This is an example of how American legal culture communicates in legislation. But it is not the only example. An even more pedantic way to forever legalize ear notching would be to create a specific punishment schedule that lists approved and disapproved punishments. Drug laws do something like this: they list schedules of controlled substances by their technical names, defined scientifically by chemical elements or properties.[28] If your drug is on the list, the law speaks to it; if not, it doesn't. Accordingly, a punishment schedule written in the same way might be the best way to legally prescribe certain punishment practices forever into the future. Similarly, one could consult the Federal Sentencing Guidelines or the Internal Revenue Code for more examples of how "legalistic" the culture is.[29]

My point is that the law reads this way because modern, positivistic culture treats legislation as speaking solely for itself. That is why the enacted law often sets forth a definition section, so lawyers can receive better direction to the sense of a terms being used. It's why comprehensive codes are enacted and administrative regulations are promulgated—so the details of law can be filled in. It's why well-written legal contracts have all sorts of complicated clauses, so parties can't wiggle very much.

By contrast, the real Eighth Amendment that was passed into law says only this: "Excessive bail shall not be required, nor excessive fines imposed, nor cruel and unusual punishments inflicted."[30] That's it. That's the whole thing. And it's no wonder, then, that non-originalists rightly believe that the specific practice of ear notching was never legislated upon—just as the specific practice of excluding women from equal protection was never legislated upon when the Fourteenth Amendment was passed.

What originalism doesn't understand is that not allowing the enacted law to speak for itself transforms the act of legislating into a fundamentally different kind of *behavior*. If there is some other expositor of the law officially hiding in the American legal system—something to reveal what it "really means"—this makes the Constitution function like a sacrament to that entity or thing. It would make the document symbolic in some way. It would turn the Constitution into a *gesture* (or a toast).

The whole reason why the fundamental law is codified—why the Constitution is enacted—is so that it can speak for itself. In modern positivistic legal culture, the law is only ever what *it* says. And for it to mean any specific concept, criteria or instantiation, to the exclusion of rivals, it must explicitly say so. You can't run to the secret meaning-checker in a legal system. All you can run to are, in the first instance, the definition sections, detailed clauses and minutia—i.e., the legalese of the law. And if that fails, you run to the judges, who are the only officially-sanctioned people to provide concepts, criteria or instantiations for text in need.

And so, the basic flaw of originalism is that it has the wrong picture of account for the current legal culture. Because it invents a secret expositor for the fundamental law, it sets forth something with the status of chieftains or elders in the system (except they are no longer living). Because of this, it flirts with an idea of "constitution" that is not legalistic. By believing the document exists only as a stead for the notions or orientations of its dead elders—or their social folkways, customs or beliefs—originalism puts forth a ritualistic or sacramental view of the Constitution. The idea is not unlike those who would use the ritual of animal sacrifice to keep and enshrine the tribal views of their fathers. Or, when two warriors cut the palm of their hands and clasp them together, signifying "blood brothers"—meaning a covenant to follow the ways of the brother-hood.

These ideas fundamentally alter what legislation really does *in practice*. The purpose of legislation is only to *regulate* culture, not to bless or *sanctify* it. Were it otherwise, law would begin to look too much like religion. So, the purpose of constitutional law could never be to bind American progeny to antiquated frameworks or arrangements. The purpose is never to keep passing along through history the ways of the fathers. Its sole purpose, rather, is only to pass along *language* from one generation to the next. And so, the only thing the framing culture left for us by way of "fundamental law" is a set of sentences that need only be complied with by thinking up the best way to *give* them meaning in the language game, not by being Amish.

§ 3. New and Old Originalism

Given all that I have said thus far, it is now possible to properly differentiate old and new originalism. The difference is not what American legal scholars often say it is: that one is concerned with "original intentions" and the other with "original meaning." Rather, the difference is not unlike the way political science can be different from sociology: one is focused upon the workings of *institutions;* the other upon *society*.

For old originalism, the key feature is to pretend to follow the directions of another entity ("boss logic"). This means, in theory, that the judge's own mind should be irrelevant, because the job consists of "following orders." The new originalism, however, rejects this picture of account. It appeals to a mass under-standing of some sort that existed in framing society and became hegemonic by the standards of its age. And this means that "ultimate law" becomes the com-prehension of that hegemonic understanding, rather than the mindreading and adoring of specific drafters or approvers (as they carry out the ritual of setting forth legal text).

Table 13.2: The Real Difference Between New and Old Originalism

Institutional-Leader Originalism	Cultural Originalism
There are X number of people assembled in some official institution (a committee, a convention, etc.). The "real law" is found in their prerogatives (in some way). The name of the game is to define who the people are and say what the prerogatives properly consist of.	An *historical epoch* is what "the real law" is. The name of the game is to fish through history at founding periods to find hege-monic cultural frameworks. Instead of idol-worshipping ("the Framers"), the behavior is the adoration of an historic age (epoch-appreciation).

So, for new originalism, the judge's mind has no choice but to become *ab-sorbed* by ways of thinking that dominated an historical past, so that he or she can pretend to be part of it. This is done because the framework is no longer the default of our existence.[31] The process here is similar to those who celebrate a genre by becoming imbibed with it [9:§2(d)].[32] Judging, therefore, becomes a celebratory task, with its central focus the founding age and its outlook [7:§3(c)].

In a nutshell, one might say it this way. Old originalism wants to follow the historic boss; new originalism wants to follow the historic *times*. Because of this, I propose that one differentiate these two belief systems along the lines of whether modernity is captured by an imagined *institutional boss* or by a *cultural-obedience*[33] from the distant past. Table 13.2 sets forth the distinction.[34]

§ 4. Not So Original

One of Wittgenstein's famous-cited ideas is that our intelligence can become bewitched by language.[35] The conversation American law professors are having about originalism seems to suffer from this condition. Consider two basic senses of the word "original." One is about being *authentic*, as in, "duplicate originals";[36] another is about being first in time, as in, "the original pioneers."

The problem is that American scholars often conflate the two. Originalism can only properly comment upon something being *first in time*. It cannot comment upon something being more authentic. The word "original," therefore, has stung various American law professors: it has bewitched and ensnarled their language games. This is why they believe that the rest of Americans—the non-originalists—espouse the inauthentic version of the Constitution, while they espouse the true one. But in point of fact, conservatives can only ever espouse something that came first, not something that is more authentic.

To remedy this situation, conservative American law professors need to stop telling people that they offer "the real meaning of the Constitution." They need to quit guilting people into believing we owe some fidelity to the way that life was culturally arranged or administered in the distant American past. Instead, they need to make it clear that they can only ever offer a *theory* of what they want a plain-language document to mean. So many problems could be avoided if conservatives would simply admit that they are only offering a *vision* of the document. So much fanaticism on the right can be traced to one central sin: people believe "the real constitution" is being cheated—when, in fact, they should only believe that their favorite *aspirations* for plain text are simply being rejected for alternatives (competitors).

One of the reasons, of course, that conservatives may not do this is because their visions cannot compete with modernity. I mean, how can you really argue for ear notching and excluding women from equal protection? The only way to rig the game, therefore, is to paint modernity as "the cheater." And so, originalism develops into a dogma about how constitutional text really can't speak for itself and how "the true law" is found in the archaeological exploits of American history—like religion searching for an ancient scroll. If only intelligent conservatives would shed this fiction, it would do so much to address the problem of "the crazies." Conservatism is at its best when it puts the breaks on modernity, as a car slows before a large bend, rather than trying to drive the car back in the other direction.

Unfortunately, however, originalism remains popular not only in the conversations of the American legal academy, but in certain segments of American political life (Tea Party).[37] It is so popular, in fact, that even liberal law professors now seem forced to speak its vernacular, using historical evidence to argue that the Constitution "really means" to enact this or that liberal social policy.[38] In essence, some are now fighting fire with fire.

And so, you have scholars of all stripes in the American academy suggesting to one another that the "true meaning of the law" is found in the secrets one can unearth about historical lives, debates, speeches and so forth—the quest for Law's Noah. I wrote this book because I desperately wanted to see this conversation end. My hope is that people who think about ideas—people who read books like this—will come to understand what originalism really is. Properly conceived, it is simply the desire to chain modernity to a specific and sterile aspect of the past. And that, to accomplish this, it must adopt some form of untenable thinking. It is because of this that originalism should really be understood as a kind of legal ideology rather than a meaningful contribution to philosophy of law.

Notes

1. Whittington argues that originalists are simply "the legal conservatives." He goes on to say how the elder conservatives are different from the current ones, with respect to their constitutional thinking [KW-2]. But this turns the word "originalist" into a kind of club or affiliation—like, e.g., the National Organization for Women or the Chicago Seven. To know what a group stands for requires a position paper. This cannot be the sense of originalism that concerns us. We already use the phrase "legal conservatives" for that. Instead, what is critical is what the juristic philosophy stands for, versus its competitors. We want to say what originalism is compared to (say) natural law or positivism, or "living constitutionalism." A better way of expressing Whittington's point, therefore, is to say of yesterday's conservatives: they espoused some version of OI-theory while also believing in supplementary ideals (e.g., judicial restraint).

2. [LS-1, 22-23, 26; RB-3, 92-93]

3. [B&F, 79-84, 95-104]. The term "mindset originalism" is used on page 104, and is described as a form of "abstract originalism."

4. Thomas B. Colby & Peter J. Smith, "Living Originalism," *Duke Law Jounral* 59 (2009): 239, 244. The authors state, "A review of originalists' work reveals originalism to be not a single, coherent, unified theory of constitutional interpretation, but rather a smorgasbord of distinct constitutional theories that share little in common except a misleading reliance on a single label."

5. Readers should be mindful of my discussion on sharp boundaries [4:§4].

6. The extent of the domain is a function of what kind of originalism it is. The domain may even have the power to re-write the provision, as in the extreme case of text-free originalism [8:§1], in which case the presence of ordinary-language would have nothing to do with it. But in the most common versions, the jurisdiction is only for "filling in the blanks," which means that ordinary language becomes its everyday venue, but is not technically part of its definition.

7. See *Thomas Bonham v College of Physicians*, 8 Co. Rep. 107a, 114a C.P. (1610) (Bonham's Case).

8. Notice that, even in the case of text-free Originalism [8:§1], the concern is with the events surrounding the great enactment. By asking the lawgivers (in theory) whether the enactment is in need of being promulgated again, this, at least, shows reverence for both the act of promulgation as well as the promulgators. It says, in short, that the only "real law" is that which arises out of the historical *event* that legislated it. One wants to say: it's like the giving of birth. One day, the institutions gave birth to the law, and what it forever means is somehow connected with that event.

9. Note that this is true even for a statutory provision. If a judge uses legislative history to say "what the law means," this is an originalist gesture. Although we don't speak of it this way, it is every bit the same behavior. The key ideas: (a) the text cannot speak solely for itself; and (b) its guarantor or secret expositor lies in the events at the origin of its birth.

10. Or as Gregoire Webber says it:

> Tradition, like the constitutional practices that are a part of it, knows no founding moment. It may know of a defining moment or a paradigm case, but the tradition itself cannot be so reduced. In many ways, the defining moment is only so identified after the fact and is incorporated into the evolving tradition. An original constitution, by contrast, is authoritatively identified at the moment it is founded. . . . The fixed reference—the founding—discloses an authoritative choice as to what the constitution shall be. [GW, 152-153].

11. This can get tricky. Consider the Common Law Thesis in [12:§1(d)]. It said that any "mystery rights" enacted by the Constitution were limited to the common law in existence at the time the provisions were passed. Is this argument originalist? Only if it says that this is the true meaning of the text as revealed by the *Framers* or the *society* that legislated it. In other words, it only counts if it says that the text truly means this by virtue of what the Framers or their society desire. Otherwise, it's just a straightforward argument for what judicial test to put in place, like any other [13:§1(c)].

12. What they are really doing is being "artistic"—they are doing what Dworkin imagines when he thinks of completing the chain novel [RD-1, 228-38]. They are adding another chapter in the story. Note that this is in the nature of an art. Whether it is carried out well involves connoisseur judgment [Chapter 7].

13. Of course, we must not confuse two things. One is where professors *x*, *y*, and *z* advance an argument while calling themselves "The Originalists." If we treat originalism as being whatever position *x*, *y* and *z* take when calling themselves by their moniker, we have made the idea into a social club. Cf. "The Hell's Angels." To know what the Angels believe, we'd have to wait for a position paper. So, the point is never what *x*, *y* and *z* say (per se), it is where their arguments fit within the community of juristic belief.

14. The term "living constitution" here is local to its use. It does *not* mean this: "The

Constitution should be like the Declaration of Independence. We should be like Britain. What is 'constitutional' is only how the institutions are said to work and what is publically cherished." Rather, the term means more like what Dworkin has espoused.

15. In fact, a non-originalist would never accept the old solution as being "the original" or "the true"—it would only see it as being a prior installment of a thing for which many installments are possible. It would be like saying of a person who happened to eat steak for dinner on the first day of the week, that it was somehow the "original" or "true" dinner. It doesn't make sense. If "dinner" is what must be decided, steak must come to us as an alternative that competes with all the others, irrespective of its standing as being first chosen. And this is also true if we like it so much that we choose it every night. Each night it comes, it must do so by its own accord.

16. This is because the argument does not deny that a plain-language document is up for grabs in certain ways. As such, the person is simply putting forth his or her candidate for selection under the auspices of its own merits, and *not* because the law grants it any favors. It's like a heavy-weight champ who fights into the later years: the veteran still has to win the bout.

17. Joan Biskupic, *American Original, The Life and Constitution of Supreme Court Justice Antonin Scalia* (Sarah Crichton Books, 2009), 7.

18. The provision in question is the Eighth Amendment, which reads as follows: "Excessive bail shall not be required, nor excessive fines imposed, nor cruel and unusual punishments inflicted." U.S. Const. amend. VIII.

19. One may wonder why in such a case he isn't a "pragmatist." It is better in this situation to speak of him *being* pragmatic—as we all can be in given situations—rather than impute his membership in the pragmatism school (orthodoxy). Besides, the term pragmatism sometimes means the idea of *not* having a school (orthodoxy), which clearly cannot be said of Scalia.

20. See "The Originalist," an interview of Antonin Scalia by Calvin Massey for Legally Speaking, in *California Lawyer, A Daily Journal Publication* (January 2011), http://www.callawyer.com/story.cfm?eid=913358&evid=1. "Legally Speaking" is a series of in-depth interviews with prominent lawyers, judges, and academics, co-produced by California Lawyer and UC Hastings College of the Law.

21. This point is relevant to Mitch Berman's views. If one reads Berman as saying only that originalists like history in their jurisprudence more than others, this would be fine, though it wouldn't be a good definition. The issue isn't the extent to which history is urged; it is the claim that history gets to provide the *truth* of plain words. An originalist is one who pretends that history makes the Constitution more articulate than it really is. Short of this, the weight that history looms over us is a function of one of two things. It either comes to us *apologetically* by those who weep for it, or it comes because it is still "good" on the merits. Only the last option is permissible.

22. Consider how prevalent self-inflicted bodily mutilation is today (body piercing, tattoos). Consider all of the various body parts that are being "pierced." Now, imagine a culture where 70% of the convicted population already self-mutilated their bodies significantly. In this culture, would a state-imposed mark be so bad? Would it be understood the same as a culture that did not self-mutilate so often? This is the way a living constitutionalist thinks. The issue has nothing to do with the arrangements of the past and everything to do with present arrangements.

23. I don't mean to include arguments about "following precedent" here. A person

might argue that it is tumultuous to change a long-standing precedent. It upsets things. This is really a straightforward argument about the transaction costs involved in judicial change. This doesn't say, by itself, that we owe some duty to the past, as if we are said to owe it to "forefathers" or something. It doesn't give us a guilt trip. It doesn't say "how dare you?" It merely says law needs to factor in stability when it calculates change. And so, some might say the change is too important to avoid—the time has come—while others might say it isn't worth the cost of the adjustment. These are ultimately the kinds of arguments that accountants make. This isn't my concern in the paragraph.

24. Whittington's position that history must be "authoritative" for judges seems *not* to be apologetic. This is because history is said to come to us as a legal mandate. He writes, "Originalism regards the discoverable meaning of the Constitution at the time of its initial adoption as authoritative for purposes of constitutional interpretation in the present" [KW-2, 599].

25. To see a modern example of Classical Legal Thought, consider Alabama Supreme Court Associate Justice Tom Parker's 2011 specially-concurring opinion in *Ex parte E.R.G. and D.W.G*, which denied grandparent visitation rights for the following reasons (among others):

> The family was the first of all human institutions. One man and one woman came together in covenant before God, and they, with the children God gave them, became the first human social structure. . . . There was no state: no one person had been given civil authority over another, to punish evil and to prevent oppression. Nor was there a church to provide structure and order in the worship of the Creator. Both of these necessary institutions would come later—indeed, they were prefigured in the discipline and worship of the family—but the "sacred" relationships . . . within the family came first [p. 35-36].
> . . . The Christian doctrine emphasized the role of parents in directing their children's growth and development. From the birth of the first child, children were recognized as being a gift to parents from God (Gen. 4:1, 25; see also Psalm 127:3, stating that "children are a gift of the LORD"). Speaking through Moses, God instructed children to honor their parents ("Honor your father and your mother, as the LORD your God has commanded you, that your days may be prolonged and that it may go well with you . . . ." Deut. 5:16), and parents to teach their children ("These words, which I am commanding you today, shall be on your heart. You shall teach them diligently to your sons . . . ." Deut. 6:6-7). Building on the natural concern of parents regarding their children's future, the book of Proverbs encouraged parents to "[t]rain up a child in the way he should go, [e]ven when he is old he will not depart from it." Proverbs 22:6. The Apostle Paul reminded the Ephesians of this parental responsibility, instructing them to "not provoke [their] children to anger, but bring them up in the discipline and instruction of the Lord." Ephesians 6:4. And throughout Scripture, the relationship between parents and their children is used as an analogy to the relationship of God with His people ("But as many as received Him, to them He gave the right to become children of God . . . ." John 1:12), emphasizing the significant and permanent nature of that relationship" (all Scripture quotations are from the New American Standard Bible) [p. 40-41]. Available online: http://www.alabamaappellatewatch.com/uploads/file/35to67.pdf (accessed June 12, 2012).

26. Also, the mere fact that a scholar takes an approach to the Constitution that uses history does not make him or her "originalist." Barber and Fleming use the term "broad originalist" to refer to scholars who seem to believe that Dworkin's approach would work best if it merely replaced philosophy with history [B&F, 99-116]. The idea is that, when

making constitutional text the best it can be, we should only select historically-guided meaning. This view is *apologetic historicism*. Although it bears a close relationship to originalism, it is not, strictly speaking, an originalist viewpoint. Barber and Fleming's view is stated below:

> The broad originalist believes that Dworkin's chief problem is his emphasis on doing the right thing (as left-liberals see it) at the expense of what American constitutional history and traditions indicate the right thing is. Broad originalists believe the cure for Dworkin's abstract arguments for rights (especially rights of privacy or autonomy) is greater respect for historical beliefs and practices. They therefore recommend a "turn to history" in constitutional theory, and by a turn to history, they mean in part a turn away from Dworkin's philosophic approach. [B&F, 102].

27. To see what I mean by the word "positivistic" in this sense, see Chapter 5, note 10. I simply mean that the lawyering culture in America requires everything to be "spelled out" in legislative or administrative rules.

28. Drugs are classified in five steps: from Schedule-1 through Schedule-5. Some drugs are illegal per se; others merely require a prescription. See the Controlled Substances Act, 21 U.S.C., §811.

29. See *Federal Sentencing Guidelines Manual*, 1998 ed., West Group (1997).

30. U.S. Const. Amend VIII

31. I don't mean to imply that the culture of 1789 is completely alien to us. Surely, *some* aspect of that culture still survives today in our daily lives, on its own. What I mean is that part of the culture that grew foreign to us, and therefore needs taught (studied) to be understood again.

32. C.f. experts on the Romantics in literature or of the medieval mind. In each of these cases, the person who is an expert must come to understand the feelings and outlooks of people who lived in a certain age and whose beliefs or deeds came to form the epoch or genre in question. To some extent, their minds must "get lost" in another age—another way of thinking.

33. Notice that I don't use the term "generational obedience" here for several reasons. The issue isn't that we are asked to be obedient to a prior generation. During any point in history, more than one generation exists, each being defined by political struggles both within and against others. The term "culture" is more sweeping; it's deeper than any one generation's choices (preferences). The difference is whether one merely *elects* meaning or *behaves* it. When meaning comes through *behavior*, it comes in the form of letters, speeches, language, daily routines, assumptions, social arrangements, etc.—and it substantially infects the entirety of the polity. It is, in short, what makes culture itself exist. Culture is the way meaning *behaves*. This is deeper than simply saying "a generation's choice."

34. The enthymematic point, of course, is that all versions of originalism exist merely to use the past in a way that stifles, stagnates or controls modernity. That seems to be the basic objective. Scalia argues that the whole purpose of a constitution "is to prevent change—to embed certain rights in such a manner that future generations cannot readily take them away" [AS-1, 40]. Whittington echoes this sentiment: "Fixing constitutional principles in a written text against the transient shifts in the public mood or social condition becomes tantamount to an originalist jurisprudence" [KW-1, 53]. And Gregoire Webber concurs: "An original constitution is not tradition—it does not evolve" [GW, 153].

See also [OV, 1248], noting "'Originalism envisions a constitution that adopts permanent, not evolving values," citing Antonin Scalia, "Originalism: The Lesser Evil," *U. Cin. L. Rev.* 57 (1989): 849, 862.

35. "Philosophy is a battle against the bewitchment of our intelligence by means of language" [LW-14, 64, §109].

36. This is for identical documents that are both signed, instead of one being just a copy.

37. "Originalism is popular. Four in ten Americans favor it. Not all Tea Partiers are originalists, but the movement is fairly described as populist movement inclined toward originalism." Jill Lepore, "The Commandments: The Constitution and its Worshippers," *The New Yorker*, Jan 17, 2011, 6.

"[Originalism] is discussed on talk radio and in best-selling books, in blogs and in newspaper columns; in presidential campaigns and at water coolers." Jamal Greene "On the Origins of Originalism," *Tex. L. Rev.* 88 (2009): 1, 17. See also, Ozan Varol, noting how the originalism debate "has swept the United States" [OV, 1241-42], and Eric A. Posner, "Why Originalism Is So Popular," *The New Republic*, Jan 14, 2011, online: http://www.tnr.com/article/politics/81480/republicans-constitution-originalism-popular (accessed June 12, 2012).

38. [JB-1; JB-2]. See also, Cass R. Sunstein, "Originalism for Liberals," *The New Republic*, Sept. 28, 1998, 31; and Eric A. Posner, cited above, on page 2: "[M]any liberal law professors have thrown in the towel, endorsing originalism or a version of it but arguing that the original sources indicate liberal rather than conservative constitutional norms."

Appendix

The Philosophical Investigation

The following is a thought experiment written in a Wittgensteinian format. The central purpose is to answer a single question: what does it mean to say that one violates "the original meaning of the Constitution"?[1]

Readers unfamiliar with Wittgenstein's post-Tractarian method of philosophizing must to be cautioned about the format. It involves short, numbered remarks. It relies heavily upon imaginative scenarios, simile, and juxtaposing forms of expression against other ways of speaking. Problems are approached in a *seriatim* process. You hold everything else still while chiseling at the one thing that is troubling you. After that is exorcised, you take on the next piece of the conundrum. The entire project feels like chopping down a tree, one branch at a time.

In many respects, reading this method is not too removed from reading Psalms or a kind of poetry. The project isn't a reading exercise; it's a *thinking* one. The reader must take an active part in reflecting about each numbered remark, in succession, as they chisel toward their central observations. The method is perspectival in this sense: it asks that the reader go through the same transformation in thought that the author goes through.

The Central Problem

Imagine that the following scenario is true. One day, the youth generation of the 1960s adopts its own written declaration. It's called the Declaration of Justice (DoJ). The provisions are drafted and approved during a ceremony at Woodstock, wherein all relevant participants consent to the document. They have a ceremony that instills a sense of legitimacy, so that the document takes on a sanctified ethos. And the main of American youth culture therefore sincerely and lastingly bind themselves to all the precepts stated in the document. And this obligation is then passed along to children (and their children), so that the entirety of those who accepted the original ceremony, and their lineage, today feel morally obliged to follow the DoJ. Imagine further that one of the central provisions, called Article I, says the following:

"Materialism shall not corrupt the spirit."

This provision is known as the Free Spirit Clause. To the 60s generation, it meant the following ideas: (a) don't be too greedy or selfish; (b) do not buy ostentatious luxury items like gold, furs and expensive cars; and (c) do not place the desire for material goods and wealth above the desire for basic decency toward others.

Generation X

Now let's suppose something strange happens. The children of the 60s generation who are in power today—called "Generation X"—read the DoJ with a completely different interpretation. They do not deny that the spirit should be free; they simply believe it is not threatened by the accumulation of material possessions. In fact, they think material possessions enhance inner happiness and that Pareto trades allocate social utility better. They cannot even imagine a world without their gadgets or technology, let alone an America without consumerism. They say that competition makes the spirit more vigorous and that material possessions help comfort in a way that is down-to-earth and pragmatic. So, they say that they accept the command of the DoJ, but reject their parent's political tastes.

1787 Generation

Now let's imagine that the DoJ is sent back in time, through a time portal, to American society in 1787. The majority read the Free Spirit Clause this way:

> This must be an endorsement of the philosophy of dualism. It says in a colorful parlance, "Do not let those radical elements in the Enlightenment who see every substance as being physical succeed in pushing Cartesian dualism by the wayside." What it means, properly translated, is: do not abandon the idea that there are souls, spirits, "inner light" inside humanity and an ethereal nature to consciousness. The argument must be that this philosophy is important to the future, or else they would not have sent it to us. It is a sign that we must always carry with us the mind/body problem in philosophy. It is a bold statement that the human essence cannot be reduced to a physicalist machine.

I call this the *Descartes Interpretation*.[2] It should be contrasted with still one more interpretation offered by devout Ascetical Christians[3] in 1787. They read the Free Spirit Clause as mandating poverty and humility. It requires people to wear dark clothing in public and be free from possessions. They see the clause as endorsing God's desire for a Christian life of outward poverty and devotion. I call this the *Ascetical-Christian Interpretation*.

Discussion

1. The key questions: (a) which interpretation violates the Free Spirit Clause, and (b) what does it mean to say that there is a violation?

2. My thesis: before we can say whether there is a "violation," we need to know what is being asked. Do we want to know whether the *language* is being violated or whether a cultural arrangement is being violated? Because if one means the former, one means to ask only whether the language culture could support a particular way of speaking. But if the latter, one simply means to ask whether or not the times have changed.

Polysemy

3. The *Descartes Interpretation* has the wrong sense of "materialism."

4. It's as if they went to the store and bought the wrong *kind* of thing. Imagine going to the store with instructions to buy "spirits" and coming back with Halloween costumes instead of alcoholic beverages. One rightly disappointed with the purchase would say of such a thing: they didn't get the idea.

5. Their mistake exists even though they are obedient to the logical structure of the sentence. The structure commands that "materialism" be in check relative to "spirit." (We might denote this as M < S). They perform this logical operation, but upon fundamentally mistaken "quantities."

6. It's not that the Descartes Interpretation misunderstands the *intention* of the sentence. Rather, it has misunderstood the *grammar*. And this is because a fatal sense of "materialism" has plugged them into the *wrong conversation*.

7. Consider this riddle. Jesus says the following in Matthew 19:24: "Again I tell you, it is easier for a camel to go through the eye of a needle than for a rich man to enter the kingdom of God" [NIV, 1984].

One interpretation: the phrase "eye of a needle" is only figurative: it refers to the gated entrance of the city of Jerusalem. This says it was difficult for camels to go through the opening in the gate. It means that rich people will have *trouble* squeezing through, but it still can be done.

There is a polysemy problem here: one does not know if the person means the eye of a real needle or the entrance of the city [6:§3]. For one to interpret this parable correctly, one needs to clear up the polysemy.

8. And so it is with constitutions.

Telephones or Slogans?

9. Generation X and their parents do not suffer from "a foreign language problem." They know what each other's words mean.

If you told your kids, "Don't let money get in the way of happiness," and they became greedy tycoons and said, "I didn't"—there would not be the slightest issue with regard to language. The only issue would be what made them happy.

10. Imagine a group of specialists who investigate what the words "spirit" and "material" refer to by looking at dictionaries and how school children were taught. And they conclude that the usage of the words is virtually identical between the two generations. In short, talking across time is no different here than talking from *within* it.

So, if someone said, "Materialism doesn't corrupt the spirit," people would understand well enough that they could vigorously disagree about the matter.

11. This appeal uses *telephone logic*.[4] It says that where one can successfully communicate across time using the same words—but having different opinions—that each understands the language.

12. Here's the alternative. You look to the meaning of a declaration from the perspective of those associated with calling forth its gesture. Here the logic is almost sacramental. The goal is not linguistics, but a spirituous attachment to a set of behaviors that a group had in mind when celebrating a particular artifact. This makes the declaration similar to a chant, flag, gesture, slogan, symbol or even prayer.

The goal is to say that the Free Spirit Clause is not simply its words, but is a culturally iconic sacrament to a set of generational proclivities—a cheer, as it were, for a way of life. This, I call, *slogan logic*.

13. Note that one could *innocently* use slogan logic in law. One could say, "The American Constitution represented the ascendency of Enlightenment ideals and a radicalism for its age," describing why. But this does not say that we, today, must live chained to the prior age's state of mind. This assertion is not *prescriptive*. It only means that we can better appreciate the Constitution as one might a piece of art. We can see a *cultural orientation*.

14. But there are some who take this another way. They mean to say that the Free Spirit Clause in some way *legally* adopts the social mindset of the times.

Cultural Originalism?

15. Imagine someone saying the word "peace" or giving the "peace sign" to another in the 1960s, versus a freshman college student in the 1980s doing that. Think of how the life experiences could be different. Think of how the person in the 1980s lives without the draft, without an insane war where people from their neighborhoods have come home dead; without a counter-culture, without protesters being beaten by police; without the same generational camaraderie or drug culture, etc. Here we might say: the *sense* of the peace sign is remarkably different—it no longer carries with it the same sort of experiential ethos. Imag-

ine the person from the 80s getting a lecture from a parent on what the expression "peace" was really all about.[5]

16. And so, the argument becomes thus: when the Free Spirit Clause was celebrated in 1969, all understood that people were not to be too commercialized, too materialistic, too greedy, too selfish, etc. And this cultural orientation was specifically projected upon the clause itself, so that it carries a sort of halo.

17. What is one to make of this idea? Consider the following:

> When the Free Spirit Clause was enacted, the drafters and approvers threw away gold watches as they participated in the ritual of destroying a BMW with a sledge hammer. Out of this ritual the words were written "materialism shall not corrupt the spirit." And cheers followed. As it was broadcast on television, all young people elected to follow in like kind. They renounced certain items reflecting prosperous culture. Diamonds were thrown away. No more gold accoutrements. No luxury vehicles. When historians looked upon these gestures, they proclaimed, "the original meaning of Article I is to renounce the possessions of luxury culture." That is the "true meaning."

18. This only seems to say that the parent generation celebrated an idea with certain gestures. This is the way they arranged it.

19. What gets handed to Generation X—the sentences of the document or the things that their parents liked for them? It would be like telling children they were forced to like the things their parents did. Imagine someone saying to their child, "You have to like this television show."

20. Because the Free Sprit Clause doesn't tell the children not to buy gold, diamonds or BMWs, the behaviors of the parent generation are only *antics*. They are a social arrangement that celebrates a rule for an uncorrupted spirit, not the meaning of the sentence, "Materialism shall not corrupt the spirit."

(The simple way to say this: if they wanted to forever ban BMWs, they needed to write that in the document).

21. When, in language, is the meaning of something dictated by its social arrangement? Think of names for dances. For one to Twist correctly, one needs to gyrate segments of the anatomy (the hips) in a certain specific way. So if a law required kids to "Refrain from doing the Twist when dancing," a person could look at historic bodily behavior for reference.

But the words of the Free Spirit Clause are *not* like dance-words.

22. Even slogans do not carry with them their specific arrangements. Imagine that American culture is 40% gay and that 70% of the culture wants gay rights. Imagine that there is a slogan among gays that says, "Out of the closets and into the streets."

Now imagine that, one day, another group picks up the slogan: those having negative self-esteem. Think of other groups that might pick it up: fathers who are being overlooked by society as custodial-worthy, nurturing parents. Obese people who live in an objectified, beauty-driven culture.

23. What, then, is the "original meaning" of the slogan, "Out of the closet and into the street?" Some may say it is about sexual orientation. In fact, that is *not* the original meaning; it is only the first *arrangement*. The "original meaning" is a misnomer; there is only meaning, period. And the meaning is simply to stop being quiet about something and start promoting it.

24. Compare: "Don't tread on me." "Give me liberty or give me death!" What are the original meanings of these expressions?

The account I am presenting is that the question is confused. There is no "original meaning;" there is only the framework of the language and any of its social arrangements. The arrangement Patrick Henry had in mind is quite different from what the gay rights movement had in mind when using the same exact expression—or what Martin Luther King Jr. had in mind. Yet, *all* are obedient to the language.

25. Were it otherwise, the law would turn into a *gesture* or *sacrament*. The idea is to transmit to its progeny the cultural heritage of the forebears. (Notice the religiosity).

26. Under this view, one really doesn't need a constitution—passing the crown of the kings of old or the Ring of Barahir[6] would also do the trick. Just as a chieftain might pass along his war dress or a mantle of some kind, so too could the passing of a cultural order occur through a similar kind of sacrament.

(Is this similar to asking a devout Catholic what communion means?).

27. But how do you accurately come to know the cultural inheritance? You recreate the original psychology. You would have to study the culture, the ways, the beliefs, etc. You would adopt the clothing and symbolism. You would attempt to "live the ideas." You would have to become a "student of the age," so to speak.

This is probably similar to what some actors do to become the characters they play. (Compare: Colonial Williamsburg).

28. This inculcation isn't passed along by handing over a set of general sentences that say "read this." It requires much more: instruction, dress, imagination—even theater to some extent. I want to say that it requires "play."

29. But what is the format of the instruction? It seems that aside from the behavior of *showing*—e.g., the father teaching the son his ways—it would also be the reading of narratives (stories).

30. Imagine if law was communicated the same way that religion was, through narratives and parables:

> One day they assembled in the field to celebrate their music and their new way. Therein they forswore against worldly goods and shared with one another their belongings and joy. Whilst in the said communion they also promised to pass their Word and their Ways onto their progeny in like kind. And on the day they

so affixed and bound their kin, they did set forth the proclamation, "Material-ism shall not corrupt the soul," to which all in near and far pledged their sur-render.

31. Why wouldn't one learn about the Constitution this way? Because the cul-tural understanding of the Framers was neither foreign to their world nor in need of being transmuted as a religious experience. The point of the law is to *regi-ment* culture, not to *sanctify* it.

32. The Constitution does not set forth narratives that describe the correct way to live (what to eat, how to punish, how to treat others). It sets forth flexible, simple sentences.

The Relevance of Law

33. The Free Spirit Clause isn't even needed for the 60s generation to regulate (and celebrate) themselves. Let's say someone shouted from the microphone at the stage at Woodstock: "Long live our principles and ideas; pass them on to your kids." And let's say it is televised, and people all over say, "Yes let's do that." What would be the difference in how the kids are taught to live?

   It seems that there would be no difference in how *either* the 60s generation or Generation X lived with respect to "materialism and the spirit."

34. If the DoJ had only said, "Teach your children well," one would imagine that *neither* the 60s generation nor Generation X would have changed their out-looks. It would have all been precisely the same. Yet, in all cases, each is obedi-ent to the law.[7]

35. If this is true, why bother to even write down the fundamental law? (Chris-tianity was an oral tradition for some time).

36. One answer is that constitutional sentences *can* be efficacious across culture and time to the extent that its language allows.[8] No one is saying that language cannot be followed. What is being said is that the following is governed by the language game rather than the social arrangements made by the first generation. If generations want their social arrangements or outlooks to govern forever (the-oretically), they need to specifically enact them.

37. I'm also not saying that past social arrangements are irrelevant to future ones. To the contrary, one would assume they share an important relation: the new generation has "a guide," so to speak.

38. If the the DoJ had only said, "Teach your children well," Generation X may not have addressed the balancing of materialism and spirit at all. Future genera-tions would not have even *addressed* the elder generation's problems.

39. It would be like saying to an eighteen-year-old leaving home to enter the real world, "Do your best," versus adding, "Make sure you have good nutrition." The adding of the more specific thing requires the teenager to address the nutri-

tion issue. And if that means the teenager selects the Atkins protocol over what the parents favor (e.g., Zone diet), that is perfectly acceptable. What is not acceptable, however, is for the teenager *not* to confront the nutrition issue—which is what the command requires.

40. All that constitutions really say is for subsequent generations to pick the most appropriate social arrangement. "Pick out the best 'cruel-punishment' product. Socially arrange your best idea for 'reasonable search.'"

41. It would be the same as if one sent a child to college and said, "Dress well, do your best, get good grades, pick a good major and buy your textbooks." Although one could imagine scenarios where these commands are violated, one can equally imagine all sorts of different ways to comply.

42. "But hasn't Generation X turned the Free Spirit Clause into a truism? Isn't it now superfluous, lifeless and inoperable? Hasn't it been 'deactivated'"?

No. It still commands that those whose spirits are seen as "corrupted" by material culture must shun such a thing. I'm thinking here of the difference between J.R. Ewing[9] and Alex Keaton.[10] Couldn't Alex say he followed the DoJ?[11]

Technical Jargon

43. Imagine this claim: "corrupted spirit" in the Free Spirit Clause means having too many luxury items, by *definition*. Note the similarity: "Marriage is between a husband and wife"; "Corrupted spirit is having gold and diamonds."

44. This maneuver no longer makes "corrupted spirit" an empirical matter. It says something circular: if one has too many possessions, one is "corrupted" no matter the state of affairs.

If this maneuver were allowed, it could turn the whole Constitution into its own technical-language field.[12]

45. In medicine, it is common to name a disease based upon symptomology. So, when symptoms x, y and z appear, one calls it "syndrome something," which denotes only that x, y and z have all appeared together.

46. Axiomatic jargon cannot exist in social organizations unless it is *defined*. That is the only way for the language community to pass it on. The terms require training and policing. Imagine the medical field trying to communicate without having formalized its jargon. Would it resemble the field of healing rather than medicine?

47. The law handles this by *codifying* jargon. You would find a definition section. Drug laws define controlled substances by chemical and pharmaceutical names.

48. Consider these words: "A water molecule has two hydrogen atoms covalently bonded to a single oxygen atom," H_2O (Scientific Jargon). "A triangle is a

polygon with three corners or vertices and three sides or edges which are line segments" (Mathematical Jargon).

49. Now compare this word: *Schedule-II Controlled Substance.*[13] What is this?—Exactly what the legal definition lists, and nothing more. In fact, if something *should* be listed, it cannot count until the legislature re-writes the law.[14] One could call this *grocery-list jargon*: you must associate the word with a specific inventory of "groceries."

50. Imagine that the legislature in the 1960s passes a list of banned consumer goods and calls it the "corrupted spirit list." The name of the list is understood to stand for *this list.*

51. If the law had only said "goods that corrupt the spirit are banned," one could only interpret this to mean that a list must now be *created* by those wanting to follow the law. And if one generation forms such a list, there is nothing in language that prohibits another from forming a different one.

52. Note this legal convention: "Words are given their plain meanings unless otherwise stated."

53. There is also the problem of *anthropology*. One cannot simply declare that words are axiomatic; this has to be *shown* in the language culture. You would have to see it in the consumer culture. You would have to see BMW dealers advertising products that say, "Corrupted spirit for sale." Or, there would be an entire segment of the marketplace selling "corrupted spirits" (gold, diamonds, furs, etc.). If one doesn't see this as a language phenomenon, it would be telling.

54. Imagine a child being taught the word arrhythmia. One day his father comes home from the doctor and says, "I have arrhythmia." The child says, "What is that?" And the father replies, "Oh that is when the heart beats out of rhythm." And then imagine that, later in life, the child is playing in a teenage rock-and-roll band with fellow schoolmates. One day, when the drummer is playing erratically, the child says, "The band has arrhythmia," denoting the "off" drum beat. (And he is not joking).

This is how ordinary language works. If, in fact, arrhythmia meant "off-beats," there would be a family resemblance—percussion arrhythmia, cardiac arrhythmia, auto arrhythmia (gears miss), dancing arrhythmia (out of synch), tire arrhythmia (need a wheel balance), clock arrhythmia (time is off), etc.

55. If arrhythmia took on this sort of understanding, it would seem the same as "not in synch."

Imagine the father coming home and saying, "My heart isn't in synch." The child says, "What is synch?" And the father replies, "My heart beats out of normal rhythm." The child then later says of the rock band: "The drummer isn't synched." What is it about the language game that allows the child to more easily speak of the band as being out of synch, but not having arrhythmia? Why can't arrhythmia share the same language space?

56. Only medicine as a community uses the term, and the lay public only receives it when going to the doctor or reading about medical problems. It therefore always retains a medical context.

"Marriage"

57. The school-boy or technical sense of "bachelor" is "an unmarried male."[15] This makes "bachelor" the sum of its parts: (males) plus (unmarried).

Note the curious results. Is the Pope a "bachelor?" Let's say the law said, "No bachelors in the sorority house," and someone excluded the Pope—would that be the correct meaning of the law?

If someone says "yes," it is only because he or she takes "bachelor" as an axiomatic task. If someone else said "no," it is because they take the idea as not being axiomatic. What we have here are competing *senses* of bachelor.[16]

58. The same sort of game can be played with the idea of "marriage." One might say in ordinary use that marriage is a contractual arrangement between two adults[17] to form a family partnership between them.[18] But then, someone comes along and says, "Marriage is between a husband and a wife." What does this say?

It says that "marriage" should function in language like "bachelor" when offered in an axiomatic sense. Trouble is, it sounds peculiar—like it's swimming upstream. (This is why it sounds like a political slogan).

59. The fact is that people can easily say, "So and so is married," and *not* mean to preclude gender, like the words actor/actress gender-preclude.[19]

60. The term "marriage" requires you to arrange something. If the Constitution had said, "Citizens have the right to marry," you would need to make choices:

– Cohabitation for sufficient time (common law marriage)?
– Does it emancipate certain minors (a 15-year-old can marry)?
– Performed with the "right" ceremony and vows?
– Recognized from other jurisdictions (full faith and credit)?
– Qualifications (capacity, blood relatives, etc.)
– Grounds for annulment, etc.

61. These choices are nothing but a menu. One could have marriage constructed in all sorts of ways, so that each arrangement is only an *example* of the idea.

Cf., a menu for dinner. There are x number of meals to choose from. A person selects this entre, that side, this appetizer and that drink. That constitutes "dinner." Dinner each night can be a different arrangement of the choice. This is exactly what marriage law does, except it is the state that is eating.

Cf., a department store for fashion. Imagine a store that sells various items: dresses, jewelry, watches, shoes, pants, etc. Much of what "fashion" amounts to is the piecing together of store items: this dress, that earring, etc. There are lots of ways to be fashionable (lots of combinations). This is what marriage law is, except that it is the state that is doing the dressing.

62. If you were talking on the telephone to someone in 1787 and said in a fun sort of parlance, "My two cats are married; they just love one another so much"—you would be perfectly understood. Indeed, you might get a laugh and a reply like: "That reminds me of how Old Red was with our bunny rabbit—bless his heart."

And because this is a valid play in the language game, it is consistent with the meaning of the word "marriage."

If a constitution created the right to marry 200 years ago, but did not specify the social arrangement, the judges of each generation could select something different, yet *still* be obedient to the so called "original meaning." Just as a different customer in a restaurant is obedient to the (original) idea of "dinner" when ordering differently from the menu night to night.

Original Meaning is a Fallacy

63. Here is what I want to say: there is no "original meaning of the law," as is often said. Rather, there is only the first social arrangement—the first attempt to dress behavior.

64. If there was truly an "original meaning," there would have to be an authority to educate and show what it meant. People would regard it as a foreign language problem.

Imagine seeing an impressionistic painting for the first time and thinking it's nothing but scribbles. You need to be acculturated to what impressionistic art is doing before you can get an eye for it. If the meaning of the Constitution was this "original," it would require social teaching—like, say, the word of God might, when it was first heard. It would itself engender a new vocabulary.

65. Let's imagine two janitors. The rule they must obey is: "Mop the floor." Note how curious it would be if one were to say at work, "Ted was the first ever to do this job, and this is the way he mopped. We must always follow Ted's approach and never deviate." Why would one ever think that the law is how Ted mops rather than "Mop the floor?"

66. Note this peculiar claim: "The First Congress knew best what the Constitution really meant." But what did the people really know (spell it out)? What are the secrets that they allege?

What the First Congress really knew is a lot like what someone knows when they commit insider trading on the New York Stock Exchange. One might say the First Congress is only the Martha Stewart of the law. This doesn't mean the Congress knows more about law's meaning, it only means that it knows about how to capitalize upon certain social arrangements at a discreet point in history.

67. The major confusions of "new originalists" boil down to this: (a) they can-

not distinguish polysemy from a Wittgensteinian family-resemblance; and (b) they think language as a system is a picture or a logic, rather than an anthropology. In short, what is wrong is that they do not understand Wittgenstein.

68. There is no original meaning; there is only the grammar of plain words that call for the meaning to be socially arranged.

Notes

1. An earlier version of this work was presented at the 2009 Law and Society conference (Denver).

2. The reason why the main of 1787 culture reads the Free Spirit Clause this way is because, quite simply, it lives within an agrarian society that pre-dates Karl Marx and that has not properly experienced industrialization, finance capitalism, mass consumerism, shopping malls and credit cards. The only analog the society might have is found in the excesses of wealthy aristocrats and monarchs, not something pervasive of the mainstream American culture.

3. Asceticism and religious poverty was sometimes preached in some Christian circles, because "renunciation of material goods and a life based upon a lack of material needs makes possible a more intense form of discipleship or religiosity." *The Encyclopedia of Christianity*, vol. 4, ed. Erwin Fahlbusch (Wm. B. Eerdmans Publishing Company, 2005), 307.

4. It was either at the 2009 Law and Society meeting or the 2010 Midwest Political Science Association meeting that Larry Solum characterized my views as having presented an "intelligibility thesis," which I thought was an improvement upon "telephone logic." Elsewhere, I explicitly adopt this way of speaking.

5. This could apply to any cultural symbol from the 1960s, such as what tie-dyed clothing stood for, or what "real protest" was all about.

6. A reference to a ring in J.R.R. Tolkein's *Lord of the Rings*. It is the ring worn by Aragorn, son of Arathorn.

7. I am not saying that law is irrelevant. Had the DoJ enacted a provision that said "Never buy gold or diamonds or luxury cars," there would have been serious consternation on the part of those within Generation X who approvingly received the DoJ from their parents, and who did not want to contradict themselves when they said they were following it. Hence, there would have been a moral conundrum: the language would be clearly against their desires. Either there would be guilt with the breaking of the rule, a movement to re-write it, or perhaps the rejection of the DoJ altogether (thereby alleviating the contradiction). So there would either be adherence, modification or conversion (leaving the faith).

8. The history of the American Constitution's Commerce Clause is testament both to the havoc that words cause subsequent generations as well as to the sins that occur when generations decide to "cheat." What I want to say here is something like: words don't break very easily; they require a major political and cultural happenstance. And even when that happens, the matter doesn't really go away. Segments of the culture feel aban-

doned or like society has sinned—or that others have cheated.

9. J. R. Ewing was a fictional character played by Larry Hagman on the CBS television show Dallas, which aired from 1978 to1991.

10. Alex Keaton was a fictional character played by Michael J. Fox on the NBC television show Family Ties, which aired from 1982 to 1989.

11. And isn't that precisely what that show was really about? Alex was the 1980s version of what the 60s youth represented, in terms of a kind of joy (idealism) that was clung to. Isn't it a fact that Alex's spirit was not corrupted by materialism even though he indulged in, rather than shunned, luxury items (BMW's etc.)?

12. Note that, when this is actually true, the legal system has to broadcast the technical sense to its membership during training. For example, when studying the defense of "cruelty" in family law, one inevitably encounters the professor hand-waving the meaning: "We don't mean ordinary-sense cruelty; we mean extreme, persistent and severe cruelty."

13. This is a term found in drug statutes. See Chapter 13, note 28.

14. It's not that one couldn't say of a drug unfairly accounted for by the list, "This drug should be a Schedule-II Controlled Substance." This says that an underlying logic exists in the classification scheme. It says, e.g., that Schedule-I substances have certain natural criteria different from Schedule-II. If, in fact, natural criteria are behind the classificatory scheme, then speaking of an aberration in "Schedule II" would have a different sort of grammar. It would be like saying: "this is a barbiturate, this is an amphetamine." It would be scientifically taxonomical (natural kind). But, absent this, the grammar changes markedly. It merely becomes one of *pointing*—it means, "the things specifically listed over here."

15. Philosophers sometimes call this an "analytic definition." See, e.g., *Harper Collins Dictionary of Philosophy,* 2nd ed. Peter A. Angeles (HarperPerennial, 1992), 294 (definition of "analytic statement," entry 2).

16. Controversies about "bachelor" may be as much about its axioms as about *whether* it must be axiomatic. Therefore, "bachelor" in today's language game may amount to a mixture of axiomatic grammar as well as the rejection of that grammar.

17. Note that it is common in matrimonial grammar *not* to speak of three or more people as being "married," because there are other names for this: polygamy, bigamy, etc. If people speak this way, it handles the problem of one being "over-married."

18. Cf., "True marriage is the meeting of mutual love." This would be a romantic or idealistic sense of marriage.

19. Think of words that actually preclude things. "Polygamy" specifically means having more than one spouse. "Bilateral" means two-sided. There is nothing in "marriage" that *linguistically* excludes gender. That is why the talk of "civil unions" doesn't really work. All that it does is introduce levels or *rank* into the current marriage grammar. Certain couples (men and women) end up with, in effect, grade-A marriages, while same-sex couples end up with, in effect, grade-B marriages.

Index

About the Author

Sean Wilson is an assistant professor at Wright State University, where he teaches courses in the areas of public law, judicial and American politics, and Wittgenstein. He has taught at many universities, including Penn State. He practiced law for ten years before becoming a faculty member. His scholarly interests include Wittgenstein, legal theory and judging, and quantitative ideology studies in judicial politics, the last of which he is a critic. This is Dr. Wilson's first book.